ways in which humor can appropriately be used in sermons. That includes blending biblical hermeneutics with a new word I have learned here: 'humor-neutics,' which invites preachers to notice and make use of the humor and irony that runs throughout the biblical narrative, and link that with their observations about the world around them. This is not a joke; this book will make for better sermons and better preachers."

—Marvin A. McMickle, President (retired),
Colgate Rochester Crozer Divinity School

"What a wonderful gift Alyce McKenzie and Owen Lynch have given us. In this enjoyable, engaging, and revealing book, McKenzie and Lynch show us that the God who is revealed in Scripture has a wonderful sense of humor and wants us to have one as well. In a time when there is much sadness and widespread lament in the church and our world, this daring, thoroughly enjoyable book invites us to smile, to see ourselves as a gracious God sees us, to laugh and to relish the gift of laughter."

—Will Willimon, Professor of the Practice of Christian Ministry,
Duke Divinity School; United Methodist Bishop (retired)

"Preachers instinctively know that humor in the sermon can serve the gospel. Preachers also know that when humor appears inappropriately in the sermon, everyone in the room is uneasy. This superb volume—the first study of humor in the pulpit in a generation—offers a theology of humor, perspectives on how humor works, points to sources for humor, marks occasions that are appropriate and inappropriate for humor, and, best of all, offers practical guidelines for using humor in the pulpit. This book will not turn preachers into stand-up comics, but it will help preachers see and express the humor that is all around us and that can bring a special spark to the sermon."

—Ronald J. Allen, Professor Emeritus of Preaching
and Gospels and Letters, Christian Theological Seminary

"Sermons would be a lot more listenable, delightful, and effective if preachers followed the advice of this witty, theoretically solid, and eminently practical book. Alyce McKenzie and Owen Lynch give readers many fine gifts in these pages, but none is more profound or welcome than their invitation to a more joyful expression of the faith."

—Thomas G. Long, Bandy Professor Emeritus of Preaching,
Candler School of Theology

"I smiled, nodded, laughed out loud, and underlined a lot as I read McKenzie and Lynch's wise and piquant *Humor Us!*, rethinking how humor works or doesn't in preaching and as the core of the life of faith. G. K. Chesterton said, 'Angels can fly because they can take themselves lightly.' Preachers will soar when they take this book seriously."

—James Howell, Senior Pastor, Myers Park United Methodist Church

Humor Us!

Humor Us!

*Preaching and the Power
of the Comic Spirit*

ALYCE M. MCKENZIE
AND
OWEN HANLEY LYNCH

WESTMINSTER
JOHN KNOX PRESS
LOUISVILLE · KENTUCKY

First edition
Published by Westminster John Knox Press
Louisville, Kentucky

23 24 25 26 27 28 29 30 31 32—10 9 8 7 6 5 4 3 2 1

Book design by Drew Stevens
Cover design by Mark Abrams

Library of Congress Cataloging-in-Publication Data is on file
at the Library of Congress, Washington, D.C.

ISBN: 9780664267018

Most Westminster John Knox Press books are available at special quantity discounts when purchased in bulk by corporations, organizations, and special-interest groups. For more information, please email SpecialSales@wjkbooks.com.

I would like to dedicate this book on humor to my students who have laughed and learned with me over the years, subjected to but never subjects of my humor.
—*Owen Hanley Lynch*

To Graham and Silas,
my self-appointed accountability partners who called me
    every afternoon to ask,
"How many pages did you write today, Gigi?"
—*Alyce M. McKenzie*

Contents

Preface to the "Preaching and . . ." Series

Preachers are not just preachers. When they step into the pulpit they are also theologians, storytellers, biblical teachers, pastors, historians, psychologists, entertainers, prophets, anthropologists, leaders, political scientists, popular culture commentators, ethicists, philosophers, scientists, and so much more. It is not that they are expected to be masters of homiletics and jacks of all other trades. Instead it is that when preachers strive to bring God's good news to bear on the whole of human existence, a lot is required to connect the two in existentially appropriate and meaningful ways.

The Perkins Center for Preaching Excellence (PCPE),[1] directed by Alyce M. McKenzie, has partnered with Westminster John Knox Press to create a book series that contributes to that work in a new way. While homiletical scholarship has long drawn on the full range of biblical and theological disciplines as well as a variety of philosophical and rhetorical disciplines, this series attempts to push the interdisciplinary dialogue in new ways. For each volume, the PCPE brings together as coauthors two scholars—a homiletician and an expert from another, nontheological field to bring that field into conversation with homiletics in a way that offers both new insights into preaching as a task and vocation and new strategies for the practical elements of sermon preparation and delivery.

This volume brings together homiletics (Alyce M. McKenzie) and humor studies (Owen Hanley Lynch). Humor has long played a role in preaching (although, as we will find, there have been many across church history who sought to rid the church and the pulpit of humor). Critical study of humor and its place and function in preaching, however, is fairly new. Indeed, as the authors show, an explosion of multidisciplinary research into humor arose during the last quarter of the twentieth century that coincided with the rise of the New Homiletic. A half-century later, it is time for humor studies to be brought into conversation with and employed for the betterment of the serious endeavor of proclaiming God's good news.

O. Wesley Allen Jr.
Series Editor

NOTES

1. Perkins Center for Preaching Excellence at SMU, "Perkins Center for Preaching Excellence: SMU," n.d., https://pcpe.smu.edu/.

Acknowledgments

We are grateful to our families who have sacrificed time with us as we have spent many Zoom and in-person hours in conversation about one of our favorite topics.

We are grateful to our students who call forth the best within us and bear with us when our classroom jokes don't quite hit the mark!

We are grateful for the chance for the Perkins Center for Preaching Excellence at Southern Methodist University (SMU) to partner with Westminster John Knox Press in this Preaching and . . . Series and for the patient shepherding through the process of editor-in-chief Robert A. Ratcliff. Unlike Alyce's grandsons, he did *not* call us every afternoon to ask us how many pages we had written that day, but his steady faith in the project and in us as the authors was invaluable.

There is risk involved when two people who are interested in everything collaborate on a subject that relates to everything. To the extent that this book resists the rabbit trails ending in cul-de-sacs that we were tempted to follow, we have one person to thank, and that, profusely: Lois Craddock Perkins Professor of Homiletics and Preaching and . . . series editor Dr. O. Wesley Allen Jr. We are deeply grateful for Wes's honest, thorough, and clarifying editing of our work. Readers will reap the benefits of his work behind the scenes to make this the best book that the two of us could offer. Any shortcomings are down to us!

We thank Sabina Hulem, our Perkins Center for Preaching Excellence at SMU administrative assistant, for her tireless support work in tracking citations in the final manuscript. And we are indebted to many scholars from a variety of fields whose work has informed this one. It's hard to come up with a metaphor that does justice to the richness and vastness of humor studies as it has developed over the last several decades. Maybe a tapestry, or a smorgasbord, or an orchestral piece to which many instruments contribute. Whichever we choose, it has been a nourishing, delightful process.

Finally, we would each like to thank the other for their contribution to the collaborative process. Owen describes Alyce as "my coauthor who made every part of this project a fun and intellectually rewarding experience." Alyce describes Owen as "my collaborator whose knowledge of humor studies, comic gifts, and profound faith are a gift to preachers and the people to whom they will offer humor-filled good news."

We hope you enjoy this tribute to the power of the comic spirit in preaching!

Alyce M. McKenzie
Owen Hanley Lynch
Southern Methodist University, July 14, 2022

Introduction

It's Saturday night, and a stand-up comedian and a preacher walk into a bar. No, wait, that's not a good setup for a joke, for two reasons. First, the stand-up comedian would already be in the bar doing an act on open mic night. Second, the preacher would not be walking into a bar on a Saturday night. She would be at home working on her sermon.

Your authors, one a communications scholar with a specialty in humor studies (Owen Lynch) and the other a preacher and teacher of preaching (Alyce McKenzie), have decided to take a walk together down the halls of history and into today's pulpits, classrooms, work-places, and comedy clubs, exploring the why, what, and how of humor. Owen is a Catholic from London, England. Alyce is a United Methodist from Pennsylvania. Both teach at Southern Methodist University in Dallas, Texas—Owen at the Meadows School of the Arts, Alyce at Perkins School of Theology.

We have partnered in writing this book because we both think that humor, whether in the pulpit or elsewhere, is a uniquely human capacity that can be used to heal or to hurt. Although it is often considered trivial, humor is a universal and essential part of human social life—hence the saying "Whenever two or more are gathered . . . there is a joke!" Indeed, after crying, laughter is one of the first social vocalizations by human infants.[1] Later in childhood, humor recognition and enjoyment are key indicators of healthy cognitive development.[2] The erosion of the capacity for humor is an indicator of cognitive decline as

1

we age.[3] It has been shown that humor is a key social attribute in communities in which people live much longer-than-average life span than in other communities.[4]

We also are convinced, each from our different faith backgrounds, that humor is a gift from God, part of what it means to be made in the image of God. Like all good gifts from God, humor is meant to be used and used fully for God's good purposes. Humor is clearly too valuable and powerful a capacity to be trivialized or set aside, especially in the pulpit. That is why we have given the book the subtitle *Preaching and the Power of the Comic Spirit.*

Throughout the book we use several terms that need defining at the outset. One is *comic vision,* by which we mean the certainty of the ultimate victory of positive outcomes over negative circumstances—of life over death, of hope over despair—that encompasses our sermons and our lives as Christians.[5] The comic vision is the conviction of the unthwartable nature of God's good purposes for creation and humankind, despite present appearances to the contrary. It affirms a celebratory context, not just as a future horizon, but as a present reality.

The term we use throughout the book to describe the inclination to view daily life in light of this comic vision is the *comic spirit.* By it we mean, not a penchant for trivializing important matters, but the openness to noticing and employing humor (and its compatriots joy and laughter) in light of and in the context of the comic vision.[6]

Related to comic spirit is *humor orientation.* This term refers to one's predisposition to recognize, appreciate, and use humor. We return to this term and how it can be measured using the "humor orientation scale" in chapter 2. A premise of this book is that one's humor orientation can be both cultivated and put to positive use in our preaching.

Centuries ago Tertullian, questioning the relationship between philosophy and faith in a treatise countering contemporary heresies, asked, "What has Athens to do with Jerusalem?"[7] In this collaborative book, we address a similar question: "What does humor have to do with preaching?"

Formal works on preaching most often warn against the use of humor in the pulpit, using a reductionist definition of it as opening with a joke that may or may not relate to the sermonic theme or biblical text(s). This warning is not unwarranted, since it is the habit of some preachers to reduce humor to the status of the guaranteed opening guffaw, a way to warm up the crowd at the beginning of the sermon. Or they may conscript a joke or quip to salvage a yawn-worthy expanse of biblical exegesis, or dive to the depths of self-deprecation in an effort to project a down-to-earth, relatable pulpit persona.

Given the ambiguity about its use in our current homiletical context, we see the need for an in-depth, practical exploration of humor in preaching. Recent research in the field of positive psychology highlights the benefits of humor, noting it can promote empathy, buffer stress, forge connections to the world, and help us cope with the incongruities of everyday life. In recent years, researchers in the fields of communication, linguistics, philosophy, psychology, management theory, rhetoric, and sociology have taken an increased interest in the origins, functions, and impact of humor. Humor is now welcomed into mainstream experimental psychology as a subject worthy of exploration and understanding. *Humor Us! Preaching and the Power of the Comic Spirit* harnesses this research in service of the sermon.

This conversation between preaching and humor is for those preachers who are so skittish about humor that their sermons have become arid lectures. At the other extreme, it is also for preachers who are standup comedian wannabes, yielding to the temptation to be more concerned with the comedy than the content of proclamation. And this book is for all those preachers in between who recognize that a "sense of humor" is essential for personal and social well-being, and who sense that unleashing the positive power of humor could make them better preachers, but don't quite know how to cultivate and use it.

Readers of this exploration of the use of humor in sermons will emerge able to engage listeners more fully by humorous, even entertaining, means. We make no apologies for that! But our primary purpose is to help preachers enlist the power of humor, in its various forms and functions, in offering our congregations deeper, more challenging, and more delightful engagement with God's good news in their everyday lives and in the wider world.

Humor Us! is divided into three parts. Part 1, "The Gift of the Comic Spirit," sets forth the theological context of our project: the conviction that humor is an integral part of both God's character and of our humanity as made in God's image. It consists of three chapters dealing with God's gift of humor, humor as uniquely human, and humor and the *imago Dei*.

Part 2 is titled "The Sermon and the Comic Spirit." In chapter 4, "Adding Humor to Our Homiletical Toolbox," we take a look at the communicational, psychological, and social benefits of enlisting humor in service of the sermon. Chapter 5, "Strategies for Using Humor in Our Sermons," offers a series of strategies for humor use in sermons, each with an example from recent sermons, both by Alyce and other preachers' recent sermons. Chapter 6, "Three Theories of Humor," introduces readers to superiority, relief, and incongruity theories of how humor functions. Chapter 7—"The Two Frames: Comedy and Tragedy"—places preachers' use of humor in the context of the comic vision: that death will be overcome by life and that we don't have to wait until the next life to experience joy and laughter. This chapter paves the way for our later treatment of preachers as those who are characterized by a comic spirit, as they become more attuned to humor and gain the freedom and skill to employ it in their sermons. "Foes and Fans: Humor through the Centuries"—chapter 8—is a portrait gallery of humor's historic detractors and, more recently, its promoters.

Part 3 turns to "The Preacher and the Comic Spirit." Chapter 9—"The Preacher as Jester, Fool, and Sage"—lifts up three models of historic humorists and highlights what preachers can learn from each type. Chapter 10—"The Preacher as Comic Spirit"—reveals the contribution of humor to the preacher's faith, self-confidence, and relationship with the congregation. "The Preacher's Knack for Noticing Humor in Inscape and Landscape" (chapter 11) equips preachers to notice humor in their inner lives (inscape) and their congregational and community context (landscape). Chapter 12—"The Preacher's Knack for Noticing Humor in the Textscape: Humor-neutics 101"—hones their attentiveness to biblical humor. The final chapter, "The Preacher as Last Comic Standing: Crafting Original Humor," offers strategies from comics on incorporating observational humor and storytelling into sermons.

Humor Us! can be read on one's own or studied in groups with other preachers. To maximize its usefulness in varied settings, we have placed "To Ponder" discussion breaks throughout the chapters.

Humor Us! Preaching and the Power of the Comic Spirit grows out of its authors' shared respect for the gift of humor. In the pages that follow, we unwrap that gift, from both social-scientific and homiletical perspectives, describing the various means by which preachers can exercise their comic spirit. We hope that preachers will learn to use humor better to invite listeners into a shared experience of the presence of God, the Creator and orchestrator of the comic vision, the original and ultimate bringer of life out of death. Now, kindly humor us by reading on!

NOTES

1. Rod A. Martin and Thomas Ford, *The Psychology of Humor: An Integrative Approach* (London: Academic Press, 2018).

2. Marti Southam, "Humor Development: An Important Cognitive and Social Skill in the Growing Child," *Physical and Occupational Therapy in Pediatrics* 25, no. 1–2 (2005): 105–17, https://doi.org/10.1080/j006v25n01_07.

3. Wingyun Mak and Brian Carpenter, "Humor Comprehension in Older Adults," *Journal of the International Neuropsychological Society* 13, no. 4 (2007): 606–14, https://doi.org/10.1017/s1355617707070750.

4. "Blue zones" is a label used to describe regions of the world where a higher-than-usual number of the population live much longer lives. A key and common trait of centenarians within these blue zones is a happy disposition and a keen and eclectic sense of humor accompanied by much shared laughter. See Dan Buettner, *The Blue Zones: Lessons for Living Longer from the People Who've Lived the Longest* (Washington, DC: National Geographic Books, 2010).

5. Many authors, borrowing from Dante's medieval masterpiece, have applied the term "the divine comedy" to the eschatological perspective of our Christian faith: the vision that death, tragedy, and sorrow are to be seen in the context of indestructible life and joy, epitomized for Christians in the resurrection of Jesus from the dead. We explore the contrast between the classic categories and plots of comedy and tragedy in chap. 7, "The Two Frames: Comedy and Tragedy."

6. Our choice of the term comic spirit was inspired by Conrad Hyers's *The Comic Vision and the Christian Faith: A Celebration of Life and Laughter* (Eugene, OR: Wipf and Stock, 2003), 10. In another work Hyers states, "Terms such as comic vision and comic spirit point to a certain perspective and attitude toward life that are important to a full humanity. They belong to the image of God in which we are created and to the image of Christ in which we are to be re-created" (*And God Created Laughter: The Bible as Divine Comedy* [Atlanta: John Knox Press, 1987], 6).

7. Wendy E. Helleman, "Tertullian on Athens and Jerusalem," in *Hellenization Revisited: Shaping a Christian Response within the Greco-Roman World*, ed. Helleman (Lanham, MD: University Press of America, 1994), 361–81.

PART ONE

The Gift of the Comic Spirit

1

God's Gift of Humor

"Laughter is the closest thing to God's grace."
—Attributed to theologian Karl Barth (1886–1968)[1]

A WORKING DEFINITION OF HUMOR

R. Escarpit, a psychologist, titled the first chapter of his book on humor "On the Impossibility of Defining Humor."[2] We would love to begin our study with a laser-sharp, universally accepted definition of humor, but Escarpit is right: humor is a slippery phenomenon to define. It reminds Alyce of a game she used to play with her youth group when she was a youth pastor in Pennsylvania years ago. It was called "greased watermelon football." A watermelon that had been coated with lard was the football. There is no way the game ever ended well for the watermelon! We have higher hopes for this study of humor for preaching than for it to end up in broken chunks on the ground!

Although there may be no universally accepted definition of humor, we use the following working definition by Hebrew Bible scholar Athalya Brenner to guide our work: *humor* is "the capacity to cause or feel amusement." A *sense of humor*, then, is "the faculty of perceiving humor and enjoying what is ludicrous and amusing and may express joy, merriment and amusement, but, on the other hand, also mockery, derision and scorn."[3] As individuals, we differ in our personal use and appreciation of humor as well as the degree to which we find things funny. We also differ in how often, when, where, and in what company and type of social situations we attempt to use humor in our everyday

9

life. This predisposition to appreciate but also to create humor is termed one's *humor orientation* and can even be measured using a humor orientation scale. We talk about this in the next chapter, where we encourage you to assess your own humor orientation.[4]

While all may not agree on a single definition of humor, we can all recognize successful use of humor by the laughter or smile it produces. We know it when we see it. Successful humor can be recognized by the response to it, in that humor requires a receiver or audience to confirm something to be funny or humorous. As Shakespeare stated, "A jest's prosperity lies in the ears of him [*sic*] that hears it, never in the tongue who him makes it."[5]

Part of what makes humor so difficult to define is that humor that is successful in one cultural context may not elicit laughter or even a slight smile in another. Humor is found in all cultures, but *what* is considered to be funny is by no means universal. Opinions about the degree to which something is funny (or not) are relative to individual taste, a particular social group's ethos, and wider social context and cultural mores.[6] When we repeat something we found to be funny to an audience that does not laugh, we name the problem as "an inside joke" or "You had to be there." But in the right context and the right in-group, humor can evoke laughter that is contagious and binding. When enjoyed by a group, humor invites us to suspend personal agendas and practical concerns that can lead to overseriousness and conflict, and revel in the joke or oddity together as a community, be it a community of two or two thousand.[7]

While our working definition of humor ("the capacity to cause or feel amusement") is simple, we acknowledge the complexity of humor: that while humor is universal to humans, we all have individual humor orientations. Successful use of humor depends on context.

AN APPRECIATION OF HUMOR

Mystic Evelyn Underhill says, "For lack of attentiveness, a thousand forms of loveliness elude us every day."[8] The same could be said of humor all around us. Humor scholars agree that we create humor when we perceive it. Incongruities and situations become funny when we interpret them as funny. Recognition and appreciation of humor are key to activating it in everyday life. And for that, one needs what is widely referred to as a "sense of humor." We hope this book will sharpen preachers' ability to both appreciate and create humor, not just in general, but with regard to its homiletical potential.

In a book Alyce wrote several years ago called *Novel Preaching,* she earnestly advised preachers to exercise what she called a "knack for noticing."[9] She encouraged them to develop the habit of close attentiveness to their inner lives (inscape), outer lives (landscape), and biblical text (textscape), searching for signs of God at work. She is embarrassed to admit that she never once mentioned attentiveness to humor. Looking back, she wonders, *What was I thinking?* to make such a glaring omission. Or, better yet, *What was I not thinking?* She was making the all-too-common mistake preachers make of underestimating humor, reducing it to the opening joke or quips sprinkled over the sermon to spice its otherwise bland exegetical expanses. She was regarding humor as a condiment, rather than a God-given human capacity deserving of a central role in the preparation, content, and delivery (embodiment) of sermons. She had an underdeveloped appreciation for the comic spirit and its role.

Owen came to a deeper appreciation of humor's social role in his first in-depth, yearlong, participatory ethnography (a process where the researcher embeds and fully participates as a member of an organization or social group) of a hotel kitchen.[10] As he worked alongside the chefs, he began to realize how central humor was to their everyday sensemaking and workplace processes. This made him wonder why humor is so often left out as a glaring omission in organizational and ethnographic accounts. He has never encountered a social context where humor is fully absent or trivial. So he paid special attention to humor's use in the kitchen (and many social contexts since), recognizing that humor is a unique form of communication because it elicits an observable response (laughter) demonstrating a common interpretation. When chefs laughed at a joke or made fun of a manager (many times without the manager realizing it), their laughter was shared, uncontrollable, immediate, and impossible to fake. It demonstrated a common understanding among the social actors (the chefs) in their workplace environment. By paying close attention to humor, Owen also began to realize that humor's use was not trivial banter but was a significant part of the social construction of work and professional identity. He focused on it as a communication act that reveals how the chefs (then doctors, teachers, and management consultants) used everyday humor to make sense of their surroundings, shape their labor processes, maintain their professional autonomy and identity, and resist managerial control of their craft.[11]

We took different paths to get here, but Alyce and Owen have both arrived at a place where we enjoy, respect, and honor humor and the place it has in our lives and our fields. As we shall see in chapter 8, many philosophers, theologians, and preachers across the centuries have not shared such an appreciation of humor. Some of the warnings of these detractors concerning ways humor can do damage need to be taken seriously. But we are arguing that humor, when used respectfully and ethically, is serious business and deserves to play a significant role in the proclamation of God's good news.

Homiletician David Buttrick defines the purpose of preaching this way: "Preaching 'transforms' our identity by giving our stories a beginning and an end. As we locate our lives within the greater narrative of Jesus and his life, death, and resurrection, our story is transformed by this encounter with God-with-us."[12] This is an apt description of the victorious future comic vision folded back into our present-day lives, in which we are called to activate the comic spirit and notice the humor that abounds within and all around us.

HUMOR AS COMPANION TO FAITH, HOPE, LOVE, AND JOY

There is certainly no defense against adverse fortune which is, on the whole, so effectual as an habitual sense of humor.

—Unitarian Minister and Abolitionist
Thomas Higginson (1823–1911)[13]

Conrad Hyers, scholar of religion and humor, notes that "it was an unfortunate omission on the part of the early church not to have included humor among the seven cardinal virtues and humorlessness among the seven deadly sins."[14] We wouldn't elevate humor, wielded by flawed human beings, to the status of a virtue, those godly states of mind and heart Paul in Galatians 5:22–23 calls fruits of the Spirit (love, joy, peace, patience, kindness, generosity, faithfulness, gentleness, and self-control). While virtues generally have a positive impact, humor is a double-edged sword that can hurt or heal, build up or deride, be used for good or ill.[15] Literary critic Terry Eagleton reminds us that the word "sarcasm" come from an ancient Greek term meaning "to tear the flesh."[16] We affirm, however, that when rightly motivated, humor can be used in a virtuous fashion. Let's consider ways that humor can help create conditions that activate the virtues of faith, hope, love, and joy.

In terms of *faith*, a sense of humor can help us look beyond our foibles and failures to reliance on a forgiving, gracious God. Indeed, theologian Reinhold Niebuhr viewed humor as a prelude to faith. "What is funny about us," he said, "is precisely that we take ourselves too seriously."[17] Humor helps us laugh at ourselves, realize our limitations, and entrust ourselves to God's life-affirming power in the face of injustice and the prospect of death. In this regard it is closely related to humility, the least respected virtue in our culture, which associates it with weakness, and the most respected virtue in Scripture.

With regard to *hope*, a sense of humor can be a sign of hope even in trials—in the crucible of trial the gold of humor can be forged. It has been empirically demonstrated that humor can positively affect psychological and physical well-being and that a sense of humor is a major component of high-hope individuals.[18] One well-known example is a 2003 study in which researchers reported a significant increase in hopefulness among a control group that watched a humorous video compared to a group that did not.[19]

A considerable amount of literature and research on the subject of hope has been produced in the past two and a half decades. As psychologist and renowned hope researcher Charles Snyder has eloquently stated, "A rainbow is a prism that sends shards of multicolored light in various directions. It lifts our spirits and makes us think of what is possible. Hope is the same—a personal rainbow of the mind."[20] Humor is one of those shards of light that can lift our spirits, help us endure what is before us, and imagine possibilities that lie ahead.

Romans 5:1, 3–5 offers a theological context for hope, what we might call Paul's "hope cycle." "Therefore . . . we also boast in our sufferings, knowing that suffering produces endurance, and endurance produces character, and character produces hope, and hope does not disappoint us, because God's love has been poured into our hearts through the Holy Spirit that has been given to us." As an aspect of God's character, humor is part of what the Holy Spirit seeks to pour into our hearts to set in motion a cycle of hope rather than despair.

With respect to *love*, the apostle Paul reminds us, "If I speak in the tongues of mortals and of angels, but do not have love, I am a noisy gong or a clanging cymbal" (1 Cor. 13:1). Humor without love can devolve into mean-spirited sarcasm and cynicism. But when well-intentioned humor is combined with love, relationships are more likely to flourish.

Humor's role has been studied in initial interactions of randomly paired people within controlled situations to see how it affects the forming of relationships.[21] In one experiment, a group of people who did not know each other was introduced and placed in a humorous situation while people in a control group were introduced to one another during a nonhumorous task. Those meeting in the humorous situation reported having a higher sense of closeness and decreased uncertainty with each other than those in the control group reported. As Oscar Wilde notes, "Laughter is not at all a bad beginning for friendship."[22]

Moving from friendship to romantic relationships, research psychologists have found that what is called "affiliative humor"—humor that is not targeting anyone and is focused on generally amusing topics—leads to satisfaction in couples' relationships in harmonious as well as conflictual situations. By contrast, the use of "aggressive humor"—humor that targets others and puts others down—leads to disaffection and dissatisfaction in the relationship and decreased the likelihood of a dispute being resolved in a satisfactory manner.[23]

Avner Ziv has studied humor and its role in marital satisfaction. His work finds that marital satisfaction is related to perception of a partner's humor more than the spouse's own humor. In other words, if you find your spouse funny or think they find you funny (or better yet, both!), your marriage is more likely to make you satisfied.[24] Humor and loving connections among humans are closely related.

Owen remembers a student who had a particularly quick wit and took his senior seminar on applied humor research. She had just started dating someone new and confessed she had broken up with her last two boyfriends because there was no "humor chemistry." Owen came up with the idea of her taking her date to a comedy club to see if he and she laughed at the same jokes, and especially if he laughed at female comedians she appreciated. The experiment seemed to turn out well since she and the man became engaged, then married, and at this writing are still living and laughing together.

We have discussed humor in relation to faith, hope, and love. Finally, what about *joy*? Joy is not identical to humor, though they often walk hand in hand. Joy is a state of mind and heart, neither reducible to emotions nor dependent on circumstances. This kind of joy sustains us in the midst of despair. Says the prophet Nehemiah, "Do not be grieved, for the joy of the LORD is your strength" (8:10). The joy of the Lord is given to us by God, not something we produce from within ourselves.

Theologian, poet, and civil rights activist Howard Thurman offers this eloquent affirmation of the giftedness of joy:

> What is the source of your joy? There are some who are depen-
> dent upon the mood of others for their happiness. . . . There are
> some whose joy is dependent upon circumstances. . . . There are
> some whose joy is a matter of disposition and temperament. . . .
> There are still others who find their joy deep in the heart of their
> religious experience. . . . This is the joy that the world cannot give.
> This is the joy that keeps watch against all the emissaries of sadness
> of mind and weariness of soul. This is the joy that comforts and is
> the companion, as we walk even through the valley of the shadow
> of death.[25]

While joy is a different gift than humor, humor can be an expression of that gift and can in turn enhance it. C. S. Lewis explores this relationship between humor and joy in *The Screwtape Letters*. He presents a correspondence between two devils: Screwtape, an experienced tempter, and his nephew Wormwood. Screwtape is advising Wormwood on how to tempt his assigned human ("the Patient") into sin and hell. The senior demon laments the power of humor and joy to sustain the soul: "Fun is closely related to joy," says Screwtape. There needs to be an element of fun, of joy, of hilarity in the malaise of all the pressures we feel every day. Screwtape calls this dynamic "emotional froth," explaining that the devil does not know the indwelling cause of such joy and that it produces nothing good for hell's agenda. In tempting humans, says Screwtape, emotional froth should always be discouraged.[26]

In his medieval masterpiece *The Divine Comedy*, Dante depicts the residents of hell as experiencing self-love that collapses the soul into a black hole of ambition and insecurity. Hell is a deadly serious place. By contrast, for Dante, the residents of heaven experience the joyous, soul-expansive power of the kind of love that is based on recognition of our own foibles and our need for one another. As Dante exclaimed in approaching the eighth level of heaven, "I seemed to see the Universe alight with a single smile."[27]

A sense of humor, with its companions playfulness and laughter, can contribute to a stubborn joy even in desperate conditions, to heaven in the midst of hell. We see such defiance in Christian martyrs cracking jokes on the way to pyre, rack, and chopping block. In the third century, St. Lawrence, being burned to death on a grill over hot coals, is said to have called out to his executioners, "This side is done. Turn me over and have a bite."[28]

To Ponder

In this discussion of the relation of humor to faith, hope, love, and joy, we have identified several ways humor can function in our lives and, potentially, our sermons. Humor can help us to

—Laugh at our foibles and shortcomings.[29]
—Disrupt rigid social expectations and overseriousness.[30]
—Recognize our need to rely on God.[31]
—Endure painful circumstances with hope and joy.[32]

Which of these statements resonates most with you? Can you think of an example of how it has been true in your life? How you might activate it in a sermon?

HUMOR AS INTRINSIC TO THE CHARACTER OF GOD: GOD HAS A SENSE OF HUMOR!

> Humor is an aspect of divine character . . . and an element of the Apostle Peter's declaration "that you may participate in the divine nature" (2 Pet. 1:4).[33]
> —Theologian Brian Edgar

Being attuned to humor, playfulness, and a sense of the absurd in life around us is a hallmark of a posture in life we call the *comic spirit*. It is also an integral part of the character of God.

It all begins with creation: "God saw everything that [God] had made, and indeed, it was very good" (Gen. 1:31). "Everything" includes humor!

And it doesn't end with creation. God's subsequent interactions with humankind depict one who specializes in the dynamics of reversal and incongruity on which a sense of humor and a comic vision thrive. We meet God, who makes a fine art of overturning human expectations, showing again and again that divine foolishness is wiser than human wisdom, that divine weakness is stronger than human strength. As Paul reminds us, "God chose what is foolish in the world to shame the wise; God chose what is weak in the world to shame the strong; God chose what is low and despised in the world, things that are not, to reduce to nothing things that are . . ." (1 Cor. 1:27–28). Paul draws again on this sense of reversal in the Christ hymn in Philippians (2:4–11). But this view of God's sense of humor as revealed in reversal is not limited to Paul. Luke presents Mary as ecstatically giving prophetic witness to the reversal of status of the weak and the strong in the Magnificat (Luke 1:46–54).

Central to many biblical stories and teachings and to the theological understandings that have grown out of them is the deflation of human pomposity, exaltation through humility, and demotion through arrogance. These are consistent themes that a comic spirit notices and that have characterized comic literature, including parts of the Bible, for centuries. We believe they are at the core of God's character and the divine relationship with humankind.

For example, in the book of Proverbs and in parts of the biblical wisdom literature more broadly,[34] Wisdom, understood as an aspect of the character of God, is personified as a woman, standing at the crossroads, calling young fools and those who are no longer young and ought to know better onto her path of wisdom (Prov. 1:20–33; 8:1–21). As a personification of divine Wisdom she delights playfully in the entire created world and is instrumental in its creation:

> When he marked out the foundations of the earth,
>   then I was beside him, like a master worker;
> and I was daily his delight,
>   rejoicing before him always,
> rejoicing in his inhabited world
>   and delighting in the human race.
> —Proverbs 8:29b–31

The thirty chapters of the book of Proverbs, with its pithy advice on human relationships, personal conduct, and community responsibility, are presented as issuing from Wisdom's lips. And when the Wisdom of God speaks, we learn something from her about God's humor. Wisdom is capable of laughing at our calamity when we do not follow her divine invitation[35] and exposing the folly of human beings who tend to be meddlesome, lazy, lustful, and arrogant.[36]

Early Christians saw similarities between Woman Wisdom at the crossroads calling disciples onto the path of wisdom and Jesus inviting followers to embark on the Way (Matt. 11:28–30; John 14:6). John's Prologue attributes the qualities of Proverbs' Woman Wisdom to the masculine Logos (Word). Matthew equates Jesus with Heavenly

Wisdom (23:34). Paul, describing the cosmological role of Christ in
1 Corinthians 8:6, draws on the vivid picture of Wisdom as contributor to creation in Proverbs 8:22–31ff.[37] Woman Wisdom comes to be
associated with the divine in Jesus, the second person of the Trinity,
and, by some later theologians, with the Holy Spirit.[38]

These connections between Woman Wisdom and Christology mean
that when Jesus as "Wisdom-in-Person"[39] speaks, we learn something
of the humor of the God he represents on earth. Jesus clearly included
humor in his homiletical repertoire. Though the scriptural record does
not present Jesus as a teller of gut-buster jokes, the parables present him
as having a keen sense of the ridiculous. He used a wicked wit to expose
the folly of trusting in wealth, superficial religiosity, and lukewarm dis-
cipleship. He painted absurd scenes of a camel trying to squeeze through
the eye of a needle, putting a lamp under a bushel, putting new wine
into old wineskins, and cleansing the outside of a cup while leaving it
filthy inside. He compared the reign of God to a mustard tree when no
such plant existed. Such parables would have clearly evoked a wry smile
among those attracted to Jesus and anger among his privileged, powerful
adversaries.

Alyce heard of a preaching professor who posed this question on
the first day of class: "Who is the greatest preacher of all time?" After
a silence long enough to become awkward, one brave student raised
her hand and hazarded a guess: "Jesus?" "Correct!" said the professor.
"Next question: Why don't we preach like Jesus?" If we did, in addition
to learning how to preach prophetically and pastorally in new ways, we
would know how to wield humor's power to deflate human pretension
on the way to introducing hearers to the God of humor and joy.

A follow-up question that draws even closer to our subject matter
than "Why don't we preach like Jesus?" is this: Why don't we preach
the God of Jesus? If we did, we would be proclaiming a God who has a
sense of humor! Why don't we preach a God who has a sense of humor?

Psalm 104:26 is a psalm of praise that describes a God who created
all things, all nature and creatures, the skies and the sea, and "Leviathan that [God] formed to sport in it!" A God who formed a giant sea
serpent to sport in the sea has to have a sense of humor—the mental
image alone is worth a smile if not a laugh.

Likewise, it seems God created humans to sport on the land. A God
who created human beings, placing them in a garden and giving them
both free will and the temptation to misuse it, has to have a sense of
mischief and humor. What did God think would happen when those

humans met up with that snake? The scene in Genesis 3 is usually read in terms of the tragic results that come upon the human race. However, the snake redefining disobedience as the legitimate exercise of free will has a comic element. Incongruity, the discrepancy between how we expect or wish things to be and how they are, was born in the garden of Eden! Incongruity, as we shall see, is a key dynamic in humor.

After creation, in one scenario after another, we begin to see God's sense of humor at work. A God who initiated God's covenant with a geriatric couple who conceive and birth a son whose name, Isaac, means laughter has to have a sense of humor.

A God who chooses an obscure group from a backwater region to be God's chosen people has to have a sense of humor. We are reminded of Tevye's sly comment to God from the musical *Fiddler on the Roof:* "I know, I know. We are your chosen people. But, once in a while, can't you choose someone else?"

This God, as casting director for the Bible's odd dramedy, shows what we would call questionable judgment in God's choices of protagonists. People who are too old (Abraham and Sarah), too young (Jeremiah), con artists (Jacob), good-looking but shallow (Saul), dynamic leaders but who don't always think with their brains (David), vulnerable women who survive by any means they can and are disrespected by society (Rahab), a peasant couple from a backwater village (Mary and Joseph), fishermen with no particular education or training, women unlikely to be believed as the first preachers of the Resurrection, archenemies of the gospel (Paul), and on and on.

Over and over again in Scripture, God displays the divine habit of reversing our expectations and upending the status quo. Such a God embodies a keen sense of the incongruity and reversal that are keys to much humor: becoming incarnate in a poor family, unable to provide for God's son in conventional kingly fashion; choosing everyday people as his emissaries; teaching about finders weepers, losers keepers; being executed as a criminal; and, in the resurrection, replacing the expectation of the finality of death with that of life. The Song of Solomon, in describing human love, asserts that "Love is strong as death" (8:6). The resurrection's message at the core of God's comic vision is that divine love is stronger than death. And so is divine humor.

Alyce has personal experience of God's sense of humor: calling a painfully shy adolescent girl (no, this is *not* a lead-in to Mary; this is about Alyce) to the very public vocation she has lived out for the past forty years. She would resent it and call it a cruel use of divine humor if it hadn't turned out to be such a spiritually rewarding, though sometimes harrowing ride. Over the years, Alyce has come to realize she had nothing better to do with her time.

Owen had the opposite experience. It was not that he experienced God's sense of humor in his vocation so much as his own sense of humor helped him experience and find a deeper place for God in his life. He finds humor in most things. He relies on humor in his research, his teaching, and especially in his ethnographic and social impact work to reduce social distance and to learn local meanings. His life focus changed in part due to his (re)reading C. S. Lewis's *Mere Christianity* a decade ago. It was not Lewis's argumentation or theology that grabbed Owen's attention. It was Lewis's style; the trustworthy persona he established through his wit and observations that resonated with Owen. Lewis's style got past Owen's usual analytical and skeptical approach and helped him consider important questions as if posed by a friend. One of the reasons Owen is enthusiastic about this book, *Humor Us!*, is that he believes that people who have the proper combination of a profoundly reflective personal narrative, a hopeful comic vision, and charitably wielded humor are uniquely qualified to take on today's flippant, cynical mindset—which thrives on division and is often expressed through the extremes of egotistical superiority humor. As Lewis describes it, this is "a humor that puts people down as we stand on their heads in triumph."[40]

Earlier we mentioned Psalm 104:26, where we are told that God created the sea and Leviathan to sport in it. The Talmud (*Avodah Zarah* 3b) teaches that God's schedule comprises daily activities assigned to four quarters of the day, including one devoted to "playing with Leviathan"! What a divine example of work-life balance! For the rabbis, playfulness is a fundamental attribute of God. Moreover, Jewish teachings advise human beings committed to realizing a more godly personality to recognize that humor is a vital part of our perception of the world. We do not have to take everything so seriously. The Talmud teaches that God, in divine omniscience, maintains the ultimate "sense of humor."[41]

To Ponder

When the women came to the tomb with spices and ointments in Luke's Gospel, they found the stone rolled away from the tomb and no body inside. Two men in dazzling clothes appeared and asked them, "Why do you look for the living among the dead?" (Luke 24:5). This account epitomizes the reversal at the heart of the gospel, the comic vision of the victory of life over death, faith over fate, hope over despair. Can you think of a way in which you have experienced this comic vision, this dynamic of divine reversal in your life? Or discussed it in a recent sermon?

NOTES

1. Quoted in James Martin SJ's *Between Heaven and Mirth: Why Joy, Humor, and Laughter Are at the Heart of the Spiritual Life* (New York: HarperCollins, 2011), 15.

2. R. Escarpit, *L'humour* (Paris: Presses Universitaires de France, 1963), quoted in *On Humour and the Comic in the Hebrew Bible*, ed. Yehuda T. Radday and Athalya Brenner (Sheffield: Almond Press, 1990), 23.

3. Athalya Brenner, "On the Semantic Field of Humour, Laughter and the Comic in the Old Testament," in *On Humour and the Comic in the Hebrew Bible*, ed. Yehuda T. Radday and Athalya Brenner (Sheffield: Almond Press, 1990), 39. This definition is especially appropriate for this book as its author is a biblical scholar but also, and perhaps more importantly, it largely agrees with field humor studies.

4. Melissa Wanzer, Melanie Booth Butterfield, and Steven Booth Butterfield, "The Funny People: A Source Orientation to the Communication of Humor," *Communication Quarterly* 43, no. 2 (1995): 142–54.

5. William Shakespeare, *Love's Labour's Lost*, act V, scene ii, lines 934–36.

6. Owen Hanley Lynch, "Humorous Communication: Finding a Place for Humor in Communication Research," *Communication Theory* 12, no. 4 (2002): 423–45, https://doi.org/10.1111/j.1468-2885.2002.tb00277.x.

7. John Morreall, "Philosophy of Humor," in *The Stanford Encyclopedia of Philosophy* (Winter 2012 edition), ed. Edward N. Zalta, https://blogs.baruch .cuny.edu/literatureandthebrain/files/2017/01/humor-1.pdf.

8. Evelyn Underhill, *Mysticism: A Study in the Nature and Development of Spiritual Consciousness* (Grand Rapids: Christian Classics Ethereal Library, 1999).

9. Alyce McKenzie, *Novel Preaching: Tips from Top Writers on Crafting Creative Sermons* (Louisville, KY: Westminster John Knox Press, 2010), chaps. 1–3.

10. Owen Hanley Lynch, "Kitchen Antics: The Importance of Humor and Maintaining Professionalism at Work," *Journal of Applied Communication Research* 37, no. 4 (2009): 444–64, https://doi.org/10.1080/00909880903233143; Lynch, "Kitchen Talk: Cooking with Humor: In-Group Humor as Social Organization," *Humor: International Journal of Humor Research* 23 (2010): 127–60, https://doi.org/10.1515/humr.2010.007.

11. Owen Hanley Lynch, *Humorous Organizing: Revealing the Organization as a Social Process* (Saarbrücken: VDM Publishing, 2007); Zachary A. Schaefer and Owen H. Lynch, "Negotiating Organizational Future: Symbolic Struggles in a

Fiscal Crisis," *Journal of Organizational Ethnography* 4, no. 3 (October 12, 2015): 281–305, https://doi.org/10.1108/joe-07-2014-0017.

12. David G. Buttrick, *Homiletic: Moves and Structures* (Philadelphia: Fortress, 1987), 17.

13. Tryon Edwards, *A Dictionary of Thoughts* (United States: F. B. Dickerson Company, 1908), 238. Thomas Wentworth Higginson (1823–1911) was an American Unitarian minister, author, abolitionist, and soldier. He was active in the American abolitionism movement during the 1840s and 1850s, identifying himself with disunion and militant abolitionism. He was a member of the Secret Six who supported John Brown.

14. Conrad Hyers, *And God Created Laughter: The Bible as Divine Comedy* (Atlanta: John Knox Press, 1987), 5.

15. Brian Edgar, *Laughter and the Grace of God: Restoring Laughter to Its Central Role in Christian Spirituality and Theology* (Eugene, OR: Cascade Books, 2019), 19–20.

16. Terry Eagleton, *Humour* (New Haven, CT: Yale University Press, 2019), 42.

17. Reinhold Niebuhr, "Humour and Faith," in *Holy Laughter: Essays on Religion in the Comic Perspective*, comp. Conrad Hyers (New York: Seabury Press, 1969), 140.

18. High-hope individuals are those who remained committed to goals and believe that their circumstances could improve despite the uncertainties and setbacks of life.

19. Alexander P. Vilaythong et al., "Humor and Hope: Can Humor Increase Hope?," *Humor: International Journal of Humor Research* 16, no. 1 (January 4, 2003), https://doi.org/10.1515/humr.2003.006.

20. Charles R. Snyder, "Hope Theory: Rainbows in the Mind," *Psychological Inquiry* 13, no. 4 (October 2002): 240–75, https://doi.org/10.1207/s15327965pli1304_01.

21. Barbara Fraley and Arthur Aron, "The Effect of a Shared Humorous Experience on Closeness in Initial Encounters," *Personal Relationships* 11, no. 1 (March 2004): 61–78, https://doi.org/10.1111/j.1475-6811.2004.00071.x.

22. Oscar Wilde, *The Picture of Dorian Gray* (Leipzig: Bernhard Tauchnitz, 1908), 16.

23. Bethany Butzer and Nicholas A. Kuiper, "Humor Use in Romantic Relationships: The Effects of Relationship Satisfaction and Pleasant versus Conflict Situations," *Journal of Psychology* 142, no. 3 (May 2008): 245–60, https://doi.org/10.3200/jrlp.142.3.245-260.

24. Avner Ziv and Orit Gadish, "Humor and Marital Satisfaction," *Journal of Social Psychology* 129, no. 6 (December 1989): 759–68, https://doi.org/10.1080/00224545.1989.9712084.

25. Howard Thurman, *Deep Is the Hunger: Meditations for Apostles of Sensitiveness*, 1st ed. (Richmond, IN: Friends United Press, 1951), 160–61.

26. C. S. Lewis, *The Screwtape Letters* (London: HarperCollins, 2001), 54.

27. Dante Alighieri, *The Divine Comedy, Paradiso* 27:4–5, quoted in Hyers, *And God Created Laughter*, 6.

28. Martin, *Between Heaven and Mirth*, 72.

29. Humor prods us to step away from our ridiculousness at times and laugh at ourselves. It invites us to laugh together in ways that can help communities build identity and survive hardship.

30. Humor provides a break from the rigidness or monotony of everyday life; our laughter even sometimes temporally immobilizes us. See Wallace L. Chafe, *The Importance of Not Being Earnest: The Feeling behind Laughter and Humor* (Amsterdam: John Benjamins Publishing, 2007), 1–181. Laughter, especially shared laughter, is a signal that the situation, even a tension-filled moment, is not actually dangerous and we are safe to enjoy it with each other. See Peter McGraw and Joel Warner, *The Humor Code: A Global Search for What Makes Things Funny* (New York: Simon and Schuster, 2014).

31. A sense of humor in the context of faith can help us look beyond our foibles and failures to reliance on a forgiving, gracious God.

32. A sense of humor, with its companions playfulness and laughter, can produce a stubborn joy even in desperate conditions.

33. Brian Edgar, *Laughter and the Grace of God: Restoring Laughter to Its Central Role in Christian Spirituality and Theology* (Eugene, OR: Cascade Books, 2019), 4.

34. Two apocryphal books in which wisdom looms large are the Wisdom of Sirach (or Ecclesiasticus) (200–175 BCE) and the Wisdom of Solomon (50 BCE).

35. Woman Wisdom is not all sugar and spice. She promises those who do not heed her call to "laugh at your calamity; / and mock when panic strikes you" (Prov. 1:26).

36. H. J. Flowers, "The Humour of the Book of Proverbs," *Baptist Quarterly* 6, no. 7 (January 1933): 312–17, https://doi.org/10.1080/0005576x.1933.11750289.

37. Alyce M. McKenzie, *Preaching Biblical Wisdom in a Self-Help Society* (Nashville: Abingdon Press, 2002), 170.

38. Leo D. Lefebure, "Sophia: Wisdom and Christian Theology," *Christian Century*, October 19, 1994, 953. See also Ben Witherington III, *Jesus the Sage: The Pilgrimage of Wisdom* (Minneapolis: Fortress Press, 1994), chaps. 1 and 2.

39. Witherington, *Jesus the Sage*, chap. 4.

40. C. S. Lewis, *The Problem of Pain* (Grand Rapids: Zondervan, 2001), 43.

41. Daniel Feldman, "Does God Have a Sense of Humor?," *Jewish Action*, May 23, 2013, https://jewishaction.com/religion/jewish-law/does-god-have-a-sense-of-humor/.

2

Humor as (Uniquely) Human

There is nothing like a gleam of humor to reassure you that a fellow
human being is ticking *inside a strange face.*
—Novelist Eva Hoffman[1]

Our ancient forebears were onto something when they classified the
human being as the "laughing animal." Although the Latin for this clas-
sification is *Homo ridens*, the idea itself goes back further to the fourth
century BCE with the Greek philosopher Aristotle. He considered
laughter to be a specific and crucial characteristic of humans, though by
no means the sole defining characteristic.

Modern scholars have affirmed this ancient view. As we noted in the
previous chapter, anthropologists and biologists have recognized that
humor is universal, in that humorous activity is found in all cultures.[2]
While the capacity for humor is part of our genetic makeup, there are cultural differences in its perception, appreciation, and use.[3] Not all humans,
in part due to cultural influences, think the same things are funny. Both
nature and nurture make us into the laughing animals we are.

"LAUGHING ANIMALS" AND ANIMALS THAT LAUGH

Infants, in all geographical locales and all cultural contexts, smile and
laugh for the first time around three months of age, long before they
learn to say their first word. So regular is this phenomenon that psychologists consider the presence or absence of an infant's smile and
laughter to be an indication of healthy cognitive development or the
lack thereof.[4]

Anyone who has been on a crowded airplane and in the company of an infant knows there is nothing more enjoyable than a baby giggling. On the other hand, it can be quite disagreeable if this same baby begins to wail for the remainder of the flight. This is why the game of peeka-boo can be a high-stakes enterprise in a crowded airplane. This situation illustrates the fact that a baby's laughter is primarily related to surprise or something sudden and unexpected that turns to joy.[5] The sudden expressive face that can elicit a giggle from an infant might also induce a cry. At this stage of life, both responses are natural and involuntary.

A human's laughter, as an involuntary physical response at the stage of infancy, cannot be distinguished from laughter found in other animal species. Biologists have studied the laughter of squirrel monkeys, whose vocal sounds are genetically innate, existing in their species even if raised in isolation from others of their kind.[6] Their vocalizations resemble human laughter. Similarly, laughter can be observed in apes as a physically induced response to tickling.[7] And such behavior is not just found in primates. As any pet owner can tell you, animals have a sense of play and exhibit laughing-type behavior at times. Even lab rats have been found to be ticklish.[8] One can hardly avoid chuckling when imagining a first-year lab assistant being assigned rat-tickling duty and wondering if the joke is on them or the rat.

A number of scholars theorize that humor evolved from mock-aggressive play in prehuman apes, with laughter serving as a play signal. Adolescent apes exhibit a facial expression of baring the teeth in a non-threatening way as a signal of mock aggression clearly understood by all parties as a nonthreatening prelude to chasing and play fighting. Some ethnologists argue that this is the origin of the human (*Homo sapiens*) smile. Ape hooting or "laughter" is a verbal expression of physical enjoyment and sends the message that the play aggression is benign, not to be escalated or misinterpreted as real.

Peter McGraw and others see this play behavior in apes to be evidence of the evolutionary origin of our humor and a support of what is called the *benign violation theory* of humor: that humor is a violation of an expectation that is simultaneously determined to be safe.[9] If they are correct, what we find humorous, like irony, is just a more complex and evolved cognitive form of the same impulse that drives the benign physical violation of ape play.

Humor scholar John Morreall describes the experience of benign violation in this way: we experience something that violates our understanding of how things are supposed to be, but we suspend a negative response (concern for our safety), and enjoy the oddness of what is occurring. Benign violation found in ape play expands to safe violations or oddities of the cognitive, imaginary, and linguistic type.[10]

The reason for mentioning animals laughing in ways similar to infants is to offer evidence of the evolutionary origin of human humor—but the origin only, because humor in humans, as we advance beyond the infancy stage, becomes much more than an involuntary physical response to stimuli. Humans as they age, unlike other animals, develop the capacity to stand back from themselves and their situation enough to develop a sense of humor or a perception of the comical. As Conrad Hyers puts it, "Donkeys can bray, but only humans can laugh. If one has ever ventured to tell a joke to one's dog or cat, . . . one senses the importance of the distinction."[11]

When you laugh at something because you *think* it is funny, that's *cognitive humor*. Such cognitive humor is uniquely and universally human. In evolutionary terms, it is a development that extends beyond the physical response of animals with lesser cognitive abilities or development to an intellectual response of humans with more. In theological terms, it is unique to humanity because we are made in God's image, and there are gifts and responsibilities singular to us. We do not wish to offend any squirrel monkeys that are reading this book, but we contend that, unlike laughter alone, the comic spirit is an exclusively yet universally human trait. We have established that infants laugh, and we don't want to offend any infants reading this book either. But what is of more interest for our purposes is how such laughter is just the beginning of humans finding different things to be humorous for different reasons at different stages of their intellectual development.

STAGES OF HUMOR DEVELOPMENT

Readers may be familiar with Piaget's cognitive development model, which highlights four stages of intellectual growth: sensorimotor (eighteen to twenty-four months), preoperational (two to seven years), concrete operational (seven to eleven years), and formal operational (adolescence through adulthood). Research psychologists have identified four analogous stages for cognitive humor development, in which children follow basic universal stages, and as they develop cognitively and socially, so do their humor appreciation and use.[12]

The first two stages occur between eighteen and thirty-six months and are closely related. The first involves "incongruous action with objects," such as when a child playfully puts a bucket on his head as if it were a hat. The second is related but involves developing language skills a few months later. It involves "incongruence in labeling of objects." At this stage, the child is amused by calling the bucket on his head "macaroni."

When Owen's daughter Caelan was four years old, she would crack up whenever she heard someone say the word "eyeball," regardless of the context. She simply found the word itself amusing, perhaps because the word "eyeball" at face value seems nonsensical (the eye is not a ball). In this response, we can see the beginnings of linguistic play or incongruence of labeling, similar to the stage when preschoolers find it humorous when you call something by a different or silly name.

This wordplay and joke structure blossom into the third stage around the age of three. This stage involves "conceptual incongruity," that is, the twisting or violating of some element of a known concept that is found to be amusing. This is the beginning of finding humor in puns and might be referred to as the knock-knock stage, because children at this age are becoming more skilled and appreciative of wordplay. The same daughter who found "eyeball" to be the height of hilarity as a preschooler, as the model would suggest, progressed to knock-knock jokes shortly thereafter. Before she had mastered puns, she had mastered the rhetorical structure of knock-knock jokes and could create her own. One of her favorites involved using her father's name:

> Knock, knock.
> Who's there?
> Owen.
> Owen who?
> Owen, will you open the door?!

It did not take long for this joke to give way to "Orange you glad I didn't say 'banana'?"

The fourth stage of humor development takes place around the ages of seven to eleven and involves "multiple meaning." In this stage children begin to recognize and appreciate the concept of a paradox, or incongruity, where they find amusement and humor in something that can be interpreted to be one thing and simultaneously mean another, even its opposite. For example, at this stage we can begin to find humor and enjoyment in the famous image (optical illusion) of an old woman and

Figure 2.1

a young woman at same time by William Ely Hill, first published in *Puck*, a humor magazine, in 1916 with the witty title of *My Wife and My Mother-in-Law*.

Humor theory names this fourth stage as the culmination of humor development, but we know that human facility with humor continues to grow long after we have reached the age of eleven. Yet such growth is really just variation on the theme of the fourth stage. Our ability to recognize and play with multiple meanings for the sake of amusement becomes more and more sophisticated. As we mature, humor also comes to serve purposes beyond amusement. A child learns, plays, and develops a sense of humor, and it becomes an important part of one's personality as an adult—how they see and make sense of the world and become a unique, yet social person, a paradox in itself. Indeed, as noted earlier, as humans age we develop the capacity to stand back from ourselves or situations in which we find ourselves and recognize incongruity in them and the multiple ways we can make sense of it. This capacity provides amusement but also helps us cope with incongruity in life and the world.

For example, Owen has a friend who is a coach. He supported and championed his wife's career but confessed to Owen that he often wished that she just wasn't as successful as she was. He recognized the incongruous nature of the jealous feelings since he loved her and wanted the best for her, and he felt tremendous guilt. Owen's initial response to his friend was to tell him a classic Catskill joke: "There are two elderly women in a Catskill resort. One of them says, 'The food here is terrible.' The other responds, 'Yeah, I know, and such small portions!'" Owen and his friend both laughed; the joke relieved the tension, and they transitioned into a discussion of the ways that life and especially relationships are full of contradictions and opposing impulses or feelings. The discussion was loaded with humor as well as serious self-reflection. Finally, the coach compared his situation to one of his players being happy for the win but wishing they had gotten to score the winning goal. Owen agreed and told him he used to say the same thing to his soccer coach, until his coach reminded him that he was the goalie!

Owen's friend recognized his ego-based feeling was natural and was able to laugh at himself and his own failings versus feeling debilitating guilt. Also, by using humor he was able to relate to the players he coached whose feelings he saw as natural and part of team sports and, to the right degree, healthy. Owen used humor to help him empathize with his friend and to be able to discuss with his friend the same essential lessons we could learn from cognitive dissonance theory and relational dialectics. Absurd, multiple meanings and contradictions are part of social life. Through humor they are made accessible and relatable.

There is nothing new about this. In the Bible we find the example of Sarah coping with the absurd incongruity of conceiving a child in her nineties with laughter that resolves into God's impossible possibility whom she names "Isaac," which means, "He laughs." As Sarah explains, "God has brought laughter for me; and everyone who hears will laugh with me" (Gen. 21:6).

To Ponder

Think of a recent occasion when you personally experienced contradictory impulses or an incongruous situation that was difficult. Were you able to use humor to make sense of it and resolve the tensions that result from these conflicting impulses? How might you translate such use into homiletical strategies that employ humor, not to deflect from addressing such impulses or situations, but to engage them in deeper ways?

HUMOR ORIENTATION

We have established that humor is uniquely human, yet that a sense of humor is also learned and culturally defined. Communication scholar John Meyer argues that the idea of a person having a "sense of humor" implies that it is all or nothing, that any given individual either has or does not have a sense of humor. It is more accurate to say that different individuals have different degrees of a sense of humor.[13]

By *sense of humor* we mean the degree to which one appreciates humor. We can be sure that different people in the pews will respond to humor in sermons with different levels of appreciation and engagement. Another term, *humor orientation* (HO), refers to the level not only of a person's appreciation (sense) of humor but more markedly to the degree to which a person creates humor. Preachers have different levels of natural ability in creating and using humor homiletically. When we consider humor in sermons, then, it is helpful for preachers to know their own level of humor orientation. HO is a concept developed by Melanie and Steve Booth-Butterfield[14] and is meant to describe how often one engages in humor creation and seeks out humorous social interactions as part of making their way in the world.

To measure a person's HO, the Booth-Butterfields created a questionnaire examining one's communication competency and willingness to engage in humor in everyday situations. The questionnaire focuses on how funny one thinks others consider them to be and then places the person on a continuum from low HO to high HO.

People with high HO naturally have a high humor appreciation (sense of humor) but not all people with high humor appreciation report having a high HO (creation of humor).[15] Owen's business partner, for example, is easy to make laugh and appreciates Owen's humor (well, most of it!). Owen's partner has a strong sense of humor (appreciation for humor). However, he does not often create humor on his own and thus scores lower on the HO scale. Owen, by contrast, has a high appreciation of humor, as seen, for example, in his ethnographic work where as a participatory action researcher he is drawn to study the way humor functions in various groups, which have included chefs, ex-felons on parole, middle school teachers, the homeless, and paramedics. His ability to appreciate their unique and diverse humor—especially their inside, sometimes edgy humor[16]—demonstrates that he not only "gets the joke" but is open to learning their in-group sensemaking processes.[17] But he also has a high HO, using humor frequently to amuse his spouse (or attempt to), empathize with his friends, and teach his students.

Preachers should value and aim for having a high HO for a number of reasons. Researchers have demonstrated a correlation between high HO and conversational and nonverbal competency, meaning that people who have high HOs are likely to put people at ease and get them talking more freely.[18] Similarly, people in positions of authority (e.g., physicians) with high HOs have been shown to be perceived as more credible by those with whom they communicate (e.g., patients).[19]

It's encouraging to know that one's humor orientation is not set in stone. Humor production is a complex cognitive skill, but people can *learn* to be situational high HOs when they speak to others, whether in teaching, making business pitches, or preaching.[20] In other words, low or moderate HOs can learn to "pick their spots and act funnier than they really are" to serve specific purposes.[21]

Our intention in this book is to help preachers increase their HO by urging them to use a comic mode or frame as a lens for viewing the world, to work on developing a knack for noticing humor in everyday situations and Scripture, and to experiment with communicating that humor to others, especially in sermons.

To Ponder

Complete the questionnaire and score your own humor orientation. If you are really brave, then have someone you know well (and can forgive easily) score you.

1. Strongly Disagree 2. Disagree 3. Neutral 4. Agree 5. Strongly Agree

___1. I regularly tell jokes and funny stories when in a group.

___2. People usually laugh when I tell jokes or funny stories.

___3. I have no memory for jokes or funny stories.

___4. I can be funny without having to rehearse a joke.

___5. Being funny is a natural communication style with me.

___6. I cannot tell a joke well.

___7. People seldom ask me to tell stories.

___8. My friends would say I am a funny person.

___9. People don't seem to pay close attention when I tell a joke.

___10. Even funny jokes seem flat when I tell them.

___11. I can easily remember jokes and stories.

___12. People often ask me to tell jokes or stories.

___13. My friends would not say that I am a funny person.

___14. I don't tell jokes or stories even when asked to.

___15. I tell stories and jokes very well.

___16. Of all the people I know, I am one of the funniest.

___17. I use humor to communicate in a variety of situations.

Scoring: After administering, recode (reverse score) items 3, 6, 7, 9, 10, 13, 14; then sum (add all 17) and then average (divide by 17).

High HO = 5–4.1
Medium HO = 4.0–3.1
Low HO = 3.0–2.1
No HO = 2.0–1.0

NOTES

1. Eva Hoffman, *Exit into History: A Journey through the New Eastern Europe* (London: Faber & Faber, 2014), 113.

2. Mahadev L. Apte, *Humor and Laughter: An Anthropological Approach* (Ithaca, NY: Cornell University Press, 1985); William F. Fry, "The Biology of Humor," *Humor: International Journal of Humor Research* 7, no. 2 (1994), https://doi.org/10.1515/humr.1994.7.2.111.

3. Guo-Hai Chen and Rod A. Martin, "A Comparison of Humor Styles, Coping Humor, and Mental Health between Chinese and Canadian University Students," *Humor: International Journal of Humor Research* 20, no. 3 (January 21,

2007), https://doi.org/10.1515/humor.2007.011; Rod A. Martin and Thomas Ford, *The Psychology of Humor: An Integrative Approach* (Burlington, MA: Academic Press, 2018).

4. Caspar Addyman and Ishbel Addyman, "The Science of Baby Laughter," *Comedy Studies* 4, no. 2 (January 2013): 143–53, https://doi.org/10.1386/cost.4.2.143_1.

5. John Morreall, *Taking Laughter Seriously* (Albany: State University of New York Press, 1983), 41.

6. Uwe Jürgens, "Neuronal Control of Mammalian Vocalization, with Special Reference to the Squirrel Monkey," *Science of Nature* 85, no. 8 (August 1998): 376–88, https://doi.org/10.1007/s001140050519.

7. Marina Davila Ross, Michael J. Owren, and Elke Zimmermann, "Reconstructing the Evolution of Laughter in Great Apes and Humans," *Current Biology* 19, no. 13 (July 2009): 1106–11, https://doi.org/10.1016/j.cub.2009.05.028.

8. Brigitte Osterath, "Playful Rats Reveal Brain Region That Drives Ticklishness," *Nature*, November 10, 2016, https://doi.org/10.1038/nature.2016.20973.

9. Peter McGraw and Joel Warner, *The Humor Code: A Global Search for What Makes Things Funny* (New York: Simon and Schuster, 2014).

10. Our understanding of the link between the study of animals, specifically chimpanzees' behavior and signaling, and the possible link to current human humor communication and behavior is much informed by John Morreall's writings. See, e.g., "It's a Funny Thing, Humor," *Philosophy of Humor Yearbook* 1, no. 1 (2020): 33–48.

11. Conrad Hyers, *And God Created Laughter: The Bible as Divine Comedy* (Atlanta: John Knox Press, 1987), 17.

12. Doris Bergen, "Development of the Sense of Humor," in *The Sense of Humor: Explorations of a Personality Characteristic*, ed. Willibald Ruch (Berlin: De Gruyter Mouton, 2010), 329–58, https://doi.org/10.1515/9783110804607-016; Paul E. Mcghee and Mary Frank, *Humor and Children's Development: A Guide to Practical Applications* (New York: Routledge, 2014).

13. John Meyer, *Understanding Humor through Communication: Why Be Funny, Anyway?* (Lanham, MD: Lexington Books, 2015), 51.

14. Steven Booth-Butterfield and Melanie Booth-Butterfield, "Individual Differences in the Communication of Humorous Messages," *Southern Communication Journal* 56, no. 3 (September 1991): 205–18, https://doi.org/10.1080/10417949109372831.

15. Booth-Butterfield and Booth-Butterfield, "Individual Differences in the Communication of Humorous Messages."

16. This is *resistance humor*, usually aimed at the monotonous, nonsensical, or stressful conditions of work and social life. Sometimes it is directed at authority or restrictions in one's life (especially, for example, with those on parole) or at the overwhelming aspects of a certain occupation's day (like paramedics).

17. Owen Lynch, "Cooking with Humor: In-Group Humor as Social Organization," *Humor: International Journal of Humor Research* 23, no. 2 (January 2010), https://doi.org/10.1515/humr.2010.007.

18. Andy J. Merolla, "Decoding Ability and Humor Production," *Communication Quarterly* 54, no. 2 (June 2006): 175–89, https://doi.org/10.1080/01463370600650886.

19. Melissa Bekelja Wanzer, Melanie Booth-Butterfield, and Kelly Gruber, "Perceptions of Health Care Providers' Communication: Relationships between Patient-Centered Communication and Satisfaction," *Health Communication* 16, no. 3 (July 2004): 363–84, https://doi.org/10.1207/s15327027hc1603_6.

20. E.g., see Melanie Booth-Butterfield and Melissa Bekelja Wanzer, "Humor Enactment in Learning Environments," in *Communication and Learning*, ed. Paul Witt (Berlin: De Gruyter Mouton, 2016), 211–39.

21. Steve Booth-Butterfield, "The Humor Orientation Scale: Original 17-Item Version," Persuasion Blog, July 17, 2009, http://healthyinfluence.com/wordpress/2009/07/17/the-humor-orientation-scale-original-17-item-version/.

3

Shaped in God's Image

Humor and the *Imago Dei*

A sense of humor is the only divine quality of man [*sic*].
  —German philosopher Arthur Schopenhauer
  (1788–1860)[1]

Humor is mankind's [*sic*] greatest blessing.
  —Writer, humorist, publisher, and lecturer
  Mark Twain (1835–1910)[2]

In the Hebrew Scriptures we learn that human beings are made in the image of God: "Then God said, 'Let us make humankind in our image, according to our likeness" (Gen. 1:26). Then God "formed man [*adam*, the human one] from the dust of the ground, and breathed into his nostrils the breath of life; and the man became a living being" (Gen. 2:7).

Theologians have devoted much time to the question of what it means to be created in the image and likeness of God. They have said very little, however, about humor and laughter in relation to that image.

HUMOR AS GOD'S GIFT

Theologian Brian Edgar, in his book *Laughter and the Grace of God*, seeks to correct that omission. Says Edgar, "The universality of humor, as an essential aspect of the person, is connected with the *imago Dei*. To be human is to be humorous and this humor is, along with all aspects of the person, to be redeemed and a part of the future eschatological life."[3]

In the biblical account of Eden, God set us in a veritable garden of gifts: nature's beauty and bounty, sexuality, companionship, food and drink, to name a few. When setting us in that garden, God also gave us the gift of free will. The rabbis taught that within the heart of the human being reside both the evil inclination (*yetzer harah*) and the good inclination (*yetzer tov*). Clearly, we have a pattern of using God's good gifts for selfish ends that separate us from one another and from God. Theologians throughout the centuries have attributed our human tendency to misuse the good gifts of God to original sin, labeling the eviction from the garden of Eden the fall of humankind.

Conrad Hyers says the fall includes the "fall of humor." He explains, "The fall is, if anything, the loss of laughter, not the loss of seriousness. Adam and Eve fell when they began to take themselves, their 'deprivations,' and their ambitions too seriously."[4]

In his book *Between Heaven and Mirth: Why Joy, Humor, and Laughter Are at the Heart of Spiritual Life,* Jesuit priest Father James Martin tells of how he went around making talks about his first book, a look at twenty saints who had shaped his life. He discovered that what drew audiences to his talks was not so much an interest in hagiography as it was the emphasis on joy.[5] Says Martin, "Many professional religious people . . . as well as some devout believers in general give the impression that being religious means being dour, serious, or even grumpy . . . but the lives of the saints, as well as those of great spiritual masters from almost every other religious tradition, show the opposite. Holy people are joyful. Why? Because holiness brings us closer to God, the source of all joy."[6]

Humor, in the right hands used for the right reasons, can foster joy. Understanding humor as a gift from God to human beings, who are crafted in God's image, we ask, why on earth would we ignore such a gift? New Testament scholar Stephen Patterson draws a portrait of God as One who both gives all and demands all.[7] We are to acknowledge, with Paul, "What do you have that you did not receive?" (1 Cor. 4:7). At the same time, we are to love God and neighbor with all we've got: heart, soul, mind, and strength. From this we can infer that God as creator and gifter of the capacity for humor expects us to use it. Thomas Aquinas, viewing humor as a solace for the spirit, regarded a reluctance to engage in it as tantamount to a vice.[8]

While rabbinic teaching occasionally endorses an ascetic of self-discipline, this counterbalancing perspective also appears: "A person will have to answer for everything that his eye beheld and he did not consume."[9] That may not be an excuse to break open that package of Double Stuf OREOs and eat them all. Rather, it is a nudging reminder that the good things God has created—in this case, humor opportunities—are not to be wasted. Humorlessness is not pleasing to God. Homiletician Fred Craddock writes, "Art is not a gift which a few people are given, but rather it is a gift which most people throw away."[10] I think he would approve of our creating a variation of his saying: "Humor is not a gift which a few preachers are given, but rather it is a gift which many preachers throw away."

In his study of the humor of the saints, Father Aloysius Roche concludes that their expression of humor is a divine gift. "Wisdom is from above, and it is the gift of the Holy Spirit; and humor is part and parcel of wisdom." For Roche, the union of the natural gift of humor and the supernatural gift of faith produces the optimistic joy of the saints.[11]

John Morreall, author of several works on religion and the comic spirit, asserts, "If we collected all the books of Christian theology, excised the handful of pages that even mentioned humor, and sent the collection to Mars, Martian readers would never figure out that the human race was capable of laughter."[12]

Your authors are on a mission to correct this humor omission, at least in terms of the pulpit. But we are not promoting just any humor or laughter. Humor can be whatever we make it. Like any good gift of God after Eden, it can be used for good or ill. Humor can and has been used to trivialize serious experiences, put others down, and scapegoat entire social groups. But in contrast to such "fallen laughter,"[13] humor in the context of the comic vision, used in keeping with the character and purposes of God, can be used to invite us to acknowledge the delightful ridiculousness of much of our human behavior, to challenge an unjust status quo, and to deal with complex issues so that they do not become overwhelming. It can foster compassion and a sense of common humanity. It can instigate positive individual and communal action. As Susan Sparks, a Baptist pastor, stand-up comedian, and author of several books on humor, puts it, "When I say humor, I am referring to joyful, therapeutic humor; humor that lifts us up. I am not speaking of scornful, hateful, or judgmental humor. Certainly humor can be misused. So can sanctity."[14]

We seek to give humor the job description its talents deserve and the title that fits its status. Its job description is no longer "to be a condiment sprinkled over the sermon." Its title is no longer "entertainer" or "distracter." Its new job description is "conveyer of the core message [entrée] of the gospel," and its new title is "gift from God."

Alyce went to a funeral recently. It lasted from 2 p.m. to 3:45 p.m. There were several testimonials. There were two meditations by two different pastors. There were three Scripture readings. There was extensive congregational singing of numerous praise songs. We preachers are taught in seminary worship courses that the focus of the Christian funeral and the funeral sermon is the gift of eternal life that a loving God offers humankind. It needs to lift up the identity of the deceased, as a beloved child of God both in their earthly life and in the ongoing life they now live with God. An exclusive focus on specific qualities of the deceased, whether positive or negative, can hijack the service and the sermon.

The focus of this almost-two-hour-long funeral was the deceased person's sense of humor. Several relatives and friends shared anecdotes of how John's humor had cheered them up, helped them put their problems in perspective, and diffused conflict at family holidays. Some repeated his favorite jokes. Others gave accounts of pranks and shenanigans in which they had participated with him. There was, to be fair, a passing mention of his faith as shown in his commitment to his family. But for Alyce, something was lacking in all of this. She wanted somebody, she didn't care who—daughter, brother, sister, pastor, friend—somebody, anybody to go to the podium, pick up the microphone, and say, "John's sense of humor and joy in life were a gift from God!" She wanted somebody to articulate the subtext: that John's sense of humor was made in the image of God's sense of humor, that John's use of humor in his dealings with family and friends was a channel for God's forgiveness and joy." She wanted somebody to give credit where credit is due! That sentiment is the golden thread of this book: an invitation to preachers to appreciate and activate our sense of humor, recognizing from whom it comes and on whose behalf we are to exercise it, giving credit where credit is due.

To Ponder

—Have you ever thought of your own sense of humor as a gift from God?
—Can you think of an example of you or someone you observed using humor in a negative way that distorted God's good gift? Describe the scenario and the impact the use of humor had. Recall our discussion of *The Divine Comedy* by Dante in the first chapter. For Dante hell on earth could be humor as self-love that collapses the soul into a black hole of ambition and insecurity. By contrast, consider how humor could express heaven on earth.
—Can you think of an example of you or someone you observed using humor in a positive way that faithfully exhibited the imago Dei? Describe the scenario and the impact the use of humor had.

HUMOR AS GOD'S GIFT TO THE SERMON

I was thinking about how people seem to read the Bible a whole lot more as they get older; then it dawned on me. . . . They're cramming for their final exam.
    —Comedian George Carlin (1937–2008)[15]

Sermons are like biscuits. They could all do with a little shortening.
    —Anonymous

Every semester in her Introduction to Preaching class Alyce offers students a list of "Top Ten Homiletical Proverbs." They are not, strictly speaking, proverbs. Proverbs are, by definition, anonymous, and she admits to having made up most of these. She thinks the students may be onto her, but they play along. One of the "proverbs" is "The Holy Spirit is available for consultation at times other than Saturday night." That is to say that throughout the whole process of sermon preparation, delivery, and reception, God is available and active, not that God will do all the work (despite Luke 12:12!).[16] She quickly offers a second "proverb": "Preparation is a sign of respect for your congregation." (She points out that the reverse is also true.)

Taken together, these two sayings convey both the availability of God and the responsibility of human beings: the initiative of God in preaching (for preaching is, first and foremost, a gift from God) and the crucial response of a human being bringing their whole selves to the scholarly, prayerful preparation. That includes one's sense of humor.

As humor is a divine gift generally speaking, it is certainly a gift from God for preaching. Preachers differ in their understanding of the interaction of divine and human in the preaching event, but there is widespread agreement that when we preach we are not just providing information about God but inviting listeners into relationship with God and that God's presence undergirds and pervades the sermonic process from preparation to embodiment (delivery) and beyond.

That doesn't translate into a guarantee that when preachers speak, they utter the verbatim words of God. What can be said about humor as a double-edged sword can be said about preaching as well—it is a gift that can be abused. We understand the "Word of God" as a metaphor for the self-communication of God, not as a literal reference to the verbatim speech of God. This means that the preacher can, at times, preach against the text, and that the Holy Spirit can, at times, preach against the preacher! To use a historical example, while the master's preacher was preaching, "Slaves, be obedient to your masters," the Holy Spirit was preaching, "Let my people go." And while the preacher was preaching, "Women shall keep silent in church," a woman in the pews that day was discerning a call to preach!

Preachers respond to the opportunity to share in the divine creative power of speech by offering our whole selves to the sermonic process. Philips Brooks, in the Lyman Beecher Lectures to faculty and students at what was then the Divinity School at Yale College in 1877, defined preaching as "truth through personality." As homiletician Jana Childers says, "His Lyman Beecher lectures at Yale called upon preachers to attend to their innards—to let the truth of God invade them. Says Brooks, 'the truth must really come through a person, not merely over his [sic] lips, not merely into his understanding and out of his pen. It must come through his character—his affections—his whole intellectual and moral being.'"[17]

It is inspiring when a preacher prays before a sermon, "Lord, help me get out of the way so your Word can be heard." But at the same time, those sitting in the pews might start checking out the red exit signs over all the doors, thinking, *Where else does the preacher have to go?* Wouldn't an even better prayer be, "Lord, help me to place everything I am and have *in your way* so You can use it to communicate with the congregation"? That includes my intellect, emotions, experiences, personality, struggles, and most certainly my God-given capacity for discerning and using the gift of humor. Christian preachers affirm that preaching is a sui generis form of communication in which God's promised divine presence interacts with the response of human preachers in their congregational/cultural context, and their preparation.

That response entails offering to God our whole selves, but also honoring the full selves of the human beings who hear our sermons; that includes their sense of humor. In the last quarter of the twentieth century a paradigm shift occurred in preaching called the New Homiletic, characterized by a turn toward the experience of the hearer. It criticized traditional preaching as being too heady and predictable to gain and maintain listener interest. It pointed out that deductive preaching's monological quality reduced the congregation to recipients of the preacher's ideas rather than inviting them to be participants in the communication process. Fred Craddock, whose book *As One without Authority* (1971) jump-started the New Homiletic, famously remarked that traditional propositional preaching reduced the congregation to javelin catchers for the preacher's ideas.[18]

Traditional preaching was deductive, moving from general to specific. It most often took the form of what has become known as the three-points-and-a-poem sermon. The preacher stated the conceptual theme of the sermon at the beginning and broke it down into conceptual sub-themes. The comic equivalent would be starting a joke with the punch line and then narrating the setup to show why it was funny. By contrast, the New Homiletic favored an inductive approach, in which the preacher began with the particulars of experience, whether from the Bible or contemporary life, and built toward the reveal at the end, leaving room for listeners' interpretations along the way and, at times, leaving the conclusion up to the listener. It encouraged preachers to take into account the experience of listeners in crafting their sermons. At the same time, it broke the rule that preachers weren't to share their own personal experiences and struggles from the pulpit. Forms of preaching that tapped into our innate love of stories began to proliferate, incorporating suspense, imagery, and plot.[19] This included new uses of humor in preaching.

In Alyce and Owen's discussions related to this project, Owen made the chronological observation that scholars began to give more respect to humor and study it for its role in social, linguistic, and psychological contexts in the last quarter of the twentieth century. Since this corresponds to the time in which the New Homiletic arose, Alyce began to wonder if the chronological simultaneity of the rising interest in humor and the New Homiletic was more than coincidence.[20] Was there some connection between the New Homiletic and the recognition of the importance of humor across multiple disciplines? We put this question to homiletician Ronald J. Allen, Professor of Preaching Emeritus at Christian Theological Seminary in Indianapolis, Indiana, in an interview.

In his words, "The New Homiletic didn't cause the resurgence of respect for humor. But it created an environment in which humor was welcome. It brought about a recertification of autobiographical experience in sermons from its neglect or rejection earlier in the twentieth century. Preachers learned that people identified with experiences of incongruity in the preacher's life. More than conveying theological and biblical concepts, the New Homiletic was about creating a redemptive experience for listeners. This involves an overturning of expectations of despair and failure with hope and new beginnings that is at the core of the comic vision."[21]

That redemptive experience, then and now, consists of challenging oppressive convention by celebrating divine grace that overcomes injustice. In offering both challenge and hope, humor has the potential to be an effective sermonic ally. Yet even several decades beyond the early 1970s, humor still is not on every preachers' homiletical toolbar beyond the guaranteed guffaw to open the sermon. Our goal in this study is to bridge the gap between the profound positive potential of humor in the pulpit and its actual use. We want to activate the comic spirit and get humor on preachers' homiletical toolbars, recognizing that, while made in God's image, we are not God and we need divine guidance in using the gift of humor.

Anne-Grethe Krogh Nielsen, who serves the Danish Lutheran Church and Cultural Center of Southern California, points out that humor is related to humility and asserts that their combination is key to preaching. "Humor, like humility, comes from the same root word in Latin for humanity: *humus*. The lowly earth is the source for all three words: humor, humility and humanity."[22]

Made in the image of God (Gen. 1:26–27) gathered up from the dust of the ground (Gen. 2:7), we preachers are humanity, humor, and humility all mixed together. We are called to combine these crucial ingredients in our recipe for humble, humor-filled preaching!

To Ponder

To quote Fred Craddock from an interview he gave in 2016 on the use of humor in preaching, "Humor is the clearest evidence of the grace of God. It brings a sense of freedom and lightness. You can laugh at yourself and others."[23] Can you resonate with this statement and think of an example of yours or someone else's use of humor in this way?

—In everyday life?
—In a recent sermon?

NOTES

1. Daniel Coenn, *Schopenhauer: His Words* (Munich: BookRix, 2014), 11.

2. Albert Bigelow Paine, *Mark Twain: A Biography; the Personal and Literary Life of Samuel Langhorne Clemens*, vol. 3 (Harper & Bros., 1912), 1556.

3. Brian Edgar, *Laughter and the Grace of God: Restoring Laughter to Its Central Role in Christian Faith and Theology* (Eugene, OR: Cascade Books, 2019), 14.

4. Conrad Hyers, *And God Created Laughter: The Bible as Divine Comedy* (Atlanta: John Knox Press, 1987), 14.

5. Hagiography is the study of the important role that hags have played in the history of Christianity. Actually it's the study of the lives and contributions of the saints. But you knew that.

6. James Martin, SJ, *Between Heaven and Mirth: Why Joy, Humor, and Laughter Are at the Heart of the Spiritual Life* (New York: HarperCollins, 2011), 2–3.

7. Stephen J. Patterson, *The God of Jesus: The Historical Jesus and the Search for Meaning* (Harrisburg, PA: Trinity Press International, 1999).

8. Terry Eagleton, *Humour* (New Haven, CT: Yale University Press, 2019), 95.

9. Jerusalem Talmud, Kiddushin 4:12.

10. Fred B. Craddock, *Overhearing the Gospel: Preaching and Teaching the Faith to Persons Who Have Already Heard*, rev. and exp. ed. (St. Louis: Chalice Press, 2002), 13.

11. Aloysius Roche, *A Bedside Book of Saints* (Manchester, NH: Sophia Institute Press, 2005), 69–76.

12. John Morreall, *Comedy, Tragedy, and Religion* (Albany: State University of New York Press, 1999), 118. Other works by Morreall include *Taking Laughter Seriously* (Albany: State University of New York Press, 1983) and *The Philosophy of Laughter and Humor* (Albany: State University of New York Press, 1986).

13. Hyers, *And God Created Laughter*, 15.

14. Susan Sparks, *Laugh Your Way to Grace: Reclaiming the Spiritual Power of Laughter* (Skylight Paths Publishing, 2010), xxv.

15. "Classic George Carlin Jokes," *New York Daily News*, June 23, 2008, https://www.nydailynews.com/news/national/classic-george-carlin-jokes-article-1.297138.

16. "Do not worry about . . . what you are to say; for the Holy Spirit will teach you at that very hour what you ought to say."

17. Philips Brooks, *Lectures on Preaching* (Grand Rapids: Baker Book House, 1969), 8. Quoted in Jana Childers, *Purposes of Preaching* (St. Louis: Chalice Press, 2004), 45.

18. Fred B. Craddock, *As One without Authority: Fourth Edition Revised and with New Sermons* (St. Louis: Chalice Press, 2001), 46. In their book *Preaching and the Thirty-Second Commercial: Lessons from Advertising from the Pulpit* (Louisville, KY: Westminster John Knox Press, 2021), Carrie La Ferle and O. Wesley Allen describe an analogous turn toward the consumer in advertising in response to a cultural shift toward multidirectional and receiver-oriented communication models.

19. For a brief history of the New Homiletic and an overview of its major initial voices, see O. Wesley Allen, *The Renewed Homiletic* (Minneapolis: Fortress Press, 2010), 1–18.

20. Around this time feminist biblical scholars and historians began to object to the dearth of recorded traditions about women's use of humor throughout history and to articulate its power to subvert oppressive gender roles.

21. Zoom interview with Dr. Ronald J. Allen, December 10, 2021.

22. Anne-Grethe Krogh Nielsen, "Pastor—The Danish Lutheran Church and Cultural Center of Southern California," https://www.danishchurchsocal .com/pastor.

23. From interview with Bill Turpie at the 2008 Festival of Homiletics on "The Use of Humor in Preaching," Day1DotOrg, "Dr. Fred Craddock on Using Humor and Emotion in Sermons," YouTube, June 17, 2008, https://www .youtube.com/watch?v=bT1DA-e2nos.

PART TWO

The Sermon and the Comic Spirit

4

Adding Humor to Our Homiletical Toolbox

Positive Benefits of Humor

The most wasted day of all days is one without laughter.
—American poet, playwright, and essayist
e. e. cummings (1894–1962)[1]

When Alyce was growing up in New Cumberland, a small town on the Susquehanna River in Central Pennsylvania, her parents expected that she and her three siblings would attend church weekly at Baughman Memorial Methodist Church. And by "expected" they meant "required." She didn't put up much of a fight. She enjoyed sitting several pews from the front and looking all around, gazing at the stained-glass window portrayal of the ascension (*Why was Jesus barefooted?*), noting the height of Mrs. Apgar's beehive hairdo (*How much hairspray did that take?*), wondering what the people who seemed to be listening raptly to the sermon were really thinking about, and whether the preacher lived in the sanctuary all week, wearing that Alvin and the Chipmunks robe and sleeping behind the altar. The moment in the service that was most awe-inspiring to her was when the preacher stepped into the pulpit and, as the house lights were dimmed, the ceiling spotlight over his head went on. And he was lit up! In her shallower moments, she has wondered if her call to ministry doesn't boil down to her desire to be the one who gets to be lit up![2]

We're way into the twenty-first century now. Jesus is still in mid-air, his bare feet still not touching the ground. But that's about all that's the same in many congregations. The preacher may well not be standing in a pulpit. They may be wearing skinny jeans, a tunic top and boots, or khakis and a button-down. Mrs. Apgar may well have been replaced by a praise band.

The congregation(s) is different, too. In surveying the congregation, both those who are physically present and those who are watching the livestream, a preacher can assume that not everyone is listening raptly to the sermon. Instead they may be texting, or checking scores or the latest promo codes for the new running shoes they are waiting to go on sale. Their (our) attention spans have shortened due to their (our) online searching habits, consisting of bursts of attention for information gathering. They (we) are losing the ability to follow a sustained train of thought related to any one subject.[3]

Even those who are listening are listening with varying degrees of internal acceptance. Preachers who have read even a couple of articles about postmodernism's effect on contemporary religion are aware that many of the people before them have shifted from seeing themselves as receivers of truths handed down by authoritative public figures and institutions to regarding themselves as co-creators of meaning gained from their own experience.

Clearly, preachers need strategies that engage listeners in communication both with the speaker and one another in the preaching event. In the words of O. Wesley Allen and Carrie La Ferle, authors of the first volume in this Preaching and . . . series, *Preaching and the Thirty-Second Commercial: Lessons from Advertising for the Pulpit*, "In today's world, audiences must be engaged as participants and co-creators of meaning if they are going to take communications . . . directed to them seriously and build a relationship with communicators."[4]

These challenges make underestimating humor, with its ability to engage and invite the audience to participate through laughter, even more unwise. It's going to take every sermonic strategy at our disposal, every tool in our homiletical toolbox, to reach congregations (both physical and virtual), of experientially oriented, authority-suspicious, serial-tasking, often biblically untutored listeners.[5] And that includes humor in the context of the comic vision/spirit! In addition to gaining and keeping the audience's attention, humor in sermons can provide diverse benefits for many aspects of human life, as demonstrated in research from a wide array of social sciences and humanities.

RESEARCH ON THE BENEFITS OF HUMOR

As the following review demonstrates, the ability to discern and use humor is a basic skill for a happy and productive life.[6]

As we have noted previously, humor is a double-edged sword. It should come as no surprise, then, that only appropriate and effective humor earns us respect and positive benefits. Used positively, humor can unite groups of people, be used to construct and maintain our social and professional identity,[7] and elevate our well-being and life satisfaction.[8] Let us consider some specifics.

Humor benefits our physical health. Engaging in humor and specifically laughter strengthens our immune system. Humor relaxes muscles and burns calories.[9] Indeed, humor has even been shown to help us recover from illness and heal faster.[10]

Humor helps us stay mentally sharp as we age. Engaging in humor is especially important as we age for the physical and social benefits mentioned earlier. Also, active humor use has benefits for maintaining cognitive acuity as we age.[11]

Humor is related to healthy cognitive and social development. Many studies link healthy cognitive and social development in children with humor, as well as examine the advancement of verbal and nonverbal humor in relation to typical versus atypical development.[12]

Humor enhances our emotional intelligence and relationships. A strong sense of humor is shown on multiple levels to be an "engaging personality trait" that has direct implications for social relationships.[13]

Humor fosters creativity. There is a significant positive relationship between high humor orientation and sense of humor and an individual's creativity in other areas.[14]

Humor can help us be open to new perspectives. A significant relationship has been proved between active humor use and critical and innovative thinking.[15] This creative thinking and problem solving also translate to the workplace and organizational behavior.[16]

Humor can be a means of coping with the unexpected and staying the course through tough times. Humor is a key aspect of an individual's ability to roll with the punches, to accept and even to enjoy incongruity and to be flexible. People with a high sense of humor are far more likely to enjoy and even seek out ambiguity.[17] This trait has a positive effect on building social relations, in work advancement, and in leadership.[18] It can reduce the likelihood of burnout in stressful and unpredictable environments.[19]

Humor benefits the classroom experience, improving student learning. Students learn more from a teacher whom they rate as funny.[20] Humorous teachers are more liked by their students and are given credibility.[21]

Humor improves speaker credibility and likability. While humor in sermons has, until recently, only been researched sparsely, research abounds with regard to its use in public speaking in general. Humor in speeches makes them both more interesting and more likely to capture attention.[22] It also leads an audience to retain information longer.[23] Similar to classroom teachers, speakers who use humor effectively increase their persuasiveness[24] by enhancing their credibility and likeability.[25]

This pile-up of humor's positive effects reminds your authors of an article on the benefits of walking.[26] So many benefits, so little time!

To Ponder

—Which of the benefits of humor could be most helpful to you in preaching sermons that help you relate to your listeners and motivate them to respond in some way?

—Discuss how effective, audience-appropriate humor could help you relate to your listeners and preach sermons that are clear and also motivate listeners to respond in some way.

THE KEY TO EFFECTIVE SERMONIC HUMOR USE: KNOW YOUR AUDIENCE

For everything there is a season, and a time for every matter under heaven. ·
    —Ecclesiastes 3:1

A word fitly spoken
    is like apples of gold in a setting of silver.
—Proverbs 25:11

In the next chapter (chapter 5) we offer a series of strategies, with examples, for harnessing these humor benefits for contemporary sermons. But first, a few ground rules for the use of sermonic humor and a cautionary tale or two. The focus of sermonic humor use needs not to be on the preacher, on what the preacher thinks is funny, or on the preacher's need to be perceived as funny. We need to be honest with ourselves about our motivation for using humor and sometimes acknowledge and suppress our craving for cleverness! The focus needs to be on the listener: who the listeners are, what they need, and how humor can assist us preachers in getting the good news heard by these particular people in this particular congregation on this particular occasion. Keeping the focus on the needs of the hearers can prevent several misuses of humor in sermons, such as trivializing profound truths,[27] using humor to compensate for lack of substantive content, and using humor (inadvertently) to belittle or exclude some listeners or groups. Preacher and author Will Willimon highlights two key guidelines for the use of humor in sermons: the effects need to be congruent with the purposes of Christian preaching, and the liturgical, congregational context needs to be honored.[28]

Humor is highly contextual. Its impact, positive or negative, depends on timing, the surrounding circumstances, and the audience to whom the humor is offered. The concept of *kairos*, a governing principle of persuasive speech, refers to the right time for the right word. Wrong humor at the wrong time in a sermon can make the proclamation of the gospel fall flat or even seem inappropriate or offensive. Homiletician Nora Tisdale advises preachers to engage in congregational exegesis as well as biblical exegesis so that their sermons are not only faithful to the text but fitting to the congregation.[29] In activating the comic spirit in our preaching, we need to consider the needs of audience members, their level of humor orientation and appreciation, and the specifics of the occasion. All these factors will determine humor's timeliness, appropriateness, and effectiveness.[30]

There are, of course, occasions where humor is not appropriate. As Mark Twain is purported to have said, "Comedy is tragedy plus time."[31] Some times are not the right times for humor. That doesn't mean we lose sight of the comic vision or jettison the comic spirit. It means that we honor the sorrow of the moment by being fully present to it.

In the early nineties while serving a church in Langhorne, Pennsylvania, Alyce conducted a memorial service for a young woman raped and killed on a business trip to Kansas City. The service was held in the conference room of the tech company where the young woman had worked. Memorial services often include times to remember the foibles of the deceased and memories of our relationship with them that are amusing and thus celebrate the gift of the deceased. This was not such a time. Looking out over the grim faces of those who not only mourned their loss of the young woman but who were angry and horrified at the way she died, Alyce knew that what was needed was the assurance of the predictable presence of God in an unpredictable and sometimes violent world. The kind of humor this book commends has no desire to intrude on sorrowful moments. There are times when humor waits respectfully outside, with bowed head.

Know Your Audience: Cautionary Tale #1. Alyce recently was guest preacher at an Episcopal church on Pentecost Sunday. Her sermon, based on Jesus coming through locked doors and breathing the Holy Spirit upon the disciples in John 20:19–29, emphasized that we can expect Jesus to visit our panic rooms where we are huddled in fear and that there is no place where Jesus will not deign to visit. She described a recent trip to the Holy Land and the guide's designation of A sites (Jesus was definitely here), B sites (Jesus may or may not have been here), and C sites (Jesus definitely was not here). One of the C sites was the Church of the Holy Sepulchre. Alyce used humor to paint a picture of the noise and chaos of the scene, buses beeping in the parking lot, guides calling for their groups, a near fistfight between an angry tourist who had waited in line for an hour to kiss the cross and a priest trying to clear the area to hold afternoon Mass. She concluded by saying, "I get why this is a C site. Jesus would never come here. It's too noisy, too hostile, too human!" The congregation laughed, but there was an uneasy undertone to it. She circled around, eventually, to affirming that there are no B or C sites in our lives, but that Jesus is definitely with us in our personal panic rooms and areas of violence and anxiety in our world. She concluded with, "You don't have to go to the Holy Land to encounter Jesus! Your interior landscape is an A site. Jesus is definitely here, and *this* is the Holy Land."

Afterward, the priest thanked Alyce for her sermon. "I appreciate the positive part of your sermon about Jesus being everywhere, but I wish you hadn't done that bit on the Church of the Holy Sepulchre and all the C sites. I'm currently working hard to gather enough people from this congregation to come on a trip to the Holy Land I'm organizing for the fall." Know your audience.

Know Your Audience: Cautionary Tale #2. On another occasion Alyce used a story of being eight and a half months pregnant with her daughter Rebecca and being surprised by a baby shower organized by the first church she served out of seminary. She described her husband, Murry, insisting that she attend a Girl Scout parents' meeting for their then eight-year-old daughter, Melissa, at church one afternoon in June. She recounted their conversation with details crafted to elicit a chuckle.

"I was sitting cross-legged on the floor of our bedroom alphabetizing baby toiletries for the new baby due in three weeks wearing a maternity top that had seen better days and jeans.

"My husband, Murry, came into the room with a reminder: 'Hon, have you forgotten the Scout parents' meeting we need to attend at four today?'

"'Can't you see I'm busy here? Besides, it's June. Scouts don't start until September. You go."

"They want full family participation," he said. "Why don't you freshen up, maybe put on a little makeup, and let's go?"

To which I replied, "I *am* wearing makeup!"

In her sermon, Alyce described driving into the church parking lot and wondering why it was so full on a Sunday afternoon in June, then walking into a fellowship hall filled with balloons, gifts, and smiling faces. She used it as an example of God's joyful story of salvation that is ongoing and that we are invited to enter. The conceptual connection was sturdy: the concept of a celebration in progress we did not initiate or plan. And it struck a humorous note with some. But as she shared the story, she realized a number of couples who were struggling with fertility issues were present in the congregation. How did the metaphor of a baby shower for the messianic banquet come across to them? Know your audience. Alyce decided to put that story into retirement—or, at the very least, to repurpose it.

Know Your Audience: Cautionary Tale #3. Alyce is proud of her developing self-restraint. She was recently invited to speak at a Catholic seminary's commencement ceremony. She had just heard a hilarious anecdote about a church communications director whose duties included preparing funeral bulletins for an Episcopal church. Since the funeral liturgy remains constant from funeral to funeral, her habit was to do a "find and replace," inserting the name of the most recently deceased person into the liturgy. This process worked well until one week a woman named Mary died and the next week a man named Steve died. Imagine the communication director's horror as the congregation, gathered to honor Steve, launched into the Apostle's Creed. "And we believe in Jesus Christ his only Son our Lord who was conceived by the Holy Spirit and born of the Virgin Steve." Alyce was soooo tempted to use that story. Why? Because she suspected it would bring a big laugh. She didn't end up using it. Why not? Because she realized her motivation was about her, not her listeners; the story didn't really fit the theme of her address; and she wasn't sure how a Protestant clergywoman telling a joke that involved the Virgin Mary would play with a Catholic audience. Wouldn't it be like a Catholic priest invited as guest speaker in a United Methodist church making fun of John Wesley? Everyone knows that only Methodists are allowed to make fun of John Wesley! She will always think of that story as the one that got away. And it's probably a good thing! If there is the slightest doubt about the appropriateness of a particular use of humor for a particular group, know your audience and take a pass.

To Ponder

—Can you think of a sermon you heard or preached in which the use of humor could serve as a cautionary tale for having not been as aware of the congregation as the preacher might have been? What could have been a better homiletical approach? Should humor have been avoided, or would a different example of humor have worked?

NOTES

1. Eric Wei, *Wise Words to Ponder: A Selection of Great Thoughts through Quotes and Verses* (Partridge Publishing Singapore, 2020).

2. Your authors know full well that "lit" has been slang for drunk for over a century. And that it now means more like "excited or excellent." We mean it in the latter sense, not the former!

3. See Nicholas Carr, *The Shallows: What the Internet Is Doing to Our Brains* (New York: W. W. Norton, 2011).

4. Carrie La Ferle and O. Wesley Allen, *Preaching and the Thirty-Second Commercial: Lessons from Advertising for the Pulpit* (Louisville, KY: Westminster John Knox Press, 2021), 138.

5. See Alyce M. McKenzie, *Making a Scene in the Pulpit: Vivid Preaching for Visual Listeners* (Louisville, KY: Westminster John Knox Press, 2018), for a more in-depth discussion of audience dynamics and sermonic responses.

6. John C. Meyer, *Understanding Humor through Communication: Why Be Funny, Anyway?* (Lanham, MD: Lexington Books, 2015); Meyer, "Humor as a Double-Edged Sword: Four Functions of Humor in Communication," *Communication Theory* 10, no. 3 (August 2000): 310–31, https://doi.org/10.1111/j.1468-2885.2000.tb00194.x.

7. John C. Meyer, "Humor in Member Narratives: Uniting and Dividing at Work," *Western Journal of Communication* 61, no. 2 (June 1997): 188–208, https://doi.org/10.1080/10570319709374571; Sarah J. Tracy, Karen K. Myers, and Clifton W. Scott, "Cracking Jokes and Crafting Selves: Sensemaking and Identity Management among Human Service Workers," *Communication Monographs* 73, no. 3 (September 2006): 283–308, https://doi.org/10.1080/03637750600889500; Owen Hanley Lynch, "Kitchen Antics: The Importance of Humor and Maintaining

Professionalism at Work," *Journal of Applied Communication Research* 37, no. 4 (November 2009): 444–64, https://doi.org/10.1080/00909880903233143.

8. Satoshi Shimai et al., "Convergence of Character Strengths in American and Japanese Young Adults," *Journal of Happiness Studies* 7, no. 3 (September 2006): 311–22, https://doi.org/10.1007/s10902-005-3647-7; Kim R. Edwards and Rod A. Martin, "The Conceptualization, Measurement, and Role of Humor as a Character Strength in Positive Psychology," *Europe's Journal of Psychology* 10, no. 3 (August 13, 2014): 505–19, https://doi.org/10.5964/ejop.v10i3.759.

9. Julia Wilkins and Amy Janel Eisenbraun, "Humor Theories and the Physiological Benefits of Laughter," *Holistic Nursing Practice* 23, no. 6 (November 2009): 349–54, https://doi.org/10.1097/hnp.0b013e3181bf37ad; Mary Bennett, "The Effect of Mirthful Laughter on Stress and Natural Killer Cell Activity," *Alternative Therapies* 9, no. 2 (2003): 38; Amy Toffelmire, "Ha! Laughing Is Good for You!— Mental Health," MedBroadcast.com, April 2009, https://www.medbroadcast.com /channel/mental-health/stress/ha-laughing-is-good-for-you; Morgan Griffin, "Give Your Body a Boost—with Laughter," WebMD, Health & Balance, April 10, 2008, https://www.webmd.com/balance/features/give-your-body-boost-with-laughter.

10. Christopher Peterson, Nansook Park, and Martin E. P. Seligman, "Greater Strengths of Character and Recovery from Illness," *Journal of Positive Psychology* 1, no. 1 (January 2006): 17–26, https://doi.org/10.1080/17439760500372739.

11. George E. Vaillant, *Aging Well: Surprising Guideposts to a Happier Life from the Landmark Study of Adult Development* (New York: Little, Brown Spark, 2002); Dan Buettner, *The Blue Zones: Lessons for Living Longer from the People Who've Lived the Longest* (Washington, DC: National Geographic Books, 2010); Wing-yun Mak and Brian D. Carpenter, "Humor Comprehension in Older Adults," *Journal of the International Neuropsychological Society* 13, no. 04 (May 18, 2007): 606–14, https://doi.org/10.1017/s1355617707070750.

12. Margaret Semrud-Clikeman and Kimberly Glass, "The Relation of Humor and Child Development: Social, Adaptive, and Emotional Aspects," *Journal of Child Neurology* 25, no. 10 (June 17, 2010): 1248–60, https://doi.org/10 .1177/0883073810373144; Paul E. Mcghee and Mary Frank, *Humor and Children's Development: A Guide to Practical Applications* (New York: Routledge, 2014).

13. Elizabeth E. Graham, "The Involvement of Sense of Humor in the Development of Social Relationships," *Communication Reports* 8, no. 2 (June 1995): 158–69, https://doi.org/10.1080/08934219509367622.

14. Christiane Humke and Charles E. Schaefer, "Sense of Humor and Creativity," *Perceptual and Motor Skills* 82, no. 2 (April 1996): 544–46, https://doi .org/10.2466/pms.1996.82.2.544; Avner Ziv, "Facilitating Effects of Humor on Creativity," *Journal of Educational Psychology* 68, no. 3 (1976): 318–22, https:// doi.org/10.1037/0022-0663.68.3.318.

15. Mcghee and Frank, *Humor and Children's Development,* 99–116; Theodore Lewis, "Creativity: A Framework for the Design/Problem Solving Discourse

in Technology Education," *Journal of Technology Education* 17, no. 1 (September 1, 2005), https://doi.org/10.21061/jte.v17i1.a.3; Saba Ghayas and Malik Farah, "Sense of Humor as Predictor of Creativity Level in University Undergraduates," *Journal of Behavioural Sciences* 23, no. 2 (2013): 49–61.

16. Josephine Chinying Lang and Chay Hoon Lee, "Workplace Humor and Organizational Creativity," *International Journal of Human Resource Management* 21, no. 1 (January 2010): 46–60, https://doi.org/10.1080/09585190903466855; Robyn McMaster, "A Dash of Humor Ups Performance and Creativity at Work," Brain-Based Biz, September 22, 2008, http://brainbasedbiz.blogspot.com/2008 /09/dash-of-humor-ups-performance-and.html.

17. Nicholas A. Kuiper et al., "Humor Styles and the Intolerance of Uncertainty Model of Generalized Anxiety," *Europe's Journal of Psychology* 10, no. 3 (August 13, 2014): 543–56, https://doi.org/10.5964/ejop.v10i3.752.

18. Laura A. Talbot and D. Barry Lumden, "On the Association between Humor and Burnout," *Humor: International Journal of Humor Research* 13, no. 4 (2000), https://doi.org/10.1515/humr.2000.13.4.419; Jessica Mesmer Magnus, David J. Glew, and Chockalingam Viswesvaran, "A Meta Analysis of Positive Humor in the Workplace," *Journal of Managerial Psychology* 27, no. 2 (February 10, 2012): 155–90, https://doi.org/10.1108/02683941211199554; Millicent H. Abel, "Humor, Stress, and Coping Strategies," *Humor: International Journal of Humor Research* 15, no. 4 (January 22, 2002), https://doi.org/10.1515/humr.15.4.365.

19. Lydia Dishman, "Secrets of America's Happiest Companies," Fast Company, January 10, 2013, https://www.fastcompany.com/3004595/secrets -americas-happiest-companies; Bruce J. Avolio, Jane M. Howell, and John J. Sosik, "A Funny Thing Happened on the Way to the Bottom Line: Humor as a Moderator of Leadership Style Effects," *Academy of Management Journal* 42, no. 2 (April 1999): 219–27, https://doi.org/10.5465/257094; Lauren Breeze, Adrienne Dawson, and Susanna Khazhinsky, "Humor in the Workplace: Anecdotal Evidence Suggests Connection to Employee Performance," St. Edward's University, 2004; Mesmer Magnus, Glew, and Viswesvaran, "Meta Analysis of Positive Humor in the Workplace"; Fabio Sala, "Laughing All the Way to the Bank," *Harvard Business Review*, September 1, 2003, https://hbr.org/2003/09/laughing -all-the-way-to-the-bank; McMaster, "A Dash of Humor Ups Performance and Creativity at Work."

20. Melissa B. Wanzer, Ann B. Frymier, and Jeffrey Irwin, "An Explanation of the Relationship between Instructor Humor and Student Learning: Instructional Humor Processing Theory," *Communication Education* 59, no. 1 (January 2010): 1–18, https://doi.org/10.1080/03634520903367238.

21. John A. Banas et al., "A Review of Humor in Educational Settings: Four Decades of Research," *Communication Education* 60, no. 1 (January 2011): 115–44, https://doi.org/10.1080/03634523.2010.496867.

22. Charles Gruner pioneered work looking at the rhetorical effectiveness of humor use. See Charles R. Gruner, "Advice to the Beginning Speaker on Using

Humor—What the Research Tells Us," *Communication Education* 34, no. 2 (April 1985): 142–47, https://doi.org/10.1080/03634528509378596.

23. George Pacheco and John Meyer, "Persuasive Humor," in *Persuasion in Your Life*, 2nd ed. (New York: Routledge, 2017), 301–19, http://dx.doi.org/10 .4324/9781315536415-13; Robert M. Kaplan and Gregory C. Pascoe, "Humorous Lectures and Humorous Examples: Some Effects upon Comprehension and Retention," *Journal of Educational Psychology* 69, no. 1 (February 1977): 61–65, https://doi.org/10.1037/0022-0663.69.1.61.

24. P. E. Lull, "The Effectiveness of Humor in Persuasive Speech," *Speech Monographs* 7, no. 1 (December 1940): 26–40, https://doi.org/10.1080 /03637754009374872.

25. Jim Lyttle, "The Effectiveness of Humor in Persuasion: The Case of Business Ethics Training," *Journal of General Psychology* 128, no. 2 (April 2001): 206–16, https://doi.org/10.1080/00221300109598908.

26. Seraine Page, "20 Fantastic Benefits of Walking Daily," TotalWellness, April 29, 2019, https://info.totalwellnesshealth.com/blog/20-fantastic-benefits -of-walking-daily.

27. An example would be a preacher equating Bartimaeus's excitement at the Son of David's coming through Jericho with his young son's excitement when he hears the ice cream truck come through the neighborhood. The technical name for this is *infra dignitatum* [beneath the dignity of].

28. William H. Willimon, "Humor," in *Concise Encyclopedia of Preaching*, ed. William H. Willimon and Richard Lischer (Louisville, KY: Westminster John Knox Press, 1995), 264. Willimon also notes that sermonic humor should emerge from interaction with the biblical text, not be imposed on it, and be natural for the preacher's own style and personality.

29. Leonora Tubbs Tisdale, *Preaching as Local Theology and Folk Art* (Minneapolis: Fortress Press, 1997), 33. This groundbreaking book put the concept of congregational exegesis on the radar screen of preachers and teachers of preaching and continues to be an influential work.

30. Steve Sherwood, "Intersections of Wit and Rhetoric: Humor as a Rhetorical Enterprise," *Proteus: A Journal of Ideas* 29, no. 1 (2013): 46.

31. Or it may have been Steve Allen, "Steve Allen's Almanac," *Cosmopolitan*, February 1957, 12.

5

Strategies for Using Humor in Our Sermons

Someone asked me if I were stranded on a desert island, what book would I bring. . . . *How to Build a Boat.*
 —American stand-up comedian, actor, writer, and film producer Steven Wright (b. 1955)[1]

One of the benefits of this study for Alyce has been that she now has language and categories for understanding how she has been using humor in sermons over the years and insights into why it has often worked, but in some cases has not! This chapter offers a series of strategies for using humor in our sermons, inspired by chapter 4's social-scientific research and chapter 6's description of incongruity and relief humor.

Each strategy is accompanied by a positive example from recent sermons, by both Alyce and others. Several examples come from a recent gathering of United Methodist clergy and laity held in Richardson, Texas.[2] In attending the event, Alyce decided to take a page out of Owen's playbook and view it as an ethnographic immersion in the use of humor. She discovered that, when one activates the knack for noticing humor (KFN) we discuss in chapters 11 and 12, it's amazing how plentiful the harvest!

Mixed in with the positive examples are a few cautionary tales about the use of humor. They are all autobiographical, since using oneself rather than colleagues in examples of humor that went awry avoids the time and expense of litigation! Our hope is that these sermonic examples encourage readers to evaluate their past use of humor as well as to brainstorm future possibilities.

HUMOR USED AT THE BEGINNING OF A MESSAGE
CAN GAIN LISTENERS' ATTENTION

Why do so many preachers caution against canned jokes, especially at the beginning of a sermon? For one thing, since jokes are memorable, self-contained units, they may be all that people take from the sermon, leaving the point behind. For another, starting with a joke (especially a hilarious, gut-buster joke [GBJ]), even if it is closely related to the sermon's theme, is a hard act to follow. What's next in your act if you've begun by pulling the rabbit out of the hat? Rules were made to be broken, though, so if the joke is brief, tightly tied to the theme of the sermon, and if what follows it matches it in vitality and listener engagement then maybe. . . . In chapter 13 we offer guidelines for including original observational humor in sermons. These may adhere to classic joke structure, but they are unique to the preacher.

While attention after a GBJ most often drops off, more subtle humor can have the opposite effect: it can ramp up sermonic interest. As Fred Craddock asserts, sometimes a sermon can start in the shallow end before inviting listeners into deeper waters.

An example of this opening use of humor comes from Alyce's sermon on Matthew 24:36–44, "Time to Wake Up!"[3] She says:

> I have two brothers and a sister. Our names in birth order are Wade, Alyce, Robert, and Susanna. Growing up, every night before bed, all four of us made sure to pray . . . that, in the morning, Mom would be the one to wake us up for school and not Dad. Mom's method was to get a washcloth and warm it and wring it out and come and sit on the edge of our bed and speak gently to us while warming our face with the washcloth.
>
> Dad's method—he had been in the navy—was to turn the lights on in our face, while slamming the wall next to the door and calling out, "Hit the deck. Hit the deck!"
>
> Actually, Dad's method got me out of bed faster. No more lying there half asleep, contemplating the possibility of getting up. His method got my feet on the floor, my clothes and shoes pulled on, my backpack, homework, and lunch money in hand, and my coat on my back. Out the door, boarding the bus by 7:35 a.m.
>
> Jesus' approach in this passage is more like my dad's wake-up call than my mom's.
>
> "Wake up and get ready. For the Son of Man is coming at an unexpected hour!"[4]

HUMOR, PLACED THROUGHOUT THE SERMON, CAN HELP LISTENERS STAY ENGAGED

John Drakeford, in his book *Humor in Preaching,* calls this use "holding your congregation without a rope!"[5]

Alyce heard a sermon by United Methodist bishop Gregory Palmer at the church conference referred to earlier. A couple of times throughout his message, "Finding Our Way in the Wilderness," he said, "I'm going to put a quarter in the meter and park here for a bit." It was a lively quip used, but not overused, as a refrain that kept us engaged. Humor can be lightly sprinkled rather than poured. It doesn't have to draw attention to itself to hold our attention.[6]

Owen heard a sermon recently in which the visiting priest, as he came to the end of the portion of his homily where he depicted the tough reality of our human predicament and turned to the good news, paused and said, "Since I'm a guest speaker here, I don't know you all that well. So I don't know how much good news you can take in one sitting. You will have to let me know later if it was too much!" The congregation chuckled and perked up, energized for the final portion of the sermon.

A humorous anecdote can enliven a sermon midway through, regathering wandering attention. Zan Holmes's story about the man and his thrice-hemmed pants that we mention later in the chapter serves that function.

HUMOR CAN PROVIDE MEMORABLE, CHALLENGING ENDINGS TO SERMONS

Homiletician Mike Graves advises preachers to place the most moving or engaging portion of their sermon last and the second-most-engaging or moving portion first.[7] Ending well is an art. There are many options in sermon endings: the summary ending in which the preacher, with economy of words, states or restates the theme of the sermon; the sermon that ends with a question that challenges listeners to respond to the sermon; the open-ended conclusion that leaves it up to listeners to contextualize the message in their own lives; the dramatic, eloquent, poetic ending in which the preacher touches emotions and calls for action; and the story ending, in which the preacher offers a story that encapsulates the theme of the sermon.[8] All of these, to one degree or another, end on a positive, practical note of how the good news makes a difference in our lives, as God challenges and empowers us to offer our witness to the world.[9]

Preachers do not use humor at the end of the sermon nearly as often as they do at the beginning. But humor can certainly qualify for last place in a sermon, contributing to a compelling, practical finale.

Let's consider humor in relation to one specific way of concluding sermons. Frank Thomas, in his *They Like to Never Quit Praisin' God: The Role of Celebration in Preaching,* in keeping with the legacy of African American preaching traditions, commends experiential preaching that ends in celebration. He recommends that the bodily, sensory responses of joy and laughter not be excluded from our sermons. Rather, they should be celebrated and planned for in sermons that move from identifying congregational members' false, negative core beliefs, reversing them by the power of the good news, and celebrating the difference that reversal makes in listeners' lives.

In that celebration, the preacher calls on congregational memories, moving stories, hymns, poetry, and so forth. In a discussion of "Materials of Celebration," Thomas says this:

> Any creative and imaginative sensory descriptive material that is capable of expressing joyous and affirmative feeling is substance for celebration. Any material based in sense appeal that puts us in touch with festive and positive emotions is suitable for use in celebration. Any material that triggers the imaginative capacity by releasing affirmation, hope, peace, joy and love in core belief . . . is material for celebration.[10]

Humor certainly deserves to be in the mix, whether in the form of a sharp-witted challenge or a warmhearted anecdote or scene.

In a sermon series titled *Up Close and Personal: Close Encounters with Jesus in the Gospel of John,* Alyce highlighted Jesus' encounters with four troubled people in John's Gospel as a means for congregational self-awareness and transformation: Nicodemus (chap. 3), the woman at the well (chap. 4), the man by the pool (chap. 5), and the man born blind (chap. 9). A story she told as part of the conclusion of the first sermon of the series and referred to in subsequent sermons was the following:

> I know a British pastor who had served his parish for quite some time and had become tired of hearing the same comments from his parishioners about his sermons at the back door. "Nice message. Enjoyed the sermon." Or sometimes, "Nice sermon. Enjoyed the message." So

he began a new practice. As he stood at the back door, as each person shook his hand and made their stock comment, he would hold onto their hand, look them in the eye and say, "Thank you, but what's different for you now?" and hold onto it until they came up with something more substantive, more specific.

He said that it brought about a remarkable change in the congregation. They all began leaving by the side door!

The sermon used humor to challenge listeners to reflect on the impact (or lack thereof) an encounter with Jesus was having on their lives. The hope is they will leave crafting their own answers to the question "What is different for me now?"

HUMOR CAN LOWER LISTENER DEFENSES WHEN EXPOSED TO A CHALLENGING OR PAINFUL REALITY THAT CALLS FOR A CHANGE IN THEIR BEHAVIOR/ACTIONS

A few years ago, Dr. Zan Holmes, preaching to an affluent, suburban nondenominational church in Plano, Texas, used a story about a man who comes home with a new pair of pants that need hemming.[11] He asks his mother-in-law to hem them. She refuses, saying she has had a long day and is tired. He next asks his wife, and she refuses for the same reason. So he hems them himself, taking off two inches, hangs them neatly over a chair in the kitchen, and goes to bed. Along about midnight his mother-in-law wakes up feeling guilty for letting him down. She gets up and neatly hems them, taking another two inches off and places them on the back of the chair. An hour or so later, his wife wakes up feeling guilty for turning down his request. She gets out of bed and takes another two inches off and leaves them on the back of the chair. When he gets up the next morning and goes into the kitchen to get the pants to get dressed for work, he finds his new walking shorts hanging over the back of the chair!

Dr. Holmes uses this story to challenge the congregation to come out of their silos and work together using their considerable affluence and influence to overcome apathy and racial prejudice and serve the needs of their community. He later segues to a positive vision of what working together would look like, telling of his dad taking him to a symphony orchestra concert as a young teenager. He portrays his disappointment as they tune up (humorously admitting that he thought this was the first number!) and then his excitement when they all play together making music and inspiring listeners.

HUMOR CAN PAVE THE WAY FOR THE INTRODUCTION OF A DEEPER, MORE DIFFICULT TOPIC

An example of the effective use of whimsical humor to pave the way for the introduction of a difficult topic is by Nora Tisdale, Clement-Muehl Professor of Homiletics Emerita at Yale Divinity School. Some years ago she preached a sermon on Palm/Passion Sunday at University Church in New Haven, Connecticut.[12] She began with a lighthearted description of the annual Azalea Parade in her hometown of Wilmington, North Carolina, that she experienced as a nine-year-old girl. She painted a picture of the streets lined with people, the marching bands, the baton twirlers, the floats with local celebrities, including the Azalea Queen, a second-tier TV star invited to be wined and dined as the parade queen each year. Someone had given Nora an autograph book, and she described running up to the main float and holding up her book to get the autograph of Shelley Fabares, then a cast member of the *Donna Reed Show* who was the Azalea Queen that year.

Her opening put listeners in a nostalgic, positive place, softening their resistance to what came next: the revelation that the Azalea Parade and Palm Sunday shared, not just a veneer of festivity, but also a deep vein of violence. Palm Sunday looks forward to the violence of the cross. The Azalea Parade looked back to a history of deep-seated ugliness and racial discrimination that was part of many contemporary communities' histories, including that of Wilmington and New Haven. The sermon's use of humor was faithful to the text and fitting to the liturgical season and day, to the location and time—Yale University and Divinity School were examining their history of racial prejudice—and to the shared experiences of many in her congregation who, like her, grew up in the 1950s and 1960s.

HUMOR CAN HELP LISTENERS BE MORE OPEN TO ACCEPTING NEW IDEAS AND SEEING THINGS FROM OTHERS' PERSPECTIVES

Contemporary congregations sometimes judge the disciples for not believing the women and accepting the good news of the resurrection. In a sermon on the resurrection appearances in Luke's Gospel, Rev. Paul Bussert, a pastor in Oklahoma, fostered congregational empathy for the disciples by showing how challenging accepting that news would have been for them.[13]

He offered a string of questions: "Would you believe me if I told you the grass wasn't green but blue? That water wasn't wet? That on the way to church gas was only a dollar a gallon? That the Cleveland Browns won the Super Bowl?" This string of ridiculously rhetorical questions helped the congregation see the disciples' point of view better and helped to set up the move to the ridiculousness, the outlandishness of life coming from death.

HUMOR CAN INVITE US INTO A BIBLICAL TEXT BY SEEING IT IN AN OFF-KILTER WAY

Episcopal author and preacher Barbara Brown Taylor is an expert at this use of humor. Many of her sermons begin with a quirky take on the text. For example, her sermon "The Yes and No Brothers," on the parable of the Two Sons in Matthew 21:28–32, begins this way:

> If there had been an inquest into Jesus' death, the parable of the two brothers would probably have been presented as one of the things that got him killed. According to Matthew, Jesus told it during the last week of his life in Jerusalem—after he had stolen a donkey to ride into town on, after he had chased the merchants out of the temple, and after he had cursed the fig tree for failing to bear fruit.

Taylor continues that then he went back to the Temple to teach and was cornered by the chief priests and elders who demanded to know who had given him the authority to do all those things. Who, they wanted to know, did he think he was? In response he tells them this story.[14]

HUMOR CAN HELP BUILD COMMUNITY IDENTITY

In a sermon preached to a large church conference of United Methodist clergy and laity on the theme of Vision for the Future, United Methodist bishop Cynthia Fierro Harvey preached from Isaiah 42:5–9, whose last verse is, "See, the former things have come to pass, / and new things I now declare; / before they spring forth, / I tell you of them." She played two clips from commercials that ran several years ago for

Direct TV. They featured a family (called "The Settlers") living as if they were in the nineteenth century, wearing homespun clothing and chopping wood, using cable while their suburban neighbors around them had Direct TV. The theme, conveyed in this amusing way, was "Don't Settle." After playing the clips, Bishop Harvey challenged us, "We are not settlers." We are people who look to a future we can barely imagine, God's future.[15]

HUMOR CAN EXPOSE OUR COMMON FRAILTIES AND FOIBLES AND HELP US LAUGH AT THEM

The "Settlers" example not only builds group identity but also helps hearers get in touch with some of our human weaknesses so that we can step back and put them in perspective. It shows our tendency to resist change. Humor helps us see ourselves from the outside and gain objectivity and the realization that we are not alone in our weaknesses.

HUMOR CAN INVITE LISTENERS INTO AN EXPERIENCE OF THEIR SHARED FAITH

Humor is not limited to showing us our common foibles. It can also depict our common positive future in God's keeping. In a sermon "Finding Faith amid Our Fears," based on Proverbs 1:7; 3:5–7, Alyce recounted a devotional she had read recently in which the author confessed that he awoke every morning in the early hours for necessary reasons and then laid back down in bed staring at the ceiling as the fear parade, each of his fears with its own float, made its way down the main street of his mind. He said what he did then was to look down the street (ceiling) in the other direction, and imagine the faith parade was coming, on a collision course with the fear floats. Each faith float had its own verse of Scripture: Psalm 46:1–3; Joshua 1:9; Psalm 118:5–6; Psalm 23:4. Alyce then concluded,

> On these floats, and many more, are the promises of our transcendent, trustworthy God on a collision course with our fears, which are no match for them. It's gonna be a fear smackdown at 3:27 a.m. We'll find out that our garden-variety fears are no match for the fear of the Lord, the Bible's code word for reverent faith, which is the beginning of wisdom.[16]

The sermon uses humor to unite the congregation, both in a common experience of early-morning anxiety and in the promises of their shared faith.

HUMOR CAN CHALLENGE INJUSTICE
AND HYPOCRISY

Rev. Mary Beth Hardesty Crouch preached an Easter sermon on Luke's version of events called "An Idle Tale."[17] She talked about how quickly the disciples discounted the women, how slow they were to believe these credible witnesses to an incredible reality—the resurrection. She drew an analogy between this biblical dynamic and the phenomenon in our culture where some are quick to believe ridiculous scams and conspiracy theories and slow to trust in reliable sources.

She told the story of Peter McIndoe, a young Arkansas man who began the "Birds Aren't Real" conspiracy theory parody by claiming that the CIA had systematically eliminated birds in the 1980s and replaced them with drones. Birds are government drone spies. And yes, there were, perhaps are, people who believe him.

The story of his scrawling "Birds Aren't Real" on a piece of cardboard and joining a group of protesters in the streets of Memphis the day after Trump's election is humorous. The fact that he began shouting out absurdities to the group: "I'm angry, and I'm here to protest! Wake up, America! Birds are not real. They're a myth! They're an illusion!" is even more humorous.[18] We often think of prophetic preaching as requiring us to yell at the powers that be. Here, the preacher simply uses humor to expose the ludicrousness of a false conspiracy claim.

HUMOR CAN MAKE THE SERMON MORE MEMORABLE
FOR LISTENERS AND FOR THE PREACHER IN
THE PROCESS OF DELIVERING THE SERMON

A hallmark of effective oral communication is that a speech be easy to say and hard to forget. Many tools in our homiletical toolboxes contribute to this: use of story, imagery, vivid language choices, and dramatic sequencing that moves from itch to scratch. Humor deserves to be included in the memorability mix. That goes both for listeners after the sermon has been preached and for the preacher while she or he is preaching it. Exercised by the preacher with a comic spirit, humor can gain and maintain listeners' attention and cause them to retain the sermon after it is preached. The same is true of preachers who need to be fully present and engaged in the material to bring the energy it deserves.

APPROPRIATE SELF-DEPRECATORY HUMOR CAN HUMANIZE PREACHERS, POSITIVELY IMPACTING LISTENERS' PERCEPTION OF THEM AND THEIR WILLINGNESS TO LISTEN

Self-deprecatory humor can be especially helpful when the preacher is addressing a controversial, challenging topic. When preachers use such humor well, listeners find them more credible, approachable, and confident.

Rev. Dr. Ronald Henderson preached the annual memorial service at the church conference referred to earlier.[19] The service began with the reading of names of those who had died in the previous year, as their pictures came on the screens at the front. Dr. Henderson opened his sermon in a somber, meditative way, sharing that he had reverently read through the names of the departed saints for the past several weeks, memorizing their names as he prepared for the service.

He then told a story of how he and his daughter were at a mall recently and a man called out his name and came over and said, "Ron, so great to see you!" They shook hands and chatted a bit in general terms. Finally, the man said, "It's always good to see you, Ron. Take care now!" and moved on.

Ron's daughter said, "Who was that?" He replied, "I don't know." She asked, "Well, what was his name?" Ron replied, "I have no idea!"

Everyone laughed. He then segued into how, while our memories are short, God's lasts forever, as will the legacy of our colleagues who are now in God's eternal embrace.

This use of humor does two things simultaneously. The use of self-deprecatory humor humanizes Dr. Henderson. It brings listeners together in shared acknowledgment, "Yes, we've all done that—forgotten someone's name and felt embarrassed." The sermon doesn't leave them us there, however. It also brings us together in shared gratitude that God's memory is better than ours!

HUMOR CAN LIFT OUR SPIRITS IN STRESSFUL, CRISIS SITUATIONS

This is the most difficult benefit of humor on which to offer advice. It's also tough to find effective sermonic examples of this use of humor because these moments arise spontaneously and are highly context-specific. Stressful situations require comic restraint so we don't blurt out something that is inappropriate or comes off as flippant.

That said, here is a positive liturgical example from a recent Sunday when Owen was attending Mass. During the entrance procession, the priest and other officiants approached the altar in a formal, ceremonial manner. One of the officiants, a seminarian who was carrying the Bible high in the air above his head for all to see, stumbled and dropped the Bible with a resounding *thunk!* The church went silent. Every eye in the church was on the Bible, now on the floor. The tension seemed to last forever while the seminarian stood frozen, not knowing what to do. The priest saying the Mass simply walked over and picked up the Bible and said, "If you think it is difficult to carry, try living up to it!" The whole church laughed and even broke into applause at his wit and wisdom. The priest placed the gospel on the altar, restoring it to its proper, sacred position, and began the Mass, "In the name of Father. . . ."

To Ponder

—Which of the fourteen homiletical uses of humor suggested above have you used (or heard used) in sermons, and which have you not?

—Have you ever ended a sermon with humor? If so, describe and discuss. If not, in what situation would you be willing to do so?

—Which of these uses of humor do you discern in Jesus' teaching and preaching? Which are missing?

NOTES

1. Team Golfwell, *Absolute Best Adult Party Jokes: A Wonderful Treasury of Exceptional Hilarious Jokes, Quotes, Anecdotes and Stories* (Team Golfwell, 2018), 121.

2. Annual Conference of the North Texas Conference, United Methodist Church, June 5–7, 2022, First United Methodist Church, Richardson, Texas.

3. Preached at Christ UMC, Plano, Texas, November 27, 2016.

4. For more options in sermon openings, see Sondra Willobee's *The Write Stuff: Crafting Sermons That Capture and Convince* (Louisville, KY: Westminster John Knox Press, 2009), 11–28. Willobee, as have others, warns against the opening joke, but commends self-deprecatory humor as an option for effective openings.

5. John W. Drakeford, *Humor in Preaching* (Grand Rapids: Zondervan, 1986), 69–77.

6. Gregory V. Palmer, "Finding Our Way in the Wilderness," North Texas Annual Conference, United Methodist Church, June 5, 2022, First United Methodist Church, Richardson, Texas. At the time of this writing he was bishop of the West Ohio Conference, UMC.

7. Graves, *Fully Alive Preacher*, 119.

8. For more on the variety of endings and how to choose and craft them, see Alyce M. McKenzie, *Novel Preaching: Tips from Top Writers on Crafting Creative Sermons* (Louisville, KY: Westminster John Knox Press, 2010), 75–77. Also see John C. Holbert and Alyce M. McKenzie, *What Not to Say: Avoiding the Common Mistakes That Can Sink Your Sermon* (Louisville, KY: Westminster John Knox Press, 2020), chap. 8.

9. For a survey of historical and contemporary sermon forms, see O. Wesley Allen, *Determining the Form: Structures for Preaching* (Minneapolis: Fortress Press, 2008).

10. Frank A. Thomas, *They Like to Never Quit Praisin' God: The Role of Celebration in Preaching* (Cleveland: Pilgrim Press, 2013), 123.

11. Sermon on Mark 5:1–20, "Are We Getting It All Together?," Chase Oaks Church, Plano, Texas.

12. This sermon, "I Love a Parade," was delivered at the University Church at Yale on Sunday, April 1, 2012. The University Church is an ecumenical campus Christian community serving the Yale and New Haven communities since 1757.

13. Sermon on Luke 24:1–12, "An Idle Tale?" At the time of this writing, Bussert serves as associate pastor at First United Methodist Church in Bixby, Oklahoma.

14. Barbara Brown Taylor, *Home by Another Way* (Cambridge, MA: Cowley Publications, 1999), 187.

15. From a sermon preached at the opening worship service of the 2022 North Texas Conference, United Methodist Church, First United Methodist Church, Richardson, Texas, June 5, 2022.

16. Originally preached at a Sunday afternoon revival service, February 1, 2015, at Smith Chapel AME Church, Dallas, Texas. It can be found in Alyce M. McKenzie's *Making a Scene in the Pulpit: Vivid Preaching for Visual Listeners* (Louisville, KY: Westminster John Knox Press, 2018), 111–19.

17. Sermon on Luke 24:1–12: First United Methodist Church, Allen, Texas, April 17, 2022.

18. 60 Minutes Overtime, "The Origins of 'Birds Aren't Real,'" CBS News, May 1, 2022, https://www.cbsnews.com/news/birds-arent-real-origin-60-minutes-2022-05-01/.

19. Dr. Ronald Henderson, at the time of this writing, serves as the director of racial equity, diversity, and inclusion for the North Texas Conference of the United Methodist Church. This sermon was preached at the Annual Conference of the North Texas Conference, UMC, on June 6, 2022, at First United Methodist Church in Richardson, Texas.

6

Three Theories of Humor

Superiority, Relief, and Incongruity

Humour is not simply an enigma, any more than poetry is. It is possible to say something relatively cogent and coherent about why we laugh. . . .
—Literary critic Terry Eagleton[1]

In this chapter we review the theories of humor widely accepted across the various academic disciplines that do humor research. We recognize that you might be tempted to say, "I know a good joke when I hear one, and I have had a good belly laugh with my friends. I don't need to learn about the theory of humor to experience it."

We quite understand why someone would be put off by a discussion of humor theory or the academic study of humor. After all, you don't need to know its ingredients and cultural heritage to enjoy a dish. But knowing them helps us to appreciate a unique dish more, and compare and contrast that dish with other foods we have had. And good luck trying to replicate the dish at home without the benefit of a recipe explaining how to prepare and serve it.[2] One can certainly use humor when preaching without knowing these three theories. But in learning the three theories, one will be able to use humor in their sermons more effectively.

Plato, Aristotle, Cicero, Hobbes, Descartes, Kant, Freud, Schopenhauer, Spencer, Bergson, and Jung all spent considerable time and ink thinking and writing about humor. All had theories on humor, why we laugh, how to use humor, or why we should avoid it. Some like Sigmund Freud[3] and Henri Bergson[4] dedicated entire books to the subject. They both felt that humor was not just essentially human but was essential for humans' well-being and civil social relations. They also thought this for totally opposite reasons, Bergson felt laughter was essential to avoid social life being overly rigid, mechanical, and conformist: humor stops the individual from becoming an automaton. By contrast, Freud felt joking was a safe way to release our repressed, hostile drives: humor stops us from becoming animalistic. Bergson and Freud are both correct. Social humor is akin to the warning beep in new cars that alerts us when we are steering too far out of our lane in either direction.

Understanding humor as a divine gift capable of use and misuse leads your authors to attribute such guidance in the use of humor to humor's Creator!

Humor's complexity evades a reductive approach. Asa Berger, a professor of semiotics and visual communication, uses the parable of the blind men and the elephant to describe how scholars from different disciplines have tried to define humor. [5] The parable focuses on a group of men who are blind each touching a different part of the immense beast and describing it in detail. Each is correct from their perspective, yet each description is incomplete. Often the parable stops there and is interpreted as a cautionary tale in that each man could be mocked for thinking they had the full likeness. But we interpret this in a positive way: each perspective is an important part of the collective description needed to appreciate the complexity of the whole elephant.

It is generally agreed that there are three broad, somewhat complementary theories of why we use humor: superiority, relief, and incongruity theory. Superiority and relief theories focus on the purpose of humor, how we use it. Incongruity theory is more interested in the why of humor: what causes something unexpected and nonsensical to be recognized as funny. Each of the thinkers we have mentioned can be placed (though not neatly) into one of these humor theories or schools. Plato, Aristotle, and Hobbes fit into superiority humor; Spencer and Freud into relief humor; and Cicero, Kant, and Schopenhauer into incongruity humor.

In an earlier work,[6] Owen argued that none of the theories offers a full and complete interpretation of humor, but taken together can provide an understanding of what humor is and why it is used. Scholars like clear definitions and distinct categories so we can operationalize, identify, and put things in their "proper" place. However, this is difficult to do with humor because the theories overlap with one another. Many things we find humorous can be seen through the lens of incongruity, relief, and superiority all at the same time. It is like salsa that is sweet, salty, and spicy all on one delicious chip. Here we define each theory of humor separately, keeping in mind that very few humorous acts or utterances are purely and only from one school.

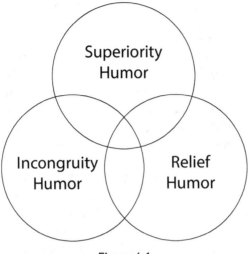

Figure 6.1

We discuss each of these theories in turn, accompanied by a brief discussion of their sermonic use to equip preachers to be more strategic about how they both discern and use humor in their sermons in the context of the comic spirit/vision.

As an interdisciplinary field of research, humor studies has exploded in the last forty years and goes under the broad title of "modern humor theory."[7] This review of schools of thought on humor will integrate applied humor studies that focus on the situational function of humor in our everyday social lives. It draws on the fields of anthropology, communication, legal theory, linguistics, management, psychology, and sociology.

SUPERIORITY HUMOR THEORY

We can laugh at, scoff at, make fun of, chide, tease, deride, mock, and poke fun at someone. These terms all position humor as something we use and direct, sometimes aggressively, at a target. This superiority view of humor positions it at best as a corrective. Humor is used to point out or emphasize that someone is inadequate according to a set of agreed-upon criteria. Laughter, from a superiority humor position, "acts as a social corrective, restraining social deviancy, tempering rigidities of character and behavior."[8] Humor, from this framework, is not "fun" but purposeful, and it is the opposite of concern and caring for others. This form of humor sets up an imbalance—a winner and a loser. Humor thus results from a sense of triumph, the vanquishing of a foe, and the laugh is the hoot of the superior in victory.

The superiority theory of humor is thought to have originated with Thomas Hobbes. Hobbes argues that human nature is rooted in our being self-serving and seeking power, fame, and glory. He sees humor as an expression of this depraved human desire: "The passion of laughter is nothing else but the sudden glory arising from sudden conception of some eminency in ourselves, by comparison with the infirmity of others, or with our own formerly."[9]

Owen had a secondary school teacher who summed up Hobbes's view of humanity as "I want what you have, for no other reason than to take it from you." Owen responded, "I don't believe that," to which the teacher said, "It doesn't much matter what you believe if the guy standing next to you does." For Hobbes, life is an arms race, humor is a weapon in that race, laughter is the weapon's bang, and the target is the victim of the joke.

A modern example of this superiority humor frame can be seen in the Darwin Awards, which describe themselves as "salut[ing] the improvement of the human genome by honoring those who accidentally remove themselves from it in a spectacular manner!"[10] This joy and laughter at the misery of others is what the Germans call *Schadenfreude*. There is an old joke that Germans have a word for everything and it is always long. The word *Handschuhschneeballwerfer*, the German word for snowballing, may take the prize. Throwing snowballs is supposed to be fun, a wholesome family activity in which no one gets hurt. After all, it is only snow and usually thrown with good intention and at a willing recipient. But as we know, sometimes people don't have good intentions and mix in a little too much ice and or they throw it at an inappropriate time or at a person who can't defend themselves.

There is a lesson here: if you are going to use superiority-type humor, follow these simple snowballing rules and everyone can join in on the fun:

—Rule one: No throwing snowballs at people who can't defend themselves or are unable to throw back.
—Rule two: Don't rain down snowballs from a lofty position. (It's not even funny when Zeus does it, and you are not Zeus.)
—Rule three: Don't ambush people with snowballs because they are a convenient target for you.
—Rule four: No rules apply to other professional snowballers.

These are essentially the rules followed by most professional comedians who, better than most, recognize the effects an icy joke can have when it hits a target. They don't use the snowball analogy, but they go by the same simple rules. It is commonly said, "In comedy you don't punch down." Don't throw a punch at someone who has less power than you or can't punch back. Only make fun of people because of what they choose to do and say, not for who they are or their physical characteristics. Don't ambush people for things they can't control.

Ricky Gervais followed these rules as he used superiority-type humor directed at the Hollywood actors at the 2020 Golden Globe Awards as they sat at tables hosted and presided over by Apple TV, Amazon, and their executives:

> Apple roared into the TV game with "The Morning Show," a superb drama about the importance of dignity and doing the right thing made by a company that runs sweatshops in China. So you say you're "woke," but the companies you work for . . . Apple, Amazon, Disney. If ISIS had a streaming service you would be calling your agents.

To Gervais the hypocrisy and exalted status of the physically present elite audience of the Golden Globes in relation to the regular audience watching at home made them fair game for his jokes.[11]

Given Hobbes's portrayal of superiority humor, does this type of humor, even following the snowballing rules, have a place in our preaching, and if so, in what way? To be honest, your authors are tempted to advise preachers to avoid it at all costs, leaving it to professional comedians.

But there are examples of harsh humor in the Bible. In Psalm 2:4 we are told that God will laugh at the kings of the earth who take counsel against him. Proverbs 1:26–27 depicts tough love as Woman Wisdom offering us a choice of wisdom or folly with clear consequences for those who make the wrong choice: "I also will laugh at your calamity; / I will mock . . . when panic strikes you like a storm." And there is Elijah's mockery of the gods of Ba'al in 1 Kings 18:27: "At noon Elijah mocked them, saying, 'Cry aloud! Surely he is a god; either he is meditating, or he has wandered away, or he is on a journey, or perhaps he is asleep and must be awakened.'" The prophets use sarcasm to unmask and debunk hypocrisy.[12]

Similarly, Jesus' vivid sarcasm exposes sin, folly, and idolatry. He compares religious authorities to whitened sepulchers (Matt. 23:27) and depicts them as those who "strain out a gnat but swallow a camel" (23:24). He challenges his everyday listeners with absurd questions that expose the irrationality of our habitual behaviors, for example, "Why do you see the speck in your neighbor's eye, but do not notice the log in your own eye?" (Matt. 7:3). He challenges prevailing assumptions that wealth is a sign of divine approval with the ridiculous image of a camel fitting through the eye of a needle (Matt. 19:24; Mark 10:25).

The Bible's humor, while acerbic, largely follows the rules of snowballing. God's mockery of God's enemies is for the sake of emphasizing God's positive and ultimate victory over all opposition, rather than mockery for the sheer fun of it. Jesus' sharp critique of those in power does not make fun of people for things they cannot help. He doesn't punch down. If anything, his humor aims up, exposing the hypocrisy of those in religious, political power.

Superiority Humor Homiletical Example

Martin Luther offers bold examples of homiletical superiority humor. He mercilessly made fun of the devil and was not afraid to poke fun at his parishioners for their presumption that they would have behaved better than biblical characters and for their sluggishness in prayer.[13]

Since none of us is Martin Luther (!), your authors suggest that contemporary preachers, when in prophetic mode, acknowledge their own complicity in perpetuating hypocrisy and injustice and that they employ the strategy of appropriate self-deprecation from time to time. Superiority humor and lack of humility make for a repugnant homiletical recipe.

RELIEF HUMOR THEORY

In the past, thinkers have focused on superiority theory. More recently, contemporary humor theorists are focusing mostly on incongruity theory. Poor old relief theory seems to just be dragged along. However, without "the relief" that humor and laughter provide, they would not be a necessary and universal part of social life. Relief theory asserts that when we joke and laugh we release physiological and psychological stress, and we break social tensions in healthy and helpful ways. This is evidenced in the sermonic samples in chapter 5 that showed humor's ability to ease tensions in stressful situations and lower congregational defenses when introducing difficult topics. Relief humor theory outlines three aspects of relief that we now consider individually here.

First, humor offers relief in *physiological* terms. On a physical level, laughter has many positive benefits, as a complex body movement that is found to ease muscle tension, break spasm-pain cycles, increase flow of oxygen and nutrients into tissues helping fight infections, and act as a modifier of neuroendocrine hormones involved in the classical stress response.[14]

Second, humor offers relief in *psychological* terms. Herbert Spencer in 1860 is credited with the first reference to humor and laughter as a socially acceptable means of releasing physical energy that builds up to contend with something stressful. He likened laughter to the safety valve on a steam pipe.

Spencer's work would influence Freud's understanding of humor.[15] Freud considered jokes to be like dreams in that they allow forbidden ideas from the unconscious to surface, and thus are healthy in release of repressed tensions. Jokes allow the truth to slip out and we are then glad, relieved to be free of it.[16] Freud concludes that humor allows for safe rebellion from constraints that can build up to cause psychic pain.

Without humor, Spencer and Freud argue, the psychological pressures and constraints of social life would be unbearable. A classic example of how this works is found in Donald Roy's study based on his ethnographic experience of a machine shop. Roy describes how the workers tolerated the "beast of monotony" and the exhausting nature of factory life by forming close-knit groups and using designated times to mark and disrupt the repetitive workday. Every day at mealtime, the *same* humorous episode occurred—one of the workers, with much fanfare and yelling, "Banana time!" took and ate a banana from another machine operator's lunch. In these brief, playful, and informal outbursts, Roy argued that the workers temporarily resisted not only the physical but also the mentally dehumanizing drudgery of their work.[17]

Prominent sociologist Erving Goffman observed that humor is often used as a face-saving behavior in negotiations to reduce psychological tension and increase trust between parties.[18] In the study "Goffman Goes to Church," researchers ethnographically observe religious services and argue that the enforcement of norms forms the basis of collective religious behaviors.[19] The researchers observed (or reported) little humor but have extensive observations into the normative complexity of religious services and how disruptions or transgression were met with avoidance, swift negative social sanctions, and enforcement behaviors by congregants and pastors alike. They conclude, "This study illuminates the gritty unpleasantries occurring every Sunday during mainline Christian services." This begs a couple of questions: Was the church's social atmosphere (sociologists call this a *social climate* or *idioculture*) so somber that pastors and people were utterly humorless?[20] Or did the research just miss the violations that were met with relief humor because sanctions were unneeded? Here may be a lesson on the benefits of a comic spirit and providing space for humor and laughter and its use in our worship services and ministry.

Finally, in addition to physiological and psychological relief, relief theory asserts that humor offers relief of *social tensions*. Generally people restrain themselves to avoid breaking social norms, and when we or others violate social norms it makes us and them extremely uncomfortable. In such cases humor can allow social normative violations to be acknowledged and the tensions arising from it to be immediately released so that a social ritual is not derailed. This social "safety valve" function of relief humor can also be observed when a "transgressor" of a norm employs humor to publicly recognize their false step.

Relief Humor Homiletical Example

A recent example occurred at a Roman Catholic Mass Owen attended. Half of the congregation stood before all the eucharistic gifts had been placed on the altar,[21] and they began to look around at each awkwardly, not knowing what to do.[22] The priest said, "Sorry, I am getting old and moving slow. Please sit." The congregation laughed, and those who stood sat back down. Once the offering ritual had finished and the priest had placed the bread and wine on the altar, he turned to the congregation and said, "Whew, I finally caught up. Please stand." The congregation laughed and stood. The congregation standing at the wrong time was a disruption to the ritual (and for the congregation, a social norm). But the joke and the laughter acknowledged the faux pas and the tension caused by this disruption, and by relieving it, allowed the structure of the Mass to be continued and maintained. The priest's skillful use of self-effacing humor even transferred the blame for the disruption to himself and made it possible for the congregation to relax. Indeed, when relief humor is used with this sort of skill, not only does one save face, they arguably lift their standing in the social setting.

INCONGRUITY HUMOR THEORY

Incongruity theory focuses on incongruity as the basis of *why* we find things humorous. From that basic understanding it proceeds to explain the function(s) incongruous humor can serve. We find things to be funny when the sensemaking process is interrupted by something unexpected, disconnected, unusual, or out of place. As Groucho Marx put it, "Humor is reasoning gone mad." The four stages of humor development discussed in chapter 2 are defined by different levels of cognitive ability in relation to the recognition of incongruity.

Contemporary humor scholarship primarily adopts the incongruity theory basis for applied humor research because making sense of incongruity (in texts or social life) is necessary for the creation and recognition of humor regardless of its intent, use, or effect. The incongruity theory of humor asserts that humor used to relieve stress or to assert superiority is secondary to the incongruity of the humor utterance itself.

The following ridiculous riddle illustrates incongruity at work. It follows the simplest joke script structure, which is when the punch line resolves an ontological contradiction.[23]

"What do you call a mushroom with money?" "A fungi to be."

The first half of the script ontologically makes no sense since mushrooms do not use money. The question creates cognitive tension (incongruity), but the absurdity sets out the expectation that it is a joke and prepares us for the resolution, the punch line. The humor of the punch line lies in the fact that "fungi" sounds like "fun guy"). The pun resolves the tension, since clearly the question is meant to be absurd and fun. Incongruity humor theory is built upon our need or desire for consistency with our internal frames and the external world or understandings. Put simply, we like things to make sense. Jokes and humor thus have a role in social life: helping us come to terms with or release the tension that ambiguity creates. As Ben Franklin reminded us, ambiguity is unavoidable: "Nothing can be certain except death and taxes." This is why we laugh at observational humor, even when it is somewhat ridiculous, as when Robin Williams observes, "Why do they call it rush hour when nothing moves?" We laugh and often say to ourselves, *That is so true!* If we cannot always have logical consistency, we learn to enjoy or play with inconsistencies or dissonance. Conflicting concepts are inevitable and they cause cognitive stress. Humor helps us accept, resolve, and reduce this tension.

Pure incongruity as nonconfrontational humor can point out the ridiculousness of a particular behavior or thought. We can see this strategic use in an example cited above: Jesus' question, "Why do you see the speck in your neighbor's eye, but do not notice the log in your own eye?" (Matt. 7:3) is as absurd as the mushroom with money, but the contrast between the sawdust speck and log drives the point home with clarity.

Incongruity Humor Homiletical Example

How might a preacher whose imagination has been sparked by Jesus' humor strategies utilize incongruity-type humor in preaching?

Let's take a look at the Beatitudes, since perhaps nowhere is Jesus' use of incongruity clearer than in these subversive sayings. Beatitudes, statements of blessing, are common in the Old Testament (see Isa. 30:18; Jer. 17:7; Ps. 1:1–2) where they express conventional wisdom— that there are positive spiritual consequences for those who wait for God (Isa. 30:18), who trust in the Lord (Jer. 17:7), and who delight in the law of the Lord (Ps. 1:2). Jesus' Beatitudes, by contrast, dial up incongruity to the point of paradox. Conditions we normally consider to be negative are presented as positive, not just in the life to come, but in this present time, surrounding the faithful with a sphere of divine presence and possibility.[24] How can the poor, those who mourn, the meek, those who hunger and thirst, and those who are hated be considered blessed or happy (Luke 6:20–23)? Matthew's version focuses more on the inward disposition of a person rather than the nature of one's outward circumstances. Still his version, like Luke's, contrasts conditions and attitudes we equate with social success and Jesus' teachings about humility and radical love of neighbor.[25]

Alyce used incongruity humor in a recent sermon on Matthew 5:3—"Blessed are the poor in spirit"—in the context of the Beatitudes as a whole. She noted that the New English Bible renders this Beatitude as "How blessed are those who know their need for God." Her sermon shone a spotlight on how this Beatitude contrasts with our habitual actions and attitudes and challenges listeners to consider how they have both bought into cultural habits and how they might embody Jesus' alternative wisdom in an everyday social situation.

When my son Matthew was in high school, he was a goalie for a Dallas-based select soccer team. He had athletic ability, and as parents we knew that team sports would be a great way to experience community and learn valuable life lessons. We attended lots of tournaments during those years. One stands out in my mind above the others. It was a Labor Day weekend tournament on a hot Sunday afternoon. I came prepared with sunhat, camp chair, and bottled water, found a shade tree, and settled in to enjoy the game. But as the afternoon unfolded, I began to shake my head in disbelief. You would not have believed the dirty play! Pulling shirts, coming in body first, kicking at the legs, trash talk—and that was just among the parents on the sidelines!

"Get us a ref who can speak English!" yelled one of the visiting player's dads. A dad from the other team moved his chair closer to our parents and began yelling instructions to his son. One of our mothers yelled over to him, "If you wanna coach, move to the other side of the field!" After the game was over, one of the dads from the other team was walking by our parents. "Where are y'all from?" asked one of our moms. "Mississippi," he replied. "Well, that explains everything!" she shot back.

Alyce then made this comment to the congregation: "This is a scene that had it all: ethnic and regional slurs, physical aggression, arrogance, a microcosm of our culture at its worst, right before my eyes." She ended with a question: "What place does 'Blessed are the poor in spirit' have on these sidelines?"

DESIRABLE DISRUPTION

We have examined the three theories of humor separately and indicated their homiletical relevance. When preachers are considering using a particular element of humor in a sermon, they would do well to consider which type of humor it most closely represents and if it then functions in the way they need it to in a particular sermon, drawing on the advice in chapter 4.

That said, matters of humor are not as clear-cut as our discussion might imply. Expressions of humor can often involve two or even all three of the types of humor discussed. A joke or spontaneous humor can emerge from incongruity and provide social and psychophysical relief, all while putting someone or something in its place.

All three overlapping and intersecting types of humor offer a "desirable disruption" to serious life and are thus a necessary part of who we are.[26] They prevent us from taking ourselves, others, or events too seriously.

Put differently, humor disables a previous serious (and perhaps flawed) frame. When instructed to take the log out of your own eye, you cannot go back to fretting or admonishing the speck in someone else's. As one scholar puts it,

> Humor's disabling function actually transforms it into a socially enabling mechanism. Any social group [or individual] is in danger of falling into a rigid pattern of social expectation or routines. Some sort of social disruption is therefore needed to enhance interest, rejuvenation, and creativity.[27]

A popular story that captures this socially disruptive power of humor concerns when Alexander the Great and his grand army met the unyielding poor hermit (the philosopher Diogenes) on the road. One of Alexander's men demanded he make way, saying, "This man has conquered the world! What have you done?" Without an instant's hesitation Diogenes replied, "I have conquered the need to conquer the world."

Humor and the exercise of the comic spirit, in the context of what we explore in the next chapter—the comic frame—have a social utility. As literary critic Mikhail Bakhtin writes in his exploration of the carnivalesque, "Certain essential aspects of the world are accessible only to laughter."[28] Medieval carnival (not to be confused with modern-day Mardi Gras, carnival, or cruise ships) as a comic framing of life is a purposeful, desired, and temporary disruption of order. We describe the specific forms that carnival took in the medieval period in chapter 8. The carnival frame turns things on their heads, forcing a shift in perspective and a (re)interpretation of that which has been taken for granted. It represents a vision of when the weak shall be strong, the poor shall be rich, and the bottom shall be on top. It temporarily disrupts, not just seriousness, but disrupts and disables the accepted basis for earthly authority, social order, and our own pomposity.

Humor and comic frame, from this perspective, encapsulates aspects of all three theories. As incongruity, it disrupts logic; as relief, it relieves tensions; and with regard to superiority, it challenges earthly based pretensions to power. Picture Jesus, King of Kings, entering Jerusalem not on a magnificent steed or at the head of a procession like Alexander, but "gentle and riding on a donkey." There is a clear carnivalesque feature to Christianity and the New Testament.[29] The unexpected switch or divergence from social order in the parable of the Good Samaritan in Luke 15 is that neither the priest nor the Levite stopped to help the wounded man on the road but the despised Samaritan. In the story of Zacchaeus, it was not King Herod or Caiaphas with whom Jesus chose to dine with but a tax collector, a thug who extorted his own people for the Romans and to enrich himself. In John 4, it is not to his disciples or to the high priest at the temple but to the disgraced Samaritan woman by the well to whom Jesus openly reveals himself as Messiah. The carnival frame reminds us not to be spiritually complacent, not to take too seriously anything we have here on earth, be it authority as with Pilate, or wealth as in the case of the rich man (Mark 10:17–27; Matt. 19:16–27), since "Many who are first will be last, and the last will be first" (Matt. 19:30).

On a recent All Saints Day, Alyce preached a sermon based on Hebrews 12:1–3, 12–13 titled "Roll Credits!" The sermon used the phrase "Roll credits" as a metaphor for finish lines in life that don't come when we expect them. Some seem to go on too long . . . like the situation of the Hebrews whose struggle threatened to outlast their faith. Others seem to end too soon, as in positive experiences that end sooner than we would like—like losing a job you love, a painful breakup, or learning of the death of a young relative.

Here is the opening to this sermon, which combines elements of disruption of logic, relief, and challenge of social convention.

Suppose it's 1973 and you are sitting on your avocado-green couch. And you have the good taste to be watching an episode of *Monty Python's Flying Circus*. Monty Python was a comedy troupe that began with a group of zany British university lads who later created a TV show that ran from 1969 to 1974. The show included inappropriate sexual innuendos and skits with absolutely no punch lines. They created a surreal comedic world that broke all the rules.

One rule they loved to break had to do with rolling the credits. Originally movie credits were printed on a roll of paper. It was then scrolled through in front of the camera. The instruction to start the credits rolling was, "Roll credits." And when did that instruction come? AT THE END!

So you are sitting on your couch in 1973 enjoying the sexual innuendos and skits with no punch lines and suddenly, ten minutes into the half-hour show, they roll credits.

Monty Python relished messing with us, flashing a signal that something has ended before we thought it should. So disconcerting!

Have the credits ever rolled too soon in a circumstance in your life? Interrupting the episode too early on? A colleague of mine some years ago was serving as a youth pastor in a small Pennsylvania town as a ministerial intern from Yale Divinity School. Granted, his heart wasn't in it and he had successfully reduced the youth group by half over the summer. Still, he wasn't expecting, as he daydreamed, staring at his shoes during Sunday morning worship, to hear his senior pastor announce, "I know you'll all join me in thanking Rick for his ministry and wishing him well on this, his last Sunday among us." You don't have to feel sorry for Rick. He went on to find his true calling teaching American history at the college level. Still, he says he could only laugh about it later.

And some early rolling credits we experience are no laughing matter. A relative's mental faculties begin to fade way too early, a well-loved colleague dies suddenly in their prime.

The sermon then moves to the situation of the Hebrews with this segue sentence:

The author of Hebrews considered his congregation's situation to be no laughing matter. They were on the brink of rolling the credits too soon in their journey of faith.

To Ponder

Look back at a couple of your recent sermons. What kind of humor or blend of humor types (superiority/relief/incongruity) have you employed?

— Have you used humor to expose hypocrisy (superiority)?
— Have you used it to release tension before introducing a tough topic (relief)?
— Have you used it to point out the incongruity between how things are and how God would like them to be (incongruity)?

Consider the answers you gave concerning the previous questions we asked you to ponder. Did any of the examples of humor in your recent sermons rise to the level of desirable disruption?

NOTES

1. Terry Eagleton, *Humour* (New Haven, CT: Yale University Press, 2019). xi.
2. A reader familiar with C. S. Lewis's *Mere Christianity* would see similarities with this paragraph and Lewis's defense on the practicality and need for

theology. Lewis, in his retelling of encounters with people who "have no time or need for theology," says he completely agrees with them. He then, with ample wit and rhetorical skill, demonstrates that for all practical pursuits they probably do. We repeat this same comic structure out of respect and some deference to Lewis. It is worth noting that Lewis wrote, "They all say 'the ordinary reader does not want Theology; give him plain practical religion'. I have rejected their advice. I do not think the ordinary reader is such a fool. Theology means 'the science of God,' and I think any man who wants to think about God at all would like to have the clearest and most accurate ideas about Him which are available" (C. S. Lewis, *Mere Christianity* [Zondervan, 2001], 153–55).

3. Sigmund Freud, *Jokes and Their Relation to the Unconscious* (New York: W. W. Norton & Company, 1960).

4. Henri Bergson, "Laughter," in *Comedy* (Cambridge: Cambridge University Press, 1996), 66–90.

5. Asa Berger was a semiotics and visual communication scholar who has a prolific publication record, including *Blind Men and Elephants: Perspectives on Humor* (London: Routledge Press, 2017). He was eclectic in his studies, focus, and methods, and often found and used humor in his work. He is quoted as saying, "I sometime describe myself, mocking myself, as someone who applies obscure theories with dubious results." This quote is from an interview: Leonhardt, Van Efferink, "Arthur Asa Berger: Understanding American Icons—An Introduction to Semiotics." Exploring Geopolitics, March 16, 2013, https://exploringgeopolitics.org /arthur-asa-berger-understanding-american-icons-an-introduction-to-semiotics/. See Arthur Asa Berger, *Blind Men and Elephants: Perspectives on Humor* (London: Routledge Press, 2017).

6. Owen H. Lynch, "Humorous Communication: Finding a Place for Humor in Communication Research," *Communication Theory* 12, no. 4 (November 2002): 423–45, https://doi.org/10.1111/j.1468-2885.2002.tb00277.x.

7. This interdisciplinary research focus on humor is often traced back to an "On Humor and Laughter" conference held in 1976. See A. J. Chapman and H. C. Foot, eds., *It's a Funny Thing, Humour: Proceedings of the International Conference on Humour and Laughter* (Oxford: Pergamon Press, 1976). The conference was built on an emerging interdisciplinary work from pathfinder humor theorists Christie Davis (folklore and anthropology), Mary Douglas (social anthropology), Willian Fry (physiology), Gary Alan Fine (sociology), Jeffery Goldstein (anthropology), Jacob Levine (psychology), John Morreall (religious studies and philosophy), Victor Raskin (linguistics), Paul Mcghee (psychology and cognitive development), and Donald Roy (organizational studies). In 1988 the International Society of Humor Studies was formed as the organizational sponsor of the annual interdisciplinary research conference. The society's journal, *Humor*, provides an interdisciplinary forum for the publication of articles on humor as an important and universal human faculty. By the turn of the new century, work also began to focus on humor's use and role in specific social and organizational contexts, the use of humor within

these spaces based on social categorizations (gender, sexuality, race, social class, and profession), and the intersectionality of these systems (see, e.g., the work of David Collinson, Janet Holmes, Owen Lynch, and Patricia Martin).

8. Eagleton, *Humour*, 41.

9. Thomas Hobbes, *The Elements of Law, Natural and Politic: Part I, Human Nature, Part II, De Corpore Politico; with Three Lives* (New York: Oxford University Press, 1999).

10. See https://darwinawards.com/, where you can vote for the person who died in the most predictable and stupid fashion. The award, like dumbest criminal, originated in early web chat rooms in 1985 and has been the subject of a series of annual "humor" books and even a movie. Wendy Northcutt, *The Darwin Awards: Evolution in Action* (New York: Penguin, 2002).

11. See Shawn Langlois, "Ricky Gervais Attacks 'Woke' Hollywood and Shreds Apple, Disney and Amazon in Savage Golden Globes Monologue," MarketWatch, January 6, 2020, https://www.marketwatch.com/story/ricky-gervais-attacks-woke-hollywood-and-shreds-apple-disney-and-amazon-in-savage-golden-globes-monologue-2020-01-05. Also see Sara M. Moniuszko, "After His Controversial Golden Globes Hosting, Ricky Gervais Defends His Humor," *USA Today*, January 8, 2020, https://www.usatoday.com/story/entertainment/celebrities/2020/01/08/ricky-gervais-defends-his-humor-after-hosting-2020-golden-globes/2842320001/, which quotes Gervais defending his jokes targeted at powerful people, whom he argues should be able to laugh at themselves.

12. See Karl N. and Rolf A. Jacobsen, *Divine Laughter: Preaching and the Serious Business of Humor* (Minneapolis: Fortress Press, 2022), 83–104.

13. See chap. 8 of this volume, "Foes and Fans: Humor through the Centuries."

14. See W. F. Fry, "The Physiologic Effects of Humor, Mirth, and Laughter," *JAMA: The Journal of the American Medical Association* 267, no. 13 (April 1, 1992): 1857–58, https://doi.org/10.1001/jama.267.13.1857; Lee S. Berk et al., "Neuroendocrine and Stress Hormone Changes during Mirthful Laughter," *American Journal of the Medical Sciences* 298, no. 6 (December 1989): 390–96, https://doi.org/10.1097/00000441-198912000-00006; Ronald A. Berk, "The Active Ingredients in Humor: Psychophysiological Benefits and Risks for Older Adults," *Educational Gerontology* 27, no. 3–4 (April 2001): 323–39, https://doi.org/10.1080/036012701750195021.

15. Freud, *Jokes and Their Relation to the Unconscious*.

16. Sigmund Freud, *Group Psychology and the Analysis of the Ego* (New York: W. W. Norton & Company, 1975). Freud is best known for his focus on the contest between the id and ego in relation to sexually repressive societal norms that he claimed caused neurotic anxiety, but it would be a mistake to limit his thoughts on humor to such.

17. Donald Roy, "'Banana Time': Job Satisfaction and Informal Interaction," *Human Organization* 18, no. 4 (December 1, 1959): 158–68, https://doi.org/10.17730/humo.18.4.07j88hr1p4074605.

18. E. Goffman, "On Face-Work: An Analysis of Ritual Elements in Social Interaction," *Psychiatry* 18, no. 3 (1955): 213–31.

19. C. M. Donnelly and B. R. Wright, "Goffman Goes to Church: Face-Saving and the Maintenance of Collective Order in Religious Services," *Sociological Research Online* 18, no. 1 (2013):154.

20. *Idioculture* is defined as a system of knowledge, beliefs, behaviors, and customs shared by members of an interacting group to which members can refer and employ as the basis of daily interaction. G. A. Fine suggests that each organization or tightly bound social group like a congregation will establish, with the influence and direction of their leader, a unique and particular idioculture or climate. Fine also suggested that in-group situated humor was a key aspect in creating and maintaining an idioculture. See G. A. Fine, "Small Groups and Culture Creation: The Idioculture of Little League Baseball Teams," *American Sociological Review* 44, no. 5 (October 1979): 733–45.

21. The eucharistic gifts are accepted by the priest from the congregation and then placed on the altar. This is the time to stand to signal the beginning of the Rite of Eucharist. The accepting and placing on the altar are usually so seamless there is no lag between accepting and starting the rite. Hence the audience confusion.

22. For those unfamiliar with the liturgy (or structure) of the Catholic Mass, the offering or "preparation of the gifts" follows the conclusion of the Liturgy of the Word and beginning of the Liturgy of the Eucharist. It is when the presider (the priest) accepts from the congregation the gifts (bread and wine) to be transformed into the Eucharist.

23. For discussion on humor script theory, which explains why and how jokes work and even how to write them, see chap. 13 of this book. Also see Victor Raskin, "Semantic Theory of Humor," in *Semantic Mechanisms of Humor,* ed. Victor Raskin (Springer, Netherlands: Dordrecht, 1985): 99–147. See also S. Attardo and V. Raskin, "Linguistics and Humor Theory," in *The Routledge Handbook of Language and Humor*, ed. Salvatore Attardo (London: Routledge, 2017), 9–63.

24. Matthew's version of the Beatitudes, in contrast to Luke's, emphasizes the inward disposition of a person, rather than the nature of one's circumstances and so is less socially subversive.

25. For a fuller discussion of the Beatitudes as subversive wisdom, see Alyce M. McKenzie's commentary, *Matthew*, Interpretation Bible Study Series (Louisville, KY: Westminster John Knox Press, 2002), chaps. 3 and 4.

26. Wallace Chafe, "Humor as a Disabling Mechanism," *American Behavioral Scientist* 30, no. 3 (January 1987): 16–25, https://doi.org/10.1177/000276487030003003; Chafe, "The Importance of Not Being Earnest: The Feeling behind Laughter and Humor," *Phonetica* 68, no. 3 (November 1, 2011): 192–97, https://doi.org/10.1159/000334478.

27. John Meyer, *Understanding Humor through Communication: Why Be Funny, Anyway?* (Lanham, MD: Lexington Books, 2015), 15. Eagleton, in his

recent book *Humour*, makes a similar point: "Humour does for adults what play does for children, namely liberates them from the despotism of the reality principle and allows the pleasure principle some scrupulously regulated free play" (19).

28. Cited in Eagleton, *Humour,* 27. From M. Bakhtin, *Rabelais and His World* (Bloomington: Indiana University Press, 1984), 48.

29. See Nehama Aschkenasy, "Reading Ruth through a Bakhtinian Lens: The Carnivalesque in a Biblical Tale," *Journal of Biblical Literature* 126, no. 3 (2007): 437–53, https://doi.org/10.2307/27638447; L. Juliana M. Claassens, "Biblical Theology as Dialogue: Continuing the Conversation on Mikhail Bakhtin and Biblical Theology," *Journal of Biblical Literature* 122, no. 1 (2003): 127–44, https://doi.org/10.2307/3268094; Hilary B. P. Bagshaw, *Religion in the Thought of Mikhail Bakhtin: Reason and Faith* (London: Routledge, 2016).

7

The Two Frames

Comedy and Tragedy

Angels can fly because they can take themselves lightly.
—British journalist, novelist, and
theologian G. K. Chesterton (1874–1936)[1]

The more thoroughly and substantially a human being exists, the more
he will discover the *comical.*
—Danish theologian Søren Kierkegaard
(1813–1855)[2]

Throughout the book, we have been using three interrelated but distinct terms. *Humor orientation* (HO) refers to one's predisposition to recognize, appreciate, and use humor. By *comic spirit* we have meant the openness to noticing and employing humor (and its companions, joy and laughter) in light of and in the context of the comic vision. This leads to the concept of the *comic vision*, which in the context of Christian theology we define as the certainty of the ultimate victory of positive outcomes over negative circumstances—of life over death, of hope over despair—that encompasses our sermons and our lives as Christians. While we have noted elements of the comic vision across the chapters thus far, in this chapter we explore this comic vision more thoroughly. We examine an approach to life (and preaching) that asserts that isolation and death do not get the last word; that adversity does not have to mean defeat; that losers can come out on top; and that life, warts and all, can be embraced as a sometimes terrifically painful but in the end promising journey. In other words, we are looking at the difference between the comic and the tragic in faith and proclamation.[3]

To be clear, humor inside or outside the Christian faith is no panacea that takes away all suffering. Trauma is a significant element of individual and corporate life that preachers need to address.[4] Holding to a comic vision of God's creation does not eliminate pain. Rather, it lets us honestly name sorrow, while recognizing the hope and even the joy in its midst. Says theologian Brian Edgar, "Tragedy, pain, and trauma are not overcome in this world by eliminating them (that is for the future kingdom, where there will be no more pain or suffering), but by finding God and divine joy in the midst of them."[5]

Comedy and tragedy's relationship began when the two met on the stage in Greece several centuries before the birth of Christ. For a while they were inseparable and knew they needed each other. Tragedies would be interspersed with comedies to demonstrate for audiences the counterbalance between both sides of life. The ancient Greeks, Shakespeare, and other dramatists took their comedy seriously. They realized that comedy is not a time-out from the world. Instead, authors through time have used it to provide another perspective on the realities of the world, a perspective that stubbornly refused to give tragedy and fate the last word. They acknowledged that this outlook was no less valid than the tragic perspective and that the two perspectives needed each other.[6]

COMEDY VERSUS TRAGEDY

Somewhere along the way in the early centuries of Christian history, however, comedy and tragedy divorced, and the unalleviated seriousness characteristic of tragedy got custody of faith. In a worldview that privileged tragedy, humor was caricatured as a trivial distraction from the serious business of living. We are arguing for the serious need for a comic spirit as a necessary counterbalance to tragedy in our preaching ministries. Religious expression at its best functions within a dialectic between an acknowledgment of life's challenges and sorrows and its humor and opportunities for joy.

Humor without faith can lead to cynicism, despair, doubt, and the loss of all that is holy.[7] On the other hand, faith without humor can fall into dogmatism, self-righteousness, and idolatry. It leads to the elevation of finite understanding to an absolute, divine status. "Ideologies, like religious dogmas, have a high level of missionary zeal and a low level of comic awareness."[8] All those who absolutize their own perspectives share in "the attempted abolition of humor in relation to themselves." Conrad Hyers points out that "a common trait of dictators, revolutionaries, and ecclesiastical authoritarians is their refusal both to laugh at themselves and to permit others to laugh at them." He adds,

"It is difficult to imagine people who have a profound sense of humor in relation to their own most ultimate convictions participating in the burning of other people at the stake—as in John Calvin's Geneva—because of a failure to subscribe to a certain formation of the doctrine of the Trinity!"[9]

Theologian Brian Edgar, in his book *Laughter and the Grace of God*, expresses what we mean by the comic vision of the preacher:

> Having a mature sense of humor . . . does not mean not being serious about life, but it does mean . . . being appreciative rather than despairing of the world; and . . . understanding that, despite appearances to the contrary, joyfulness and not tragedy is the final outcome of all things. This temperament, this sense of humor, is part and parcel of the life of faith, hope, love, and especially joy.[10]

The ancient masks of theater depict both the tragic face and the comic face as two sides of the same coin, two responses to the common human experience of incongruity: the disconnect between how we wish things were and how they are. There are many varieties of responses when things do not happen as we think they should: puzzlement, resentment, rage, despair, and amusement. In tragedies, characters respond with anger and rebellion. By contrast, in comedies they respond by not getting overly concerned. Says John Morreall, "Comedy presents incongruities as something we can live with, indeed, something in which we can take a certain delight."[11]

This living with incongruity is illustrated by the second-century BCE Roman playwright Terence, whose motto of comedy was, "I am a human being, nothing human is alien to me."[12] Maya Angelou draws on Terence in her famous speech "I Am Human" where she recognizes how hard it is to be humble, to love and forgive and come together especially for those who have trespassed against you.[13] Seeing our common humanity and having both humility and forgiveness are all easier said than done, but they are crucial components of comedy. If one cannot get past themselves and their foolish pride, if one is compelled to condemn, if the turn or trick in the plot does not lead to resolution, it will lead to destruction. If those in power or the power-hungry remain so at the end and are unrepentant and divided, then the story is a tragedy. To be human is to embrace tragedy. But to be human within the comic vision of our Christian faith is to refuse to allow tragedy to speak the final and loudest word.

THE COMIC FRAME

Kenneth Burke describes three frames of reference, that is, structures we use to organize and make sense of our personal and social experiences and to direct our social action. They are the acceptance frame, the tragic frame, and the comic frame. The *acceptance frame* simply allows us to (re)inforce current ways of thinking and social order.

The *tragic frame*, which Burke also calls the "debunking frame," recognizes that something is seriously wrong or damaging.[14] Since, in this frame, we cannot accept something or assume responsibility for it, we have two choices: we can dismiss it as not real (as some have done in the case of the COVID-19 pandemic) or we can find a scapegoat and pin our pain on them (as some have done in making death threats against Dr. Anthony Fauci). History and our current world are full of examples of this practice.

According to Burke the predominant type of humor used within the tragic frame is "burlesque humor": a mocking or targeted satire with the purpose of suppressing a behavior or even eliminating a person or a social group. This can be seen in the inhumane "humor" of the Rwanda genocide that likened people to "cockroaches."[15] It can also be seen in the 2016 presidential campaign when Donald Trump nicknamed his opponents with nicknames such as "Crooked Hillary," "Lying Ted," or "Low-Energy Jeb." Humor in the tragic frame is superiority humor on steroids—it moves from making fun to scapegoating. Burke argued that burlesque "humor" is in no way comical, but is a form of aggression and should be seen and called out as such.

Finally, according to Burke, the *comic frame* combines elements from both the acceptance and tragic frames, but offers an alternative to both by reframing the social order or some perceived wrong. The comic frame recognizes that social order and consistency of meanings are important and also that assertions made and actions taken to maintain them can be illogical or contradictory. Using the comic frame allows us to recognize oddities within others, but also those same oddities within ourselves. Foibles and personal flaws are part of our shared human experience. We are all flawed, but in the comic frame, flaws can be forgiven. The comic frame allows a welcoming back of the institution or individual, a laughing with rather than a laughing at. For Burke the tragic seeks to destroy difference and revels in assigning blame. The comic, by contrast, seeks forgiveness, acceptance, and celebration.

PLOT STRUCTURES IN COMEDY AND TRAGEDY

Tragedies most often feature lone protagonists, often with distinguished status and gifts, who encounter obstacles, battle a fatal flaw within themselves, and proceed inevitably toward isolation and defeat or death. Tragedy showcases the fatedness of the hero's fall, often highlighting the fierceness of the hero's assertion of transcendence.[16] Says Terry Eagleton, "The opposite of comedy is destiny."[17]

Comedies, by contrast, often feature a motley group viewed by others as social misfits. Like the characters in tragedies, they encounter obstacles and struggle with challenges. Rather than view these setbacks and sorrows as proof of the grim nature and outcome of life, however, comedies are willing to take the bitter with the sweet, viewing life as a risky, sometimes painful, but ultimately rewarding adventure. The plots of comedies feature characters overcoming or escaping from mishaps through a reversal of expectations culminating in a positive outcome.[18]

The plotlines of comedy and tragedy at first glance appear similar, beginning with a harmonious social situation that is then challenged or tested in some way as the action unfolds. There the similarity ends. The plot of tragedy moves inexorably toward catastrophe and increased isolation in the context of an inhospitable and capricious cosmos, typically ending with a fallen hero and a vision of disintegration, alienation, and death. Comedy, by contrast, swings up at the end with the hero happily reintegrated into her or his rightful society. Comedy's distinctive plot structure is a necessary counterpoint to the tragic form.[19]

Two thinkers who have contributed greatly to the understanding of plot structure and the comic form are Joseph Campbell and Northrup Frye. Joseph Campbell's writings on the hero's journey frame it as a divine drama, which, like life, is filled with perils, pain, and tragedy.[20] The humorous characters or tricksters, a universal mythic archetype, are typically smart and rule breaking, getting by on their cunning and wit like Br'er Rabbit of African American folktales.[21] While wise, they play the fool (examples include *Star Wars*' R2D2 and Alice's White Rabbit) in order to force a change in the hero.[22] They may reveal a character's foibles and remind them to not take themselves so seriously.

As Campbell in his own life reflected, "As you proceed through life, following your own path, birds will shit on you. Don't bother to brush it off. Getting a comedic view of your situation gives you spiritual distance. Having a sense of humor saves you."[23]

Campbell views the comedic as integral, not secondary, to the hero's journey. "The happy ending of the fairy tale, the myth, and divine comedy of the soul is to be read not as an escape from or a contradiction of the universal tragedy of man [*sic*]. It is a transformation, a transcendence. The objective world remains what it was, but, because of a shift within the subject, is beheld as though transformed."[24] The divine comedy allows for a seemingly negative or tragic sacrifice and a positive outcome to be held together at the same time.

Northup Frye, himself an ordained minister, asserted that comedies follow a U-shaped plotline (they swing up), whereas tragedies have an inverted U-shaped movement (swinging down).[25] Frye, in *The Argument for Comedy*, argues that the comic form is characterized by compassion and community, that its essential elements lie in the rise of fortune of a sympathetic or plucky underdog hero, and that in the end the unlikely but likeable hero succeeds usually through some form of trickery. This success brings a resolution and a union or coming together in a marriage or other celebratory event. Moreover, Frye suggests, "The freer the society, the greater the variety of individuals it can tolerate, and the natural tendency of comedy is to include as many as possible in its final festival."[26] Comedy is designed, says Frye, to ridicule lack of self-awareness and foolish pride. It demonstrates that ultimately confusion and separation can lead to clarity and unification.

COMEDY AND TRAGEDY ILLUSTRATED

The shape of the comic form as distinct from the tragic form comes into high relief when we take what we have learned from Campbell and Frye and consider Shakespeare, who was a master at both genres. The tragic ending of *Romeo and Juliet* is well known. Young lovers are separated by a hateful feud between their families. Were Shakespeare crafting a comedy, Romeo and Juliet would somehow overcome the feud, the families would come together for a wedding, and love would have the final word. Instead the families come together for a funeral after the two unnecessarily took their own lives simply because a letter telling Romeo that Juliet was only asleep and not dead did not reach him before news of her supposed death did.

By contrast, we find in *A Midsummer Night's Dream* characters similar to Romeo and Juliet in the sense that they are miserable and unable to achieve happiness due to the demands and interference of others.

In this plot, however, they escape into the forest, another existence, to avoid the tragedy, and under the new influence of mischief they ultimately see and accept each other and are free to love and marry as they desire, for, as Puck concludes, "all is mended."[27]

The structures illustrated in well-known Shakespearean plays are also evident in Scripture. An especially illustrative text is the parable of the Two Sons, commonly called the parable of the Prodigal Son (Luke 15:11–32). In the story, the younger son misuses his father's generosity and wealth. When a famine occurs, he finds himself isolated, hungry, and forced to take a job feeding pigs. The image of a Jewish man feeding unclean animals with food he would gladly have eaten has elements of comedy (specifically irony) and tragedy. It is unclear at this point of the story which direction, the tragic or the comic, the parable will take. The son decides in a moment of clarity to return to his father in humility (or at least the appearance of it). His father meets him with joy and immediately throws a feast and "they began to celebrate" for he, his son, was lost and is now found (15:24). This is the classic *comedic form*; the ending is a celebration of forgiveness and joyous unity.

But wait, there's more. The older son who has been working his father's field the whole time that the younger son has been gone refuses to join the celebration upon his return, a high-stakes turning point. There is risk for the older son's happiness and salvation. He refuses to give grace and forgiveness to his brother, whom he refers to as "this son of yours" (15:30), purposely not acknowledging his familial tie. The father, however, does not allow the older son's words to be final. He turns the older son's words back on him, saying that "this brother of yours" (15:32) was lost and has been found. Here the parable ends and we are left never knowing which way it turns—into a comedy or a tragedy. Is the older son's mind changed so that he joins the party (comedy), or does he turn away from the celebration, similar to those who condemned Jesus for welcoming and eating with sinners (tragedy; see 15:1–2)? Luke's use of the open ending is an invitation for the reader to decide, and—it is hoped—to act in a manner that brings the parable to a conclusion appropriate to the comic vision.

As part of the exegetical process for preaching on a biblical text, Alyce asks students what they would change about a text's ending if they could. No student has ever said that they wish the Samaritan had not stopped to help the man in need (Luke 10:30–35), the friend hadn't gotten out of bed (11:5–8), the gardener hadn't fertilized the apparently dead tree (13:6–9), and the unjust judge hadn't relented (18:2–5). No one ever says, "I wish the seeds hadn't sprouted" (Mark 4:3–8), that the vineyard owner had played it more by the book (Matt. 10:1–15), or that Bartimaeus had not followed Jesus on the way (Mark 10:46–52). We never wish for comedy to end in tragedy. We yearn for the emergence of the comic vision from the depths of the sorrows of life.

Campbell's and Frye's insights into the comic frame are instructive, not just in inspiring us to exercise the comic spirit, but also for the positive pattern they offer for strategic sequencing or forms of our sermons, referred to in classical rhetorical terms as "arrangement." Much of the homiletical theory of the past fifty years, what has been termed the New Homiletic, is patterned after the U-shaped plotline, of a move from equilibrium to disequilibrium to resolution to celebration.[28] Homileticians have articulated a variety of sermonic forms from which preachers can choose. But three components are essential to an effective form: unity, movement, and climax.[29]

One of the most common mistakes preachers, even seasoned communicators, make has to do with movement or sermonic form. It consists of our habit of returning to the bad news after we have offered the good news. Alyce calls it "backing over the spikes," using the analogy of a rental car return.[30] Just as backing over the spikes would deflate the tires, so returning to the problem once we've offered listeners the gospel deflates the sermon. With a few exceptions, sermons should move in a clean sweep from negative to positive, dark to light, despair to hope, guilt to grace, death to life, itch to scratch. Once the preacher has offered the balm of Gilead, don't pour itching powder all over the congregation! While we deal with tragedy, we do not *proclaim* tragedy—we are not called to let the curtain come down on our sermons with everyone dead on the stage. Once Jesus called Lazarus from the tomb, he did not put him back in again. Once God raised Jesus from the dead, there was no going back to the tomb. As preachers with a comic spirit preaching in the life-giving context of the comic vision, let's not mix our genres. Tragedy is a necessary complement to comedy, so we certainly don't want to end with false promises of auspicious outcomes, the stick-on-bow sort of ending that never really sticks. But in the context of the comic vision, tragedy does *not* get the last word in our lives or in our sermons. Don't make the too-common mistake of putting your sermon into reverse as you come to a close and giving the congregation whiplash.

We live in a divided, cynical time. Many people, especially young people, are overwhelmed by the immensity of the global and national issues we now face and are becoming more and more skeptical about the institutions that are charged with addressing them. This includes religious institutions perhaps most of all. We cannot reach the jaded and the cynical by ceding the field to tragedy or by attempting to distract listeners with false hope. The primary reason your authors—as a humor scholar and a homiletician—decided to collaborate in writing this book is to help preachers embrace the comic frame and spirit in their reading and preaching of the Word. The comic frame is needed to cut through the divisions and cynicism of our time and to invite everyone to the sermonic celebration.

To Ponder

—Do you ever back over the spikes in your sermons? Where do you think this tendency comes from?
—How can understanding the difference between the comic and the tragic frames help us recognize and overcome this habit?

NOTES

1. G. K. Chesterton, *The Collected Works of G. K. Chesterton*, vol. 1, *Heretics, Orthodoxy, the Blatchford Controversies.* (San Francisco: Ignatius Press, 1986), 325.

2. *Soren Kierkegaard, Concluding Unscientific Postscript,* trans. D. F. Swenson and W. Lowrie (Princeton, NJ: Princeton University Press, 1941), 413.

3. For a fuller discussion of the distinction between comic and tragic perspectives, see John Morreall, *Comedy, Tragedy, and Religion* (Albany: State University of New York Press, 1999), 21–39.

4. For recent works on preaching that addresses trauma, see Sarah Travis, *Unspeakable: Preaching and Trauma-Informed Theology* (Eugene, OR: Wipf and Stock, 2021); Joni Sancken, *Words That Heal: Preaching Hope to Wounded Souls* (Nashville: Abingdon Press, 2019).

5. Brian Edgar, *The God Who Plays: A Playful Approach to Theology and Spirituality* (Eugene, OR: Wipf and Stock, 2017), 30.

6. Morreall, *Comedy, Tragedy, and Religion*, 3, quoting from M. Conrad Hyers, "The Dialectic of the Sacred and the Comic," in *Holy Laughter: Essays on Religion in the Comic Perspective*, ed. Hyers (New York: Seabury Press, 1969), 232.

7. Hyers, *Comic Vision and the Christian Faith*, 51.

8. Hyers, *Comic Vision and the Christian Faith*, 24.

9. Hyers, *Comic Vision and the Christian Faith*, 24.

10. Brian Edgar, *Laughter and the Grace of God: Restoring Laughter to Its Central Role in Christian Faith and Theology* (Eugene, OR: Cascade Books, 2019), 15–16.

11. Morreall, *Comedy, Tragedy, and Religion*, 5.

12. Brian Richardson, James Phalen, and Peter Rabinowitz, *Narrative Dynamics: Essays on Time, Plot, Closure, and Frames* (Columbus: Ohio State University Press, 2002), 102. Terence is considered the key figure in the Roman New Comedy, adapting Greek comedy to not only Roman stage and language but also expanding the form to include social commentary, larger casts (including roles for women), and trickery and deception as key plot devices. See George Fredric Franko, "Terence and the Traditions of Roman New Comedy," in *A Companion to Terence*, ed. Antony Augoustakis and Ariana Traill (Malden, MA: John Wiley and Sons, 2013), 33–51. See also the classic work by Miola on the influence of Terence play writings; Robert S. Miola, *Shakespeare and Classical Comedy: The Influence of Plautus and Terence* (Oxford: Clarendon Press, 1994). For a recent review of scholarship on Shakespearean comedy and influence of Terence, see Robert S. Miola, "Encountering the Past I," in *The Oxford Handbook of Shakespearean Comedy* (New York: Oxford University Press, 2018), 36.

13. See "Dr. Maya Angelou: I Am Human," YouTube, March 5, 2013, https://www.youtube.com/watch?v=ePodNjrVSsk. Angelou states, "If a human being dreams a great dream, dares to love somebody; if a human being dares to be Martin King, or Mahatma Gandhi, or Mother Teresa, or Malcolm X; if a human being dares to be bigger than the condition into which she or he was born—it means so can you."

14. Kenneth Burke, *Attitudes toward History*, 3rd ed., with a New Afterword (Berkeley: University of California Press, 1984).

15. Scholastique Mukasonga, *Cockroaches* (Brooklyn, NY: Archipelago, 2016). *Cockroaches* is the story of growing up a Tutsi in Hutu-dominated Rwanda—the story of a happy child, a loving family, all wiped out in the genocide of 1994.

16. J. Cheryl Exum and J. William Whedbee, "Isaac, Samson, and Saul," in *On Humour and the Comic in the Hebrew Bible*, ed. Athalya Brenner-Idan and Yehuda T. Radday (London: A&C Black, 1990), 121.

17. Terry Eagleton, *Humour* (New Haven, CT: Yale University Press, 2019), 55.

18. Eagleton, *Humour,* 55.

19. In the story and joy of Issaac's name giving, we see the classic plot structure of comedy.

20. Joseph Campbell, *The Hero's Journey: Joseph Campbell on His Life and Work* (Novato, CA: New World Library, 2003). Also see Bill Moyers, "Bill Moyers Responds: What Would Joseph Campbell Think?," *Moyers & Company*, billmoyers.com, February 11, 2020, https://billmoyers.com/story/bill-moyers -responds-what-would-joseph-campbell-think. Moyers discusses Campbell's enduring influence on modern culture and storytelling: "It's almost impossible to overestimate the influence on modern storytelling and audiences that Campbell's reflections on *The Hero's Journey* has had."

21. Martin Janeba, "Trickster in American Folklore," University of Pardubice, 2007.

22. Lewis Hyde, *Trickster Makes This World: Mischief, Myth and Art* (New York: Macmillan, 1997).

23. Joseph Campbell, *A Joseph Campbell Companion: Reflections on the Art of Living* (n.p.: Joseph Campbell Foundation, 2017).

24. Joseph Campbell, *The Hero with a Thousand Faces* (Novato, CA: New World Library, 2008).

25. Cheryl Exum and J. William Whedbee, "Isaac, Samson and Saul: Reflections on the Comic and Tragic Visions," in *On Humour and the Comic in the Hebrew Bible*, ed. Athalya Brenner-Idan and Yehuda T. Radday (London: A&C Black, 1990), 120–21. See Northrop Frye, "The Argument of Comedy," in *Theories of Comedy*, ed. Paul Lauter (Garden City, NY: Doubleday).

26. Northrop Frye, "The Argument of Comedy," in *Shakespeare: The Anthology of Criticism and Theory*, ed. Russ McDonald (Malden, MA: Blackwell Publishing, 2004), 94.

27. "If we shadows have offended, / Think but this, and all is mended, / That you have but slumber'd here / While these visions did appear." Act V, scene 1.

28. See the earlier discussion of using humor as part of sermon endings in chap. 5.

29. Eugene Lowry's homiletical plot follows this pattern, as does the so-called valley form. See O. Wesley Allen, *Determining the Form: Structures for Preaching* (Minneapolis: Fortress Press, 2008), chap. 2, "Essential Qualities of All Sermonic Forms."

30. John C. Holbert and Alyce M. McKenzie, *What Not to Say: Avoiding the Common Mistakes That Can Sink Your Sermon* (Louisville, KY: Westminster John Knox Press, 2011), 107.

8

Foes and Fans

Humor through the Centuries

Life is too important to be taken seriously.
—Attributed to Irish essayist and
playwright Oscar Wilde (1854–1900)[1]

If you sent out an e-vite calling theologians and philosophers from the halls of history to a colloquium honoring the humor and laughter of the comic spirit, even promising adult beverages and heavy hors d'oeuvres, not everyone would respond affirmatively. Martin Luther, Francis of Assisi, and Teresa of Ávila would reply, "We will be there with bells on!" Aristotle would reply, "I'll attend, but only as a study break to refresh me to get back to serious work." John Chrysostom would decline, citing a looming deadline to finish a sermon against laughter and playfulness. Jerome would decline and articulate his disdain for the topic in the comments section. Augustine might attend, but largely to make sure that those present laughed only at the right things. Origen and Cassian would arrive to make sure no one laughed at all. Hildegard of Bingen would decline, eschewing anything so crude as bodily laughter.

It is true that some thinkers across history, secular and religious, have viewed the comic spirit (and the amusement or laughter to which it gives rise) largely in a positive light, as a uniquely human capacity that brings refreshment in the midst of our work, and that can even, in theological terms, be a present expression of our future heavenly hope.

Others have held a view that humor and laughter are morally neutral, a uniquely human capacity that can have positive effects but must be handled with caution, like a new Waterpik—which can play a helpful role in dental hygiene or can be set on too high a water pressure level and blow out a molar. Jesuit priest James Martin, in *Between Heaven and Mirth,* articulates a "morality of humor." Says Martin, "There is humor that builds up and humor that tears down, a humor that exposes cant and hypocrisy and a humor that belittles the defenseless and marginalized. . . . 'Good' or 'bad' depends . . . on how the humor deepens or cheapens the relationship with God."[2]

Over against the positive and neutral evaluations of humor has been a range of positions that reduce humor to a distraction that trivializes the serious business of living and dying in this earthly vale of tears or an expression of arrogance that denigrates others and should be suppressed.[3] Take a sweeping glance at discussions of humor across the centuries, and you will find that the Greeks and church fathers attempted to domesticate humor, the Middle Ages attempted to suppress it, the Renaissance church worked to eradicate it, and the eighteenth and nineteenth centuries offered mixed reviews. Not until well into the twentieth century did positive evaluations begin to emerge as the majority opinion.[4]

HUMOR IN ANCIENT GREEK THOUGHT

Much of the criticism of humor through the ages has resulted from its being used to put others down, what we've categorized as *superiority humor,* as described in chapter 6. Theologian Karl-Josef Kuschel labels this "Homeric laughter."[5]

Homer, in his epic poems *The Iliad* and *The Odyssey* (written between 750 and 675 BCE), depicts the gods and goddesses observing human conflicts from their lofty height, engaging in put-down humor. Eternally young and powerful, they indulge in frivolous Schadenfreude humor. In the opening scene of *The Iliad* they laugh uproariously at Hephaistos limping around the banquet hall waiting on tables. He is the god of the smithy, crippled by his father, Zeus, who in a fit of temper took him by the ankles and threw him to earth.

A scene from *The Odyssey* depicts Hephaistos taking revenge on his wife, Aphrodite, and her lover, Ares, the god of war, trapping them in their bed with an invisible net. Three male gods come—Poseidon, Hermes, and Apollo—not to offer any help or express moral outrage, but to laugh at the deceived deceivers and the clever trap the cuckolded husband has laid. They engage in stereotypical male locker-room humor. Kuschel traces this "Homeric laughter" from the beginnings of European literature. It is laughter at the expense of the weak and unfortunate.[6]

As philosophical reasoning and ethical reasoning came into their own in Greece, philosophers reacted against this frivolous, morally ambiguous brand of Homeric laughter. They began to articulate critiques of humor and the laughter to which it gives rise. Plato (428–347 BCE), working largely within a superiority theory of humor, believed there was an aggressive quality to laughter, a comic pleasure in the discovery of others' foibles. He did acknowledge that there could be a positive potential in the philosopher's laughter, but only when directed at oneself. Plato moved toward "the ethical taming of laughter," believing that laughter and ethics belong together.[7]

Many of the objections to humor and laughter through the centuries stem from three negative generalizations about humor that originate with Plato. First, engaging in humor is potentially harmful to one's character since in humor we are exposed to human shortcomings, which can rub off on us. Second, humor and laughter involve a loss of what makes us truly human: our rational faculty. We descend into silliness and irresponsibility. Third, laughter is uncharitable and antisocial since it all boils down to scorn.[8]

We contacted Plato's publicist to see if the great man would write us a brief endorsement for the back cover of our book, but were informed that he is deceased. It is just as well. He probably would have written a warning rather than a warm endorsement, perhaps something like, "Caution: Reading this book could lead to erosion of character, silliness, and antisocial attitudes." If we followed his lead, we would advise preachers to avoid using humor in the pulpit except for occasional instances of self-deprecation.

Your authors resist reducing all humor and laughter to superiority. We would replace Plato's caution with a commendation: "Warning: Reading our book could lead to increased humility, playfulness, and flexibility in your preaching." Game on, Plato!

Aristotle (384–322 BCE), a student of Plato, held a more positive view of humor and laughter than his teacher.[9] Aristotle was convinced that humor is a characteristic of human beings, which he referred to as the rational animal, that distinguishes us from animals and that has certain useful and legitimate functions. In his *Nicomachean Ethics* Aristotle asserted that every virtue exists as balanced between two extremes.[10] Only in maintaining that balance can humans find their integrity and maturity.

In terms of humor, then, he commended the virtue of *eutrapelia*, a balanced state of being between taking everything too seriously and never taking anything seriously. From the Greek for "wittiness," the term refers to the ability to jest with ease, with a good sense of humor and a good intention. *Eutrapelia* fosters a positive, playful approach to life.[11] Aristotle viewed joking and playing as activities just as necessary to the development of a genuinely human life as seriousness and hard work.[12]

HUMOR IN THE BIBLE AND THE EARLY CHURCH

In the biblical witness that Christians call the Old Testament, the Hebrew Scriptures, or the First Testament (written between 1200 and 165 BCE), divine playfulness is reflected in the creation of the world, in which Woman Wisdom is depicted as being "daily [God's] delight . . . / rejoicing in [God's] inhabited world / and delighting in the human race" (Prov. 8:30–31). The initiation of the covenant with Israel features the meaning of the name of Abraham and Sarah's comically late-in-life offspring Isaac, a name that means "laughter." Other biblical instances of humor and laughter include the mocking laughter of God at God's enemies (Ps. 2:4), the acerbic wit of the book of Proverbs (see, for example, Prov. 26:17, where meddling in the quarrel of another is compared to grabbing a passing dog by the ears!), the pomposity of Job's friends, and the peevish tantrum Jonah throws at the success of his half-hearted sermon to the Ninevites, to name just a few. Examples of iconoclastic wit abound in the Synoptic Jesus' parables and aphorisms.

Humor stood a better chance of existing within postbiblical Jewish theology than in postbiblical Christianity, due to Judaism's recognition that their birth as a people had to do with flesh-and-blood men and women with greatness and weakness intermingled. The Jewish God enjoys a good joke and delights in people's wit. For Judaism, wit and religion are not incompatible. Up until the fifth century CE the rabbis delighted in enterprising and entertaining approaches to Scripture. The decline of such approaches coincides with the political legitimatization of the Christian movement and what Hebrew Bible scholar Yehuda T. Radday calls "a humor-devastating period of deification of Scripture, a veritable bibliolatry" in which, for both Judaism and Christianity, their scriptures became "smothered in reverence."[13]

While humor seasons the pages of the Bible, it was not recognized or appreciated as the church moved into its first few centuries.[14] With the cross central to Christian faith and theology, a grim vision of the crucifixion cast a pall over any prospect of humor, all but crushing the comic spirit. A dualism was being established in which spirit, soul, and mind on the one hand were valued and physicality was devalued as the locus of sin. Monastic asceticism sought to suppress any enjoyment of the pleasures of everyday human life in the body, especially a physical response as earthy as laughter. St. Benedict in the sixth century famously banned laughter in his communities, on the grounds that boisterous laughter disturbed the decorum of the community and that laughter was most often at someone's expense.[15]

The perspective that this life is a vale of tears and that all joy must wait until the life to come drained theology of the lifeblood of humor, as the emphasis on resurrection and joy encountered early medieval dualism and asceticism. With all this sorrow and seriousness arrayed against it, humor barely stood a chance of formal expression in either the writings of early theologians or the public proclamations of the church.[16]

Indeed, this dynamic can be seen in many writings of the church fathers, who were no fans of laughter. If they could time-travel, you wouldn't find them in a comedy club. In 390, the bishop of Constantinople, John Chrysostom (nicknamed "golden mouth" for his eloquent preaching), delivered a sermon against laughter and playfulness. He saw them as pagan and far removed from Christian decorum and devotion. Admittedly, he preached in a notoriously corrupt city, but his words carry the sting of overstatement: "This world . . . is not a theatre, in which we can laugh; and we are not assembled together in order to burst into peals of laughter, but to weep for our sins. . . . It is not God who gives us the chance to play, but the devil."[17]

Jerome (342–420 CE) joined Chrysostom in condemning laughter. Origen (184–253 CE) and John Cassian (360–435 CE) concluded that refraining from laughter is a sign of virtue that should be encouraged. So maybe you would find them in a comedy club, but they would be there to practice the discipline of not laughing.

Augustine, by contrast, might drive to the comedy club and park out front, trying to decide whether or not to go inside. The reason for this picture of him wavering in the parking lot is that he seems at first glance to offer an unqualified opposition to laughter on earth. He holds the view, shared by other early Christian theologians, that human life is marked by weeping and that laughter must be postponed until we abide in heaven. He draws this conclusion about human nature based on the observation that the first thing a baby does upon being born is cry, not laugh. In this way the child becomes "a prophet of its own future misfortunes," which beset all human beings who live "in the midst of trials and temptations."[18] New parents often read the popular book *What to Expect When You're Expecting*. Thank heavens Augustine wasn't asked to write the foreword![19]

However, if that were the whole story on Augustine's view of humor, he never would have driven to the comedy club in the first place. But there he is sitting in the car, with the door open and one foot on the asphalt, trying to decide what to do. At times he writes in a manner that shows respect for humor and laughter within a limited scope. He believes that the laughter to which humor gives rise is a uniquely human ability that is a sign of rationality, as when we laugh at bad arguments or superstitious statements. But he is concerned that it can be put to good use or ill.

He places laughter in a theological context, holding that there are two types of laughter: the mocking laughter *at* Christ on the cross and the laughter *of* Christ at wickedness and its assumption of victory.[20] Christians share in the suffering of Christ when they are laughed at and mocked by the world. They share in the victory of Christ when they join him in laughter at the forces that oppose him. Even then, human laughter on this earth should be shaped by the desire for the conversion of the wicked, rather than by a superior sense of our own rectitude. Christians conform to Christ through increasing participation in his laughter. God made the devil to be mocked, not to gain victory over human beings.[21]

So after some reluctance, Augustine would get out of his car and not only enter the comedy club but take the stage to try out a set of jokes he has been working on about ridiculing the devil:

— Why will you never see the devil in an Armani suit? Because the devil wears Prada.
— How do I know that Satan runs the DMV? Because [wait for it . . .] the devil takes many forms.
— I joined a satanic cult the other day, just for the hell of it.
— Why can't the devil make money off YouTube? Because he keeps getting demonetized.
— Why do we always associate the devil with heavy metal? For all we know, the devil may like smooth jazz.[22]

Augustine would approve of contemporary preachers' use of humor in their pulpits to highlight destructive human behavior, to call out injustice, to attribute it to the force or forces that oppose Christ in the world, and to underscore that, because Christ has overcome all opposition, the opposition's days are numbered.

Just because the creeds, catechisms, and councils of the church are humor-free zones does not mean centuries passed without someone religious cracking a joke. The comic spirit and the humor to which it gave rise, in both Judaism and Christianity, occasionally managed to burst through the concrete of convention and social obedience like a stubborn flower. The Jewish festival of Purim developed a vibrant carnivalesque tradition beginning in the mid–first century. Much later, in the eighteenth century, Hasidic Judaism arose, with its recognition of a connection between humor and religion. Through centuries of persecutions, Jewish humor emerged as a survival strategy for an oppressed people.[23]

The same was likely true in Christianity outside the realm of the church's leadership and authorities. Theologian Harvey Cox argues that the comic spirit is natural to Christianity and may have flourished in the first three centuries wherever Christians were social outcasts. The earliest recorded Christian joke, for example, may be in visual form. One of the earliest representations of Christ in the catacombs was of a crucified human figure with the head of a donkey. Cox speculates that the catacomb Christians had a sense of the comic absurdity of their position. Perhaps "this band of slaves, derelicts, and square pegs realized how outlandish their claims sounded to the surrounding culture."[24]

HUMOR IN THE MEDIEVAL PERIOD

Once Christianity became the state religion, it seems this comic spirit was suppressed.[25] Whereas the Greek philosophers and Augustine had tried to domesticate and tame laughter, the medieval church tried to eliminate laughter altogether.[26] Christian writers of the period attributed laughter to pride (superiority) or flippancy (trivialization). They tended to dissociate laughter from joy. In the life to come, we would know only joy, having transcended the base bodily expression of laughter.[27] So now we can't even look forward to laughing in the life to come? What literary critic Terry Eagleton calls a "churlish suspicion of humour" sprang from political and religious authorities' unspoken recognition of the subversive power of humor and the fear of loss of social control.[28]

But remember our stubborn flower of the comic spirit pressing up through the concrete. The often subversive power of humor and laughter was suppressed but by no means eliminated through the centuries. The sixth-century Greek church developed a Holy Fool tradition, based on Paul's idea that Christians are fools for Christ's sake and the example of the socially outlandish behavior of many Hebrew prophets.[29] In this tradition, engaging in highly unconventional public behavior was an expression of piety. The Greek church still maintains the ancient custom of setting aside the day after Easter as a day of laughter because of the big joke God has played on Satan in resurrecting Jesus.[30]

Parallel to this in the medieval Western church were folk humor and traditions that overturned conventional social roles and rules, often given the name "Carnivale." Carnivale is best described as "the force that subverts and upturns everything official, authoritarian, and one-sidedly serious."[31] In medieval Europe, among the many forms Carnivale took in various towns and villages were three festivals that embodied the carnivalesque ability of humor to overturn the status quo and offer a temporary release from the constrictions of conventional social roles. Holy Innocents' Day, the Feast of Fools, and the Feast of Asses all occurred after Christmas on the days of the old Roman Saturnalia.[32] The Feast of Asses, which grew out of the Feast of Fools, was celebrated January 14, most frequently in France, in connection with the donkey bearing the Holy Family into Egypt after Jesus' birth. On Holy Innocent's Day, a young boy replaced the bishop. At the Feast of Fools, which began during the singing of the Magnificat on the Feast of the Circumcision, at the words "He has put down the mighty from their seats and exalted the humble and meek," young clergy drove the bishop and his assistants from the church, put on masks, brought out wine and food, converted the altar into a banquet table, shouted an obscene parody of the Holy Mass, and sometimes brought in a braying ass, whom they worshipped as an incarnation of the Lord of Disorder.[33] It will come as no surprise that the Feast of Fools was banned by the Council of Basel in 1431.[34]

The comic spirit's stubborn flower of humor continued to crack through the concrete of somber convention as evidenced by customs that grew up in some medieval Orthodox and Catholic traditions during the time immediately after Easter. It was celebrated as a time for joy and laughter referred to as "play day" or "Bright Sunday." Picnics, practical jokes, singing, dancing, and sermons with jokes in them exuberantly celebrated the resurrection of Jesus. Behind these liturgical traditions lay the "Easter laugh" (*risus paschalis*), as the early theologians called it. It refers to the joke God pulled on the devil, offering Christ as a ransom in exchange for humanity, hiding Christ's divinity under his human nature, and then proving too powerful for the devil to overcome.[35] Holy Humor Sunday is practiced in some churches today, transforming the Sunday following Easter, traditionally a low-attendance Sunday, into a popular observance.

The person who best embodied the humor and comic spirit of medieval Western Christianity was Francis of Assisi (1181–1226). As a young man, Francis divested himself of his family wealth and dedicated himself to imitating Jesus with joy and exuberance. For him, all creatures reflected God, and the simplest daily events were cause for celebration. Says John Morreall, "His selflessness was not based on feelings of worthlessness, depravity, or guilt, but on a healthy sense of humor about himself." St. Francis called animals and even the moon and sun "Sister" and "Brother." His own body was "Brother Ass." Poverty was his "Bride" and "Lady."[36] Legend has it that on his deathbed he thanked his donkey for his years of faithful service.

Given that description, we would not be surprised to find Francis at our comedy club. Next to him would be St. Teresa of Ávila, sixteenth-century Carmelite nun and reformer who spoke out against a deadly serious Catholicism, saying, "A sad nun is a bad nun," and "I am more afraid of one unhappy sister than a crowd of evil spirits. . . . What would happen if we hid what little sense of humor we had? Let each of us humbly use this to cheer others."[37]

With her would be several other playful saints, among them Madeleine Sophie, Jane Frances de Chantal, and Thérèsè the Little Flower. Each of them could offer sets consisting of everyday encounters that showcase their nimble wit.[38]

A few other saints would take the stage in outlandish acts of public silliness. Francis would start things off by preaching in the nude, at least until the manager rushed up and draped a blanket around him.[39] Ignatius Loyola (1491–1556), founder of the Jesuit order, who is often thought of as an austere ascetic, would surprise us by coming up and performing dances from the Basque country in Spain, his homeland. Philip Neri (1515–1595), Italian priest, called the "Humorous Saint," would interrupt his fellow saints' sets with ridiculous fashion shows: striding across the stage, having shaved off half his beard, wearing a cushion on his head like a turban or wearing a foxtail coat in the middle of summer.[40] Now St. Francis is back, clothed this time in his brown mendicant robe, preaching to the birds, scolding the swallows for chirping too loudly during Mass.[41]

While most of the humor we find in the medieval church comes from below, we would be remiss to ignore the premier theologian of the period. Thomas Aquinas, thirteenth-century Dominican priest and scholar, affirms Augustine's reservations about play and laughter and ways it can be misused, but also claims that play is a virtue and that a lack of fun in life is a vice. Says theologian Brian Edgar, "So much did Aquinas value playfulness that he argued the one who does *not* play risks falling into sin."[42] So we could picture Aquinas, maybe not performing in the comedy club, but certainly sitting at a table enjoying the show being put on by Francis and company.

HUMOR IN THE REFORMATION AND BEYOND

Once the medieval saints got offstage, Martin Luther would jump up and claim the mic. He made humor an integral part of his extensive theological reflections in his commentaries, *Table Talk,* and treatises. His comedy set would involve the humor he discerned in the Bible (the worst feature of Noah's ark was its "great and pestilential stench"), humorous connections between the Bible and life (chastising the Wittenburg congregation for thinking they would have taken better care of the baby Jesus than the Bethlehemites), facetious advice (encouraging his congregation to be as attentive to God in their prayer lives as his dog "Klutz" was to meat), and mockery of the devil at being bested by God ("He [Christ] is your devil, you devil, because he has captured and conquered you").[43]

Luther suffered from *Antechtung*, which sounds like a painful sinus condition, but is actually German for severe spiritual struggle and temptation. It was no match, however, for the combined forces of his humor and his eschatological hope: "When we are brought to life on the last day we shall spit on ourselves and say, 'Fie on you for not having been bolder in believing on Christ, since the glory is so great!'"[44]

A book on the humor of John Calvin would be a slender tome. By all reports, he was a crab. It's not easy to be of a sunny disposition when one suffers from as many physical ailments as he did. Their sheer number make the literary output of this brilliant theologian all the more impressive.

Still, Calvin's view of humor was a mixed bag. He was quite wary of the negative impact of humor when it was trivializing, time-wasting, or biting. At the same time, he put a high premium on joy as integral to the Christian life and had a certain appreciation for wit and humor in Scripture. Commenting on Philippians 3:1, he wrote,

> The Holy Spirit ... has not always avoided wit and humour, although He has kept from scurrility, which is unworthy of his majesty. There are innumerable examples in the prophets, and especially in Isaiah, so that there is not a profane author who abounds more in witty allusions and metaphors.[45]

On top of that he was capable of a certain knack for insult humor in some of his examples. One of his anecdotes went as follows: "When a certain shameless fellow mockingly asked a pious old man what God had done before the creation of the world, the latter aptly countered that he had been building hell for the curious."[46]

Dutch humanist Desiderius Erasmus, a contemporary of Luther and close friend of Sir Thomas More, wrote *The Praise of Folly* (1511), in which the character of Folly offers a humorous, satirical address to theologians and church dignitaries intended to reform the reformers. He claimed to have written it at More's insistence.

More, English lawyer, judge, social philosopher, author, and statesman, served Henry VIII as Lord High Chancellor of England from 1529 to 1532 and was the author of *Utopia*. He was an outspoken, independent wit who loved to enliven his serious writing with witty anecdotes. His writings became increasingly somber as he was drawn into the politics of the early Reformation and the machinations of Henry VIII. Fourteen months in the Tower of London can have a sobering effect, but they did not eradicate his sense of humor. On July 6, 1535, he ascended the steps to the gallows to be beheaded for refusing to recognize King Henry VIII as the head of the Church of England. Examples abound of the last words of famous people, so we know he had many options to choose from many ways to handle this situation. He could, for example, have gone the noble, dramatic route, like Sydney Carton in his gallows speech from Charles Dickens's *A Tale of Two Cities*. "It is a far, far better thing that I do. . . ." But instead, More drew humor's cloak of courage around himself and, turning to the lieutenant of the tower, said, "Assist me up. Coming down I will look after myself."[47]

Moving into the mid–seventeenth century, we observe the Puritans coming into power in England and outlawing comedy, in keeping with their attribution of laughter to original sin. They closed the theaters because of the harmful effect comedies were thought to have on audiences.[48]

In this Puritan context in which humorlessness became synonymous with holiness, humor was discouraged and even prohibited in ecclesial settings. Outside of the church, however, it found its outlet in the proliferation of joke books and irreligious practices such as mock baptisms of farm animals, blasphemous catechisms, bawdy jokes about Holy Communion, and hymns set to popular tunes.[49] Natural gas emission was a particular source of amusement, with accounts of aristocratic flatulence causing copious chortles. That's a fancy way of saying that there were a lot of fart jokes going around. While Puritans did not appreciate them, apparently just about everybody else did![50]

In the late seventeenth and eighteenth centuries many denounced humor and laughter. Lord Chesterfield, while himself a noted wit of the sophisticated variety, offered a condemnation of laughter so pompous that the word prig comes to mind.[51] He wrote, "In my mind, there is nothing so illiberal, and so ill-bred, as audible laughter. . . . It is low buffoonery, or silly accidents, that always excite laughter; that is what people of sense and breeding should show themselves above."[52] This leaves us wondering, What exactly constitutes low buffoonery? and Is there such thing as high buffoonery?

Alyce is from a denomination that has its roots in the ministries of John and Charles Wesley in eighteenth-century England. John had a deep faith, a keen mind, a relentless work ethic, and organizational brilliance. But humor? Not so much. Alyce was distressed, but not surprised to find this dreadful quote from his description of his Methodist schools: "We prohibit play in the strongest terms. . . . The students shall rise at 5 o'clock in the morning, summer and winter. . . . The student shall be indulged with nothing which the world calls play. But this rule be observed with stricktest nicety; for those who play when they are young will play when they are old."[53]

Similarly, Wesley advised his preachers, "Let your whole deportment before the congregation be serious, weighty, and solemn."[54] It's no wonder that George Whitfield, who grew up pulling pints in his father's tavern and knew how to spin a yarn, drew bigger crowds! It should be pointed out, however, that while Wesley's sense of humor was indiscernible, he never burned anyone at the stake for disagreeing with his theological positions. He should get a couple of points for that.

We'll draw this saunter through the centuries to a close for now. But we do so with the promise that in chapter 9 we will meet some key figures in the recovery of respect for humor that begins to be felt in the nineteenth century and picks up momentum by the fourth quarter of the twentieth.

When Alyce was a child, growing up with three siblings, when the four would get into a puerile altercation that involved name-calling, their dad would make them sit down in a row of chairs and make everyone go down the line and say something nice about each other. Groans would arise at these instructions. Bickering over who had to go first would ensue.

Humor isn't perfect, but since it's capable of better things than history has given it credit for, we close out this chapter by making those who have appeared in this chapter sit in a row and each say something positive about our friend Humor. What follows are paraphrases of what has gone before in the chapter rather than word-for-word quotations.

Aristotle gets to go first. He would say, "Humor and laughter can refresh the mind to return to serious work. Joking and playing are activities as necessary to developing a genuinely human life as seriousness and hard work."

Augustine's next: "Laughter and the humor which gives rise to it is a uniquely human ability that is a sign of rationality, as when we laugh at bad arguments or superstitious statements."

Now it's Aquinas's turn: "Play is a virtue, and a lack of fun in life is a vice."

Then Teresa of Ávila is up next: "A sad nun is a bad nun. Let each of us humbly use our sense of humor to cheer others."

Next Francis of Assisi praises humor for helping us to be able to take ourselves lightly.

Finally, it's John Calvin's turn. His contribution: that joy is integral to the Christian life, and we ought to appreciate wit and humor in Scripture.

To Ponder

— What are a couple of benefits of humor we covered in chapters 4 and 5 commended by various theologians and philosophers through the centuries?

— Do you find that any of the historical critiques of humor have some validity? If so, which ones?

— Which thinker(s) do you resonate with most in this chapter?

— What would you say in defense of humor to someone who believes it has no place in preaching?

NOTES

1. For more background on this quote, see Garson O'Toole, "Life Is Too Important to Be Taken Seriously," Quote Investigator, May 11, 2019, https:// quoteinvestigator.com/2015/07/26/serious/.

2. James Martin, SJ, *Between Heaven and Mirth: Why Joy, Humor and Laughter Are at the Heart of the Spiritual Life* (New York: HarperCollins, 2011), 23.

3. See Conrad Hyers, *The Comic Vision and the Christian Faith: A Celebration of Life and Laughter* (Eugene, OR: Wipf and Stock, 2003), 23–32, on the caricature of humor as trivializing or seeking to establish superiority over others.

4. Robert Darden, author of *Jesus Laughed: The Redemptive Power of Humor* (Nashville: Abingdon Press, 2008), offers a brief survey of why the church lost its ability to laugh and gradually is recovering it. See chaps. 4 and 5.

5. Karl-Josef Kuschel, *Laughter: A Theological Reflection* (London: SCM Press, 1994), 2.

6. Kuschel, *Laughter*, 2.

7. Kuschel, *Laughter*, 9–10.

8. John Morreall, *Taking Laughter Seriously* (Albany: State University of New York Press, 1983), 85.

9. Book 2 of Aristotle's work on the theory of drama, *Poetics*, deals with comedy. The trouble is, it has been lost somewhere in the halls of history. Umberto Eco's brilliant novel *The Name of the Rose* (New York: Harcourt, 1980), is a historical murder mystery set in an Italian monastery in 1327. Its plot consists of a series of murders motivated by a desire to keep it under wraps.

10. The *Nicomachean Ethics* is a series of ten books based on Aristotle's lectures at the Lyceum. Their focus was practical reflection on the creation of good living. It became a crucial influence on medieval European philosophy. Through the synthesis of Aristotelian ethics and Christian theology effected by Thomas Aquinas and others, the *Nicomachean Ethics* had a profound effect on medieval theology.

11. Brian Edgar, *The God Who Plays: A Playful Approach to Theology and Spirituality* (Eugene, OR: Wipf and Stock, 2017), 61.

12. Hugh Rahner, "Eutrapelia: A Forgotten Virtue," in *Holy Laughter: Essays on Religion in the Comic Perspective*, ed. M. Conrad Hyers (New York: Seabury Press, 1969), 187.

13. Athalya Brenner-Idan and Yehuda T. Radday, eds., *On Humour and the Comic in the Hebrew Bible* (London: A&C Black, 1990), 37.

14. See Robert Darden, "How the Church Lost the Ability to Laugh," in Darden, *Jesus Laughed: The Redemptive Power of Humor* (Nashville: Abingdon Press, 2008), 61–82.

15. Martin, *Between Heaven and Mirth*, 81–82.

16. Says religion and humor scholar Conrad Hyers, "One would never guess from reading endless volumes of religious composition that humor has anything to do with God. If God created laughter, playfulness, and humor, few

theologians, biblical scholars, or doctors of the church have ever heard about it. And if there is such a thing as the humor of God, it has never come through in our creeds, confessions, or catechisms" (Hyers, *And God Created Laughter: The Bible as Divine Comedy* [Atlanta: John Knox Press, 1987], 13).

17. John Chrysostom, *Commentary on Matthew, Homily 6.6,* quoted in Hugo Rahner, "Eutrapelia: A Forgotten Virtue," in *Holy Laughter: Essays on Religion in the Comic Perspective,* ed. M. Conrad Hyers (New York: Seabury Press, 1969), 192.

18. Gabriel Torretta, OP, "Preaching on Laughter: The Theology of Laughter in Augustine's Sermons," *Theological Studies* 76, no. 4 (November 30, 2015): 742–64, https://doi.org/10.1177/0040563915605256.

19. For a survey of church fathers' views on humor and laughter, see Rahner, "Eutrapelia," 185–97.

20. Rahner, "Eutrapelia," 185–97. During the crucifixion scene in the Synoptic Gospels, there are repeated references to Jesus being paid mock homage with a robe and crown of thorns—and being mocked, sneered at, derided, and jeered at by Herod and his soldiers, by the chief priest and scribes, and by passersby, a scene where a sardonic sign named his true identity: "King of the Jews." Laughter at the foot of the cross is cruel laughter, laughter at, certainly not with. It is what Kenneth Burke would call burlesque humor, superiority humor on steroids.

21. Toretta, "Preaching on Laughter," 760.

22. See "Satan Jokes," jokes4us.com, http://www.jokes4us.com/religiousjokes /satanjokes.html, and "Satan Jokes: 43 Best Devil Puns & Jokes from Hell You'll Enjoy," Humoropedia, July 9, 2016, https://humoropedia.com/funny-satan -jokes/.

23. J. William Whedbee, *The Bible and the Comic Vision* (Cambridge University Press, 1998), 3.

24. Harvey Cox, *The Feast of Fools: A Theological Essay on Festivity and Fantasy* (Cambridge, MA: Harvard University Press, 1969), 140.

25. John Morreall, *Comedy, Tragedy, and Religion* (Albany: State University of New York Press, 1999), 119.

26. For deeper discussion of the medieval church's antipathy toward laughter, see Barry Sanders, *Sudden Glory: Laughter as Subversive History* (Boston: Beacon Press, 1996), 130ff.

27. Sanders, *Sudden Glory,* 129–30.

28. Terry Eagleton, *Humour* (New Haven, CT: Yale University Press, 2019), 96. This subversive, socially critical ability of humor is one we need to tap into more often in our preaching.

29. See the discussion of holy fools in chap. 9.

30. Eagleton, *Humour,* 96.

31. Simon Dentith, *Bakhtinian Thought: An Introductory Reader* (London: Routledge, 1995), x. Russian philosopher and literary critic Mikhail Bakhtin (1895–1975) analyzed and celebrated these impulses as they are expressed in the novels of Rabelais and Dostoevsky.

32. Saturnalia was an ancient Roman festival and holiday in honor of the god Saturn, held on December 17 of the Julian calendar and later expanded with festivities through to December 23.

33. The Feast of the Circumcision of Christ is a celebration of the circumcision of Jesus in accordance with Jewish tradition, eight days after his birth, the occasion on which the child was formally given his name. For a description of this ritual, see Wolfgang F. Zucker, "The Clown as the Lord of Disorder," in *Holy Laughter: Essays on Religion in the Comic Perspective,* ed. M. Conrad Hyers (New York: Seabury Press, 1969), 84.

34. For a more detailed account of various Carnival rituals in medieval Europe, see Sanders, *Sudden Glory,* 127–64.

35. Brian Edgar, *Laughter and the Grace of God: Restoring Laughter to Its Central Role in Christian Faith and Theology* (Eugene, OR: Cascade Books, 2019), 38.

36. Morreall, *Comedy, Tragedy, and Religion,* 120.

37. Martin, *Between Heaven and Mirth,* 69.

38. For examples of their repartee, see Aloysius Roche, "The Wit and Humor of the Saints," in *A Bedside Book of Saints* (Manchester, NH: Sophia Institute Press, 2006).

39. Francis stripped naked in Assisi's town square to demonstrate his divesting himself of his inherited wealth.

40. These absurd actions were meant to keep him humble and avoid others putting him on a pedestal.

41. These examples are from Martin, *Between Heaven and Mirth,* 68–85.

42. Edgar, *The God Who Plays,* 11.

43. Eric Gritsch, "Martin Luther's Humor," *Word and World* 32, no. 2 (2012): 134–36.

44. Gritsch, "Martin Luther's Humor," 133.

45. John Calvin, *The Epistles of Paul the Apostle to the Galatians, Ephesians, Philippians and Colossians* (Grand Rapids: Wm. B. Eerdmans, 1965), 268.

46. John Calvin, *Institutes of the Christian Religion* (Peabody, MA: Hendrickson, 2008), 1.14.1.

47. Roche, *Bedside Book of Saints,* 72.

48. John Morreall, *Taking Laughter Seriously* (Albany: State University of New York Press, 1983), 86. They put a stop to raucous performances of medieval miracle plays in church and to the injection of funny exempla in sermons. See Sanders, *Sudden Glory,* 196.

49. Sanders, *Sudden Glory,* 205–6.

50. Writer and philosopher John Aubrey (1626–1697) in his *Lives of the Poets* recounts how the earl of Oxford, "while bowing to the queen of England . . . failed to repress a fart of remarkable proportions" (Sanders, *Sudden Glory,* 223).

51. Lord Chesterfield is a person from a long time ago with an impressive-sounding name whom many preachers like to quote (or requote from William Barclay), without providing any context, to give gravitas to their sermons. For a

long time, Alyce assumed he was a fictitious character like Sherlock Holmes but came to find out that he was actually Philip Stanhope, 4th Earl of Chesterfield (1694–1773), a British statesman, diplomat, and man of letters, and an acclaimed wit of his time, best remembered for his *Letters to His Son* and *Letters to His Godson*, guides to manners, the art of pleasing, and the art of worldly success.

52. Morreall, *Taking Laughter Seriously*, 82.

53. John Wesley, "A Short Account of the School in Kingswood, near Bristol," in *The Works of John Wesley*, 3rd ed., vol. 13, *Letters*, ed. Thomas Jackson (1872; repr., Grand Rapids: Baker, 2007), 98.

54. William Willimon, "Humor," in *Concise Encyclopedia of Preaching*, ed. Willimon and Richard Lischer (Louisville, KY: Westminster John Knox Press, 1995), 263.

PART THREE

The Preacher and the Comic Spirit

9

The Preacher as Jester, Fool, and Sage

The world is full of fools, and he who would not wish to see one, must not only shut himself up alone, but must also break his looking glass.
—Anonymous medieval French proverb[1]

In chapter 8 we used the metaphor of a flower stubbornly breaking through concrete for humor and the comic spirit finding expression despite their suppression through the ages. In this chapter we look at three specific types of such flowers to see what preachers can learn from them. We begin with court jesters in the political arena, turn to holy fools in the ecclesial setting, and conclude with the way comedians in the world of North American entertainment have become sages commenting on politics, religion, and culture. While we are not suggesting that preachers adopt the jester, fool, or comedian role wholecloth, their use of humor to offer insightful cultural, political, and religious commentary (sometimes with bold directness and sometimes with sly wit) in spite of potential consequences is instructive for our preacherly identity.

What might preachers learn from these three vocations to help us combine humor, conviction, and good news?

THE COURT JESTER

And, let me tell you, fools have another gift which is not to be despised. They're the only ones who speak frankly and tell the truth, and what is more praiseworthy than truth?
—Desiderius Erasmus, *Praise of Folly*[2]

Court fools, or jesters, have wielded their brand of offbeat, subversive humor across cultures and centuries, from ancient Rome to fourteenth-century Central Asia, to medieval and Renaissance royal courts. While most of the scholarly research on court jesters has concentrated on Europe, these eccentric characters have appeared in the courts of ancient China and the Mughal emperors of India as well as those of medieval Europe, Africa, the Middle East, and the Americas. Not always clad in cap and bells, not merely mocking and entertaining, they have fulfilled an important social role: exerting a humanizing influence on people with power and position.[3]

Every famous king had his own fool, "a licensed madman who gave the king both advice and entertainment."[4] Fools were part of the normal entourage of people of stature and were also found in traveling shows, festivals, processions, and fairs.

In ancient Rome it was the practice that a jester (*mimus*) would follow in the funeral procession of the emperor to provide diversion from the somberness of the occasion and even to mimic the dead emperor. A *mimus* named Faco accompanied the emperor Vespasian's funeral procession dressed as the emperor, mimicking his miserliness by asking bystanders how much the funeral was costing him![5]

In the sixth century a man named Bertoldo appeared at the court of King Alboin of Lombardy. Court records describe him as dwarfed, ugly, and deformed, with carrot-colored hair. He marched directly to the throne and sat next to the king. The king demanded to know who he was, where he came from, and by what authority he dared to enter the king's presence uninvited. Bertoldo replied, "I am a man. I was born the night my mother bore me. The world is my country."[6] This bold approach was typical of jesters or court fools. They were engaged as a form of entertainment and were often characterized by their comical appearance and demeanor.[7]

There are records of jesters in the courts of English kings that go back to the tenth and eleventh centuries. Initially introduced as diversions, as time went on, jesters were often influential royal advisers and confidants.

While most jesters were male, like Henry VIII's Will Somers, King James's Archie Armstrong, Queen Elizabeth's Richard Tarleton, and fourteenth-century conqueror Timur's Nasrudin, history records a few female jesters. A female fool named Mathurine flourished in the French courts of Henri IV and Louis XIII, accustomed to walking the streets of Paris dressed as an Amazon.[8]

Deeper than entertainment, jesters came to serve a truth-telling, prophetic role. They got away with speaking truth to power in situations when almost anyone else in the court would have been exiled or beheaded. A few examples can demonstrate.

A Middle Eastern king was meting out excessively harsh punishments—eight hundred lashes for this man, twelve hundred for that, fifteen hundred for the other. His jester, the folk-fool mullah Nasrudin, interrupted him with an apparently irrelevant question: "O King, do you know everything?" "Of course I do," snapped the king. "Then how could you inflict such punishment? Either you don't know the meaning of the number 1,500, or you don't know the sting of a whip."[9]

In 1386 an Austrian duke called together his council to discuss his aim to launch an attack on Switzerland. He asked the attendant fool, Jenny von Stockach, for an opinion, and she was blunt and to the point: "You fools, you're all debating how to get into the country, but none of you have thought how you're going to get out again."[10]

Charles II of England, who reclaimed the throne from Oliver Cromwell's Protestant revolution, was a noted carouser, often missing morning appointments because of hangovers. European kings evidently could say, "Off with his head," about as easily as, "Good afternoon," so courtiers were leery of pointing out any royal flaws. So it fell to Charles's fool, Tom Killigrew, to try to shame him out of his bad habits—the attempt becoming a nearly lifelong effort on Tom's part. One morning after Charles had been out most of the night, Tom walked into the royal bedroom, and Charles is quoted as saying, "Now we shall hear of our faults." But Killigrew said, "No, Faith, I don't care to trouble myself with that which all the town talks of."[11]

The fool was a stock character that Shakespeare was fond of including in his plays. Shakespeare's characters that are actual court jesters like Touchstone in *As You Like It*, Lear's Fool in *King Lear*, and Feste in *Twelfth Night* are wise and use humor and wisdom in equal measure. As Feste reveals, it is "better a witty fool than a foolish wit" (Act 1, Scene 5) and Touchstone remarks "the fool doth think he is wise, but the wise man knows himself to be a fool" (Act 5, Scene 1). Shakespeare modeled these characters after the real fools and jesters of his day, usually peasants or commoners who used their wits to outdo people of higher social standing. In Europe from about 800 CE to the Renaissance, the courts of kings and lesser nobles were all devoted to (and under the sway of) the Roman Catholic Church. A good court jester would put on little skits, with riddles and songs showing how greedy for rich clothes and other worldly goods a bishop might be, and to mock the piety of local priests given to earthly more than spiritual pursuits. The jester was careful not to mock the body of the church with its doctrines and ethical principles but to mock only church officials who did not live up to the church's high standards. Besides errant priests, the jesters publicly mocked "venal officials and nobles, and erring or corrupt or lazy rulers, together with anything deemed sacrosanct."[12]

Court fools got away with speaking truth to power by not threatening power. They were insider-outsiders, having unique access to the king, yet not being accepted as a social equal by members of the court. Unlike most advisers, they usually came from relatively humble backgrounds. This meant they were no threat to the king, and it qualified them to give rulers insights into popular feelings to which they might not regularly have access.[13]

Because jesters were peripheral to the game of politics, the king could be assured that their words were not geared toward their own advancement. Rarely were jesters much inclined to try stealing power for their own benefit (though they were not averse to winning gifts and goodies here and there). They might risk their life to tell the ruler a thing or two, but they were not revolutionary in the sense of trying to destroy the existing power structure. They preferred to change behavior as an outsider operating inside the system. "While a jester might trick the king into landing him a fat present, he wasn't likely to plot his overthrow."[14]

Court fools' license to tell the truth also came from their role as confidants to the royal rulers. Kings, queens, and emperors not only tolerated their fools but often treated them with respect and affection.[15] In an article titled "Jesters Rule," Jake Page describes how a jester would regularly sass the king, addressing him in nicknames that no other member of the royal court would dare use. Henry VIII of England (never one to turn his cheek from an insult) enjoyed the services of the fool Will Somers, who called the king Harry. The two men were exceptionally close, as often happened between kings and fools.[16]

Beatrice Otto theorizes that rulers' respect for their fools came from their experiencing the fool's honesty as the refreshing exception to the rule—someone who wasn't scared of them and who didn't mind offering unpopular advice.[17] The freedom—indeed, the expectation—of the court jester to violate the proprieties of royalty and to flaunt pomposity was experienced by the king as his own freedom. In a court full of flatterers, the jester was the one the king could count on to speak with directness and candor.[18]

The jester was also often the one through whom bad news would be passed to the king when no one else dared to tell him the truth. The jester rarely seemed to flinch from this part of his duties. The worse the news, the more creatively the fool used humor to convey it. For example, when it fell to the jester to break the news to the French king Philip of the defeat of his fleet by the English in 1340, the jester told him the English sailors "don't even have the guts to jump into the water like our brave French."[19]

Today's preachers are tasked with breaking the good news to people that sometimes first sounds like bad news. A couple of examples: A preacher might say, "The bad news is that we have to relinquish our self-focused agendas built around our own comfort and security. The good news is that we then fulfill our true purpose in life and experience a depth of joy in serving others." But a jester might say, "There is good news and there is more good news. The good news is that we have to relinquish our self-focused agendas built around our own comfort and security. But who needed all that prestige and fortune anyway? The Bible makes no mention of there being climate-controlled self-storage units in either heaven or hell! The more good news is that, without it, we are free to fulfill our true purpose in life and experience a depth of joy in serving others."

A preacher might say, "There is bad news and good news. The bad news is that sorrow and misfortune come to the wicked and the righteous alike. The good news is that God's comfort and presence surround everyone alike in times of sorrow and misfortune." But a jester might flip this around and say, "There is good news and there is more good news. The good news is that sorrow and misfortune come to the righteous as well as the wicked. And that's as it should be. Why should the wicked people hog all the misfortune? There is plenty to go around! The more good news is that God's comfort and presence surround everyone alike in times of sorrow and misfortune."

Preachers get in trouble when they offer shallow good news without acknowledging the realities of life. Our historical jesters would frown on such froth. As we saw in chapter 7, while tragedy without comedy is despair, comedy without tragedy is frivolity and false hope. To promise people wealth, health, and longevity as a reward for positive thinking, or that everything that happens to them, whether good or bad, is God's direct will, these are not promises that a self-respecting jester would allow to go unchallenged. They are precisely the sorts of illusions a jester would call out as foolish and deflate with a pointed riposte.[20]

When speaking truth to power with blunt barbs was ineffective, jesters learned the subversive strategies of irony and sarcasm. They knew how to defuse situations with witty logic. Even when that failed and they found themselves on the brink of exile or execution, they managed with surprising frequency to wriggle out of trouble with another joke.[21]

Plenty of tales show that some jesters were witty enough to talk their way out of being executed. In one instance a Chinese jester facing execution said, "I'd just like to say one thing before I die." The emperor asked what he had in mind. "If Your Majesty takes my head, it will be absolutely useless to you." The jester added that it also would be extremely painful to himself. The emperor laughed and let him go.[22]

It was in the nature of jesters to speak their minds when the mood struck them, regardless of the consequences. At such times, they were neither calculating nor circumspect. They had little to gain by caution and little to lose by candor, apart from liberty, livelihood, and occasionally even life, which hardly seems to have been a deterrent to them. They "walked the thin line between employment and execution."[23] Preachers could do well to imitate the tendency among jesters to be true to themselves and let the chips fall where they may.

By the eighteenth century fools had become increasingly out of fashion with people of enlightened tastes and were found, no longer in court and country estate, but on performing stages, and in traveling shows and fairs. These were the forebears of the stand-up comedians we know today.

THE HOLY FOOL

God's foolishness is wiser than human wisdom.
    —The apostle Paul, 1 Corinthians 1:25

We have seen how court jesters and fools were a staple social category across cultures. The same is true of the role of holy fool across religions. Generally speaking, a fool could be anyone who did not conform to a particular set of norms, who refused to join in the fray of material and political gain. The Franciscans called themselves "fools for Christ's sake," St. Francis himself being known as "God's jester." Greek and Russian Orthodox Churches canonized "holy fools." And those considered to be "mad"—sometimes called "simpletons" or "naturals"—were thought to have an aura of holiness in the Muslim world and a number of other cultures. Similar to the Franciscan use of "fools for Christ's sake," the eighth-century Indian saint and poet Cuntarar speaks of a "fool of Siva's sake." There are dervishes in the Middle East, the humorous wisdom of a Zen master in the East, and an aura of sanctity that surrounds those regarded as "lunatics" in many parts of the world. Sufis advocate folly as a means to enlightenment, call themselves "the Idiots," and use humor in their teaching to shock people and jolt them out of conventional patterns.[24] Across all these traditions, holy fools were thought to be potential mouthpieces for God.[25]

The holy fool tradition in Christian piety was inspired by the strange, symbolic actions of Old Testament prophets. We call to mind Isaiah walking naked and barefoot for three years (20:2, 3); Ezekiel lying before a stone, baking his daily barley-cake on a bed of cow dung (4:9–15); and Hosea entering into an ill-fated marriage. This tradition also has roots in Paul's teachings about being a fool for Christ. Indeed, to the outside world Jesus' teachings were foolish: forgiving your enemies, praying for your persecutors, seeking to serve rather than be served, and finding one's life through giving it away. In 1 Corinthians 1:18–31, Paul names the radical paradox, the incomprehensible incongruity of the gospel as the folly of God and Jesus' followers as fools for Christ. These verses are packed with the following paradoxical assertions:

— The message of the cross is foolishness to those who are perishing, but it is the power of God to those who are being saved.
— God has made foolish the wisdom of the world.
— God is determined to save the world through the foolishness of Paul's proclamation.
— Christ crucified exemplifies the wisdom and power of God.
— God's foolishness is wiser than human wisdom, and God's weakness is stronger than human strength.
— God chose not those possessing worldly credentials and power but those who were weak and lowly.
— Christ became for us the wisdom from God.

The holy fool tradition surfaced in the lives of the desert fathers and mothers, growing in influence in the sixth century in the Greek Orthodox Church, and finding full expression in the Russian Orthodox Church between the fourteenth and seventeenth centuries. Holy fools embodied a type of sainthood in which the expression of piety was that of publicly making a fool of oneself. The monk or priest demonstrated his humility by making himself ridiculous in his appearance and manner, becoming, in effect, a jester to the church. He humbled himself in a comic identification with the humility and humiliation of Jesus. The holy fool withdrew from worldly power and wealth, as she manifested herself both beyond and within the church, to follow in the footsteps of one hailed as a king, who wore thorns for a crown and whose throne was a cross. For example, St. Isidora wore a rag over her head, walked barefoot, and subsisted on the crumbs from the table of the Tavena-Min convent.[26]

Elizabeth-Anne Stewart points out that the motif of the holy fool is not confined to the discipline of theology. As an archetype, which she defines as "a pre-existing pattern of being which forms part of the psychic inheritance of all the human race," the holy fool exists in many of the world's religions and cultures. The type is widely found in literature and is present in the foundational myths of many people. It crops up in the lives of saints and martyrs. The common portrait of holy fools is of those who choose "integrity over security and are willing to pay the price for their choices."[27]

If there is humor in the actions and words of holy fools, it is the rigorous brand of willingness to challenge what passes for wisdom in a society. In the example of the prophets, among them Jesus, we behold a fearlessness in speaking truth to power, by means of symbolic action as well as by humor's debunking strategies of irony, exaggeration, and sarcasm. Camels and eyes of needles; specks and logs in eyes; Pharisees, respected in their communities, painted as pompous pray-ers; bosses paying all laborers the same regardless of hours worked . . . holy fools march to the drumbeat of divine wisdom, which is incongruous with human wisdom. Their lives become a testimony to how gaining one's life can look to the world like losing it, how spiritual strength can come through the appearance of weakness.

Johan Cilliers and Charles Campbell, in their book *Preaching Fools*, remind preachers that our vocation is to deliver a paradoxical, nonsensical gospel, to be fools whose identity and actions are inseparable from the folly of the cross.[28]

This particular image is tough to connect with as twenty-first-century preachers. We find it easier to blend in than to stand out, and are expected to maintain a modicum of dignity in personal and public interactions—and, most certainly, when preaching and leading worship.[29] Usually, when we make fools of ourselves publicly, it is not intentional. But there is a quirky challenge for us in the holy fool's being willing to fly in the face of public opinion and to be thought an ass or worse in honor of the one who humbled himself to ride a donkey into town!

THE COMEDIAN AS COMIC SAGE

The fear of the LORD is instruction in wisdom,
    and humility goes before honor.
    —Proverbs 15:33

Alyce, in her work on the wisdom literature of the Bible, has argued that the sage, the wisdom seeker and teacher, is a helpful model for today's preacher. Israel's sages, Jesus included, offer preachers a master class in the close observation of inner life, outer life, and biblical texts, what we are calling the inscape, landscape, and textscape.[30] How might the roles of court jester and holy fool combine with the role of sage to inform preachers' self-understanding as contemporary sages who embrace a comic spirit?

First, it should be noted that the ancient biblical sages did indeed embrace a comic spirit. They saw humor in habitual human behaviors: comparing a meddler to one who grabs a passing dog by the ears (Prov. 26:17), describing the lazy person turning in his bed like a door on a hinge (26:14), and recommending we put our hands over our mouths when we hear ourselves spouting nonsense (Prov. 30:2). Jesus' sayings about logs and specks, camels and eyes of needles, and eggs and scorpions employ two of humor's favorite strategies—exaggeration and incongruity—to contrast human and divine ways of operating in the world and to offer humor's witty, edgy challenge to the powers that be. The same can be said for his more developed parables of annoying nighttime visitors and dishonest stewards.[31] Jesus' bold use of humor that "aimed up" blurred the lines between prophet and wisdom teacher, earning him the designation of subversive sage. Humor and ancient wisdom traditions are intimate companions.[32]

But are there contemporary models that preachers might draw on for combining wisdom and humor? Owen, in his work in humor studies, has come to recognize that in our society the comic has become the contemporary sage, combining elements of jester, fool, prophet, and wisdom purveyor.

Will Rogers is a perfect early-twentieth-century example. He began in vaudeville but became the nation's premier social and political commentator. He once said, "I have a scheme for stopping war. It's this—no nation is allowed to enter a war till they have paid for the last one."[33] The simple wisdom of this humorous quip is clear as day.

Even as a political satirist, Rogers was a friend to numerous presidents and a regular guest at the White House. He was, perhaps, the last court jester invited into the throne room. In a comment that has turned out to be almost too true to be funny, he once said, "Everything is changing. People are taking their comedians seriously and their politicians as a joke."[34]

A comic who functioned as a subversive prophetic outsider later in the twentieth century was Dick Gregory (1932–2017), who rose to national prominence with satirical humor centered on current events, politics, and racial tensions. His trademark was the searing punch line. "A southern liberal?" he once said. "That's a guy that'll lynch you from a low tree." On segregation: "I know the South very well. I spent twenty years there one night."

Mel Watkins, a journalist and scholar whose books include *On the Real Side: A History of African American Comedy,* comments, "At a time when audiences expected Black performers to do minstrel skits in baggy pants and outsize shoes and use slapstick humor, Gregory broke the mold among black comedians by employing political satire. . . . He was very calm in his demeanor but very outspoken in what he said."[35] He paved the way for Richard Pryor and other Black comedians in the tradition of comic sage.

Comedians today continue to serve a truth-telling function in society and, at their best, speak truth to power, provide alternative perspectives, and remind us of our common foibles.[36] Their influence on politics is now intensified since they can speak across a wide expanse of in-person, broadcast, and digital venues. Politicians cannot afford to ignore them.

One place where the comic serves as court jester is the White House Correspondents' Dinner. Traditionally this event features a comedian whose role is to headline the event and make jokes at the expense of journalists, the administration, and the president.[37] The target is supposed to be those in power who willingly turned up to be made fun of, even openly to laugh at themselves. President Bush was ferociously roasted by the satirical Stephen Colbert at the 2006 dinner, and the president received wide praise for his ability to laugh, even vigorously, when many considered that Colbert went beyond the pale.[38]

Such formal meetings of those in power with those who humorously speak truth to power are far and few between, but people increasingly turn to comedians to make sense of political life, especially as it becomes more uncertain (incongruity function) or contentious (relief function). The "Weekend Update" segment on *Saturday Night Live* (SNL) first aired in October 1975. It is the longest-running and still the most popular sketch on the show.[39] SNL's largest audience is for episodes following political debates when the public tunes in not just to look at how SNL will humorously frame the situation, but (research shows) how to make sense of it. Research shows that SNL's framing matters and helps set public perception and interpretation of events.[40] One of the best examples of this was SNL cast member Tina Fey's impersonation of Sarah Palin, which was so exact and popular that voters misattributed Fey's satirical lines like "I can see Russia from my house" to Palin herself. That political comedy influences modern politics is seen in the fact that now mainstream news regularly reports on political comedy and even appropriates its humor and parody.[41]

SNL's "Weekend Update" paved the way for Comedy Central's *The Daily Show* hosted by Craig Kilborn (1997–98) and Jon Stewart (1999–2015) and *The Colbert Report* (2005–14), two of the most watched shows in the first decade of this century. These shows are perhaps the best example of the role of comedy as not only providing entertainment and a critique of modern politics but also becoming a trusted source of information and analysis. As millennials reported decreased trust in journalism and traditional news outlets, they reported higher trust in Comedy Central for accuracy of the news.[42] Senator John Edwards formally announced his candidacy for president on the *Daily Show*. The fact that politicians go on these shows and that audience trust in them is enhanced as a result demonstrates a blending of genres of news and satire, of wisdom and humor.

Audiences self-report that they watch such shows not only for their entertainment value but also because they regard them as equal to the actual news as a reliable source of information.[43] This was best demonstrated with the popularity of Stephen Colbert's satirical role (a character he did not break from until accepting his role as host of the *Late Show*) in the *Colbert Report* that was equally popular with conservative and liberal audience members who both identified with him and found the show equally funny. Liberals watched the show because it made fun of bombastic conservative talking heads, while the conservatives found it funny because Colbert was tricking liberals into listening to their points of view.[44] This phenomenon speaks to the malleability of humor and the ability for humor to point out the truth even when, or especially when, it is ridiculous.

Trevor Noah follows in Jon Stewart's and Stephen Colbert's footsteps in being a comic-sage. When he took over as host of *The Daily Show* following Stewart's retirement, he was largely unknown. MSNBC's *Meet the Press* interviewed him on October 31, 2018. In introducing himself, he said, "I use comedy to in some way shape and form current information . . . the same information my audience is processing. . . . I think comedy, the *best* comedy, is informed by the truth. The best comedians spoke from a position of truth."[45]

The most recent White House Correspondents' Dinner at the time of writing (May 1, 2022) was front-lined by Noah. There he not only exemplified the role of comic sage he described on *Meet the Press*, he named it explicitly. Noah made fun of President Joe Biden and other politicians with a caustic wit that would have warmed the heart of a medieval court jester. But he also spent a significant amount of time cracking jokes at the expense of the major news outlets, especially Fox News and CNN. But then he ended his comedy routine with these sage words:

> The reason we're here is to honor and celebrate the Fourth Estate and what you stand for—what you stand for—an additional check and balance that holds power to account and gives voice to those who otherwise wouldn't have one. . . . Every single one of you, whether you like it or not, is a bastion of democracy. And if you ever begin to doubt your responsibilities, if you ever begin to doubt how meaningful it is, look no further than what's happening in Ukraine. Journalists are risking and even losing their lives to show the world what's really happening. You realize how amazing it is. In America, you have the right to seek the truth and speak the truth even if it makes people in power uncomfortable, even if it makes your viewers or your readers uncomfortable. You understand how amazing that is?
>
> I stood here tonight and I made fun of the president of the United States and I'm going to be fine, right? . . . Do you really understand what a blessing it is? Maybe it's happened for so long, it might slip your mind. It's a blessing.
>
> In fact, ask yourself this question: If Russian journalists who are losing their livelihoods . . . and their freedom for daring to report on what their own government is doing, if they had the freedom to write any words, to show any stories, or to ask any questions, if they

had basically what you have, would they be using it in the same way that you do? Ask yourself that question every day because you have one of the most important roles in the world.[46]

Noah reminds the journalists to whom he is speaking of the noble nature of their vocation in our society after using humor to critique how they have been squandering that very vocation. Here he has become a subversive comic sage and moved into the role of holy fool as well. He wisely uses humor and political critique to name and live out a sacred calling.

For the past several decades social trends, at least in the United States, have shaped the advice pastors and preachers have received concerning who they should be. The 1960s told us to be prophets; the 1970s told us to be therapists; the 1980s told us to be church-growth consultants; the 1990s told us to be CEOs and player-coaches. There wasn't much mention of the role of humor in any of that. The past couple of decades have been all over the map: entrepreneurs, Bible teachers, social media influencers . . . more or less fill in the blank.[47]

Let's fill in the blank with jester, fool, and comic sage—in whatever mixture the occasion calls for. We don't need to wear a fool's cap and pointed slippers with bells on the toes like medieval court jesters. And we don't have to walk naked and barefoot through the streets of town like some of the holy fools.

But we can activate the power of the comic spirit and follow in our preaching this model of combining court jester, holy fool, and sage—unless, that is, we are willing to cede the social, spiritual role of subversive sage to the comedians. If not, let's learn from them, tempering their methods to serve God's good news. Keeping our eyes on the horizon of the comic vision, inspired by the boldness and acerbic wit of contemporary masters of comedy, let's up our humor game!

To Ponder

—What function of the jester could be applicable to your preaching in your context?

—What about the holy fool?

—In what ways are you already operating like a sage in your community and preaching?

—What lessons might preachers learn from comedians in speaking truth to power?

NOTES

1. This saying has been attributed to Nicolas Boileau Despréaux (1636–1711), a French poet and critic, but its precise origin is unknown.

2. Quoted in Beatrice K. Otto, *Fools Are Everywhere: The Court Jester around the World* (Chicago: University of Chicago Press, 2007), 96.

3. See Otto, *Fools Are Everywhere,* xv–xxiii.

4. Barry Sanders, *Sudden Glory: Laughter as Subversive History* (Boston: Beacon Press, 1996), 207. In Europe, many cardinals, bishops, and pontiffs kept jesters. There were also a number of jester-clerics. See Otto, *Fools Are Everywhere,* 171–77.

5. Conrad Hyers, *The Comic Vision and the Christian Faith: A Celebration of Life and Laughter* (Eugene, OR: Wipf and Stock, 2003), 41.

6. Hyers, *Comic Vision and the Christian Faith,* 40.

7. Retaining people with physical differences and limitations for entertainment purposes was a common practice among wealthy men in the Roman Empire. Making fun of the differently abled became a favorite indoor sport of kings during the Renaissance period, going out of fashion by the late seventeenth century as sensibilities became more refined. See Sanders, *Sudden Glory,* 218.

8. Records of male fools or clowns recount them occasionally dressing as women. See Enid Welsford, *The Fool: His Social and Literary History* (Gloucester, MA: Peter Smith, 1966), 175.

9. Otto, *Fools Are Everywhere,* 83–84.

10. Jake Page, "Jesters Rule," *Notre Dame Magazine,* Winter 2010–11, https://magazine.nd.edu/stories/jesters-rule/.

11. Otto, *Fools Are Everywhere,* 121–22.

12. Page, "Jesters Rule."

13. Hyers, *Comic Vision and the Christian Faith,* 40–41.

14. See "Interview with Beatrice K. Otto, Author of *Fools Are Everywhere,*" University of Chicago Press, https://press.uchicago.edu/Misc/Chicago/640914in .html, for an interview with the author as well as information about websites on the history of jesters and fools with information on historical jester-fools and stories of their exploits and witticisms.

15. Otto, *Fools Are Everywhere,* 246.

16. Page, "Jesters Rule." Page, editor and author, was a regular contributor to *Notre Dame Magazine* until his death in 2016. Troubled by the state of American politics, he prescribed an ancient antidote: the court jester. He believed that this remedy, once used to keep the exalted in line while seasoning the halls of power with sprinkles of levity, was needed more than ever today.

17. From "Interview with Beatrice K. Otto."

18. Hyers, *Comic Vision and the Christian Faith,* 41–44.

19. Hyers, *Comic Vision and the Christian Faith,* 43–45.

20. See John C. Holbert and Alyce M. McKenzie, *What Not to Say: Avoiding the Common Mistakes That Can Sink Your Sermon* (Louisville, KY: Westminster John Knox Press, 2011), 1–19.

21. From "Interview with Beatrice K. Otto."

22. Page, "Jesters Rule," 11.

23. Hyers, *Comic Vision and the Christian Faith*, 45.

24. Idries Shah, *Wisdom of the Idiots* (London: ISF Publishers, 2019).

25. Otto, *Fools Are Everywhere*, 32–33.

26. Vasili Novakshonoff, *God's Fools: The Lives of the Holy "Fools for Christ"* (Dewdney, BC: Synaxis Press, 1973), 5–6. The book deals with the lives of thirty holy fools.

27. Elizabeth-Anne Stewart, *Jesus the Holy Fool* (Franklin, WI: Sheed and Ward, 1999), 2.

28. Johan H. Cilliers and Charles L. Campbell, *Preaching Fools: The Gospel as a Rhetoric of Folly* (Waco, TX: Baylor University Press, 2012).

29. John Wesley, though a proponent of decorum and dignity in his own demeanor and that of his preachers, was moved to make a fool of himself in many people's eyes by preaching in the fields. There are many ways and degrees in which to embrace the preacher as fool!

30. The sages who collected and created proverbs in the book of Proverbs tended to offer wisdom that stabilized the status quo by commending moderate behavior. By contrast, Ecclesiastes and Jesus were subversive sages, using paradox and hyperbole in their wisdom sayings to undercut the status quo. See Alyce M. McKenzie, *Preaching Proverbs: Wisdom for the Pulpit* (Louisville, KY: Westminster John Knox Press, 1996).

31. See Alyce M. McKenzie, *The Parables for Today* (Louisville, KY: Westminster John Knox Press, 2007).

32. For a more in-depth look at wisdom and the sage in Scripture and today, see Alyce M. McKenzie, *Wise Up! Four Biblical Virtues for Navigating Life* (Eugene, OR: Cascade Books 2018), and *Hear and Be Wise: Becoming a Teacher and Preacher of Wisdom* (Nashville: Abingdon Press, 2004).

33. Ben Yagoda, *Will Rogers: A Biography* (Norman: University of Oklahoma Press, 2000).

34. Page, "Jesters Rule."

35. Mel Watkins, *On the Real Side: A History of African American Comedy* (Chicago: Lawrence Hill Books, 1999). This comprehensive history of Black humor sets it in the context of American popular culture. Blackface minstrels, Stepin Fetchit, and the *Amos 'n' Andy* show presented a distorted picture of African Americans; Watkins's book contrasts this image with the authentic underground humor of African Americans found in folktales, race records, and all-Black shows and films. After generations of stereotypes, the underground humor finally emerged before the American public with Richard Pryor in the 1970s. But Pryor was not the first

popular comic to present authentically Black humor. Watkins offers surprising reassessments of such seminal figures as Fetchit, Bert Williams, Moms Mabley, and Redd Foxx, looking at how they paved the way for contemporary Black comics. See T. Rees Shapiro, "Dick Gregory, Cutting-Edge Satirist and Uncompromising Activist, Dies at 84," *Washington Post*, https://www.washingtonpost.com/local/obituaries/black-satirist-inspired-other-comics-with-expert-timing-bold-humor-and-political-comedy/2017/08/19/f9360e40-854f-11e7-902a-2a9f2d808496_story.html.

36. For an exploration of American comedians from vaudeville days to the present, see Kliph Nesteroff's *The Comedians: Drunks, Thieves, Scoundrels and the History of American Comedy* (New York: Grove Press, 2015).

37. The traditions of the president attending and delivering a humorous speech at the Al Smith Dinner as well as attending the White House Correspondents' Dinner were both refused by Donald Trump. Trump did attend and performed at the Al Smith dinner in 2016 and was widely panned because, instead of using self-deprecating humor as is the expectation, he used aggressive superiority humor targeted at Hillary Clinton and other political opponents.

38. Elizabeth Benacka, *Rhetoric, Humor, and the Public Sphere: From Socrates to Stephen Colbert* (Lanham, MD: Rowman and Littlefield, 2016).

39. S. Robert Lichter, Jody Baumgartner, and Jonathan Morris, *Politics Is a Joke!: How TV Comedians Are Remaking Political Life* (New York: Routledge, 2018).

40. Ben Voth, "Saturday Night Live and Presidential Elections," in *Laughing Matters: Humor and American Politics in the Media Age*, ed. Jody Baumgartner and Jonathan S. Morris (New York: Routledge, 2008), 229–40.

41. Jason T. Peifer, "Palin, Saturday Night Live, and Framing: Examining the Dynamics of Political Parody," *Communication Review* 16, no. 3 (July 2013): 155–77, https://doi.org/10.1080/10714421.2013.807117; Angela D. Abel and Michael Barthel, "Appropriation of Mainstream News: How Saturday Night Live Changed the Political Discussion," *Critical Studies in Media Communication* 30, no. 1 (March 2013): 1–16, https://doi.org/10.1080/15295036.2012.701011.

42. Lauren Feldman, "The News about Comedy," *Journalism* 8, no. 4 (August 2007): 406–27, https://doi.org/10.1177/1464884907078655.

43. Heather L. LaMarre, Kristen D. Landreville, and Michael A. Beam, "The Irony of Satire," *International Journal of Press/Politics* 14, no. 2 (April 2009): 212–31, https://doi.org/10.1177/1940161208330904.

44. LaMarre, Landreville, and Beam, "The Irony of Satire," found that there was no significant difference between the groups in thinking Colbert was funny, but conservatives were more likely to report that Colbert only pretends to be joking and genuinely meant what he said while liberals were more likely to report that Colbert used satire and was not serious when offering political statements.

45. Trevor Noah interviewed by Chuck Todd, *Meet the Press*, MSNBC, October 31, 2018, "Trevor Noah: 'The Best Comedy Is Informed by the Truth,'" YouTube, https://www.youtube.com/watch?v=k3pzImEloFI.

46. Tom Jones, "Trevor Noah's Speech at the White House Correspondents' Association Dinner Was Funny yet Inspiring—Poynter," Poynter Institute, May 2, 2022, https://www.poynter.org/commentary/2022/trevor-noahs-speech-at-the -white-house-correspondents-association-dinner-was-funny-yet-inspiring/.

47. McKenzie, *Hear and Be Wise*, 1.

10

The Preacher as Comic Spirit

Life is a comedy to those who think, a tragedy to those who feel.
—British politician and writer Horace Walpole (1717–1797)[1]

Owen arrived early at a conference, exhausted from his flight, and made his way to the auditorium in the conference center. Finding it empty he chose a prime location in the middle of a row halfway back from the stage, sat down, leaned back, and promptly fell asleep. It was the kind of sleep that makes your head roll back, your mouth hang open slightly, and that involves some snuffling. He awoke some half an hour later, in that liminal state where you don't quite remember where you are or what day it is. All he knew was he was surrounded by the sound of laughter. Looking around, he saw that, while he had been doing his Rip Van Winkle imitation, the whole place had filled with people and they were all, simultaneously, expressing their amusement at the Sleeping Beauty in their midst. Owen is still deciding which of the three kinds of humor that was: superiority, incongruity, or relief. It felt good-natured, but he was still a bit embarrassed!

Waking up to find ourselves surrounded by humor: that is our situation as preachers in our current milieu. After centuries of being in a coma of comic disdain, we awakened in the last quarter of the twentieth century to find that others around us were already wide awake to the presence and power of the comic spirit in their respective disciplines, offering us a wakeup call.

A WAKEUP CALL IS COMING!

As noted earlier, scholars across disciplines began to show more respect for humor in the last quarter of the twentieth century. There were traces of this development in the theological world before this.

Beginning in the nineteenth century, preachers like Lyman Beecher, Henry Ward Beecher, and Timothy Dwight incorporated humor into their sermons in the cause of their theological polemics. So did Dwight L. Moody and Charles Finney, who retold biblical stories in contemporary humorous style. And, of course, African American preaching early on used humor to uplift the downtrodden and deflate the proud.[2]

A number of early- and mid-twentieth-century theologians held a positive view of humor before the burgeoning of humor studies as well. C. S. Lewis credited humor with being a faculty that helps us be aware of the difference, the incongruity, between the human and the divine: "Lack of humor is a characteristic of Hell."[3] Catholic theologian Karl Rahner praised humor and laughter as acknowledgments of our human limitation and an expression of our reverence for God.[4] Protestant theologian Reinhold Niebuhr regarded humor as a healthy means of coping with the incongruities of our own and others' behavior. The ability to laugh at ourselves is "a prelude to contrition . . . a vestibule to the temple of confession."[5] Swiss theologian Karl Barth grounded humor in the eschatological character of the Christian faith, what we are calling the comic vision. He believed it is incumbent on Christians to refuse to take the present with ultimate seriousness.[6]

These few examples serve as a foreshadowing of the blossoming academic interest in humor in the last quarter of the twentieth century. Several social psychologists and scientists have written analyses of humor during this period—what it is and why we laugh—among them, Robert Provine, Peter McGraw, and Joel Warner. Similarly, historians and literary scholars such as Barry Sanders, Michael Screech, and Ralph Wood have begun studying the history of humor and its manifestation in literature through the centuries.

These works paved the way for considerations of humor in theological disciplines. In the last half century, biblical scholars and theologians have both shown more respect for humor, not as frivolous or derogatory, but as integral to biblical and theological renderings of the relationship of God and humankind.

In biblical studies, the insight has been growing that Baudelaire's quote "Holy Books never laugh" is inaccurate. For example, according to biblical scholars J. Cheryl Exum and J. William Whedbee,

> The holy book we call the Bible revels in a profound laughter, a divine and human laughter that is endemic to the whole narrative of creation, fall and salvation, and finally a laughter that results in a wondrous, all-encompassing comic vision. . . . The passion and depth of this comic vision derive precisely from its recognition of the place and power of tragedy. . . . But the tragedy is episodic in the overarching structure of the Bible and ephemeral in its ultimate effects, though nonetheless excruciating in its reality.[7]

In the realm of theology, a number of writers whom we have gratefully drawn upon throughout this book have offered interpretations of humor, laughter, and joy as integral to our existential understanding of God and ourselves. These scholars include John Morreall, Karl Josef-Kuschel, Conrad Hyers, Brian Edgar, James Martin, SJ, and Steve Wilkens. Journalism professor Robert Darden has written an insightful study of humor's centrality to the Christian faith, in particular its role in deflating human pretension.[8]

It is important to recognize as part of this brief survey of humor studies that a significant strain of the work has been done by feminist scholars. Female humor analysts such as Alice Sheppard and Kathleen Sands have offered critiques of traditional categorizations of humor, underscoring its aggressive motivations and frequent function to ridicule and diminish women. They have sought to recover historical materials about women as humor users throughout history and to expose the denigrating stereotype that the female role is to enjoy humor, while the male role is to create it.[9]

We find similar approaches in biblical and theological works. Athalya Brenner critiques the misogynistic use of humor in biblical texts and today.[10] In her 1996 article "Ifs, Ands, and Butts: Theological Reflections on Humor," Kathleen M. Sands analyzed the socially transformative power of humor to expose the fabrication of norms related to gender and sexual identity.[11]

Feminist theologian Mary Daly, whose work called out Christianity as a religion whose fundamental concepts act to reinforce the oppression of women in a patriarchal society, urged women to "laugh out loud" as a form of resistance to constrictive gender roles. She defined the virtue of laughing aloud as the "Lusty habit of boisterous Be-laughing women: habit of cracking the hypocritical hierarchy's 'houses of mirrors,' defusing their power of deluding Others; cackling that cracks the man-made universe, creating a crack through which cacklers can slip into the Realms of the Wild."[12]

HOMILETICIANS, WAKE UP!

We have traced the burgeoning respect for and interest in humor that dates from the mid-1970s in history, sociology, psychology, literary studies, biblical studies, and theology. With all these disciplines waking up around us, we are led to ask what about us homileticians? Recent literature in homiletics portrays the field as groggy but gaining wakefulness with regard to the value of adopting the comic spirit as a dynamic of our preaching.

In the textbooks on preaching of the past several decades there are more warnings about the inappropriate use of humor than constructive demonstrations of its appropriate use. For example, John Holbert, while seeing value in humor in preaching, warns not to "overcute" oneself at the beginning of the sermon.[13] David Buttrick goes a step further to advise against using humor at all at the beginning of a sermon.[14]

Some authors, however, have moved from negative advice to positive assessments of humor, comic spirit, and comic vision in the pulpit. In 1977 Frederick Buechner, preacher, writer, and theologian, published his 1976 Beecher Lectures as *Telling the Truth: The Gospel as Tragedy, Comedy and Fairy Tale*. In the book, he describes the dynamic of preaching as pointing listeners toward the overcoming of tragedy by comedy and its lived reality in everyday life.

Baptist pastor and professor of psychology and counseling John Drakeford, in *Humor in Preaching* (1986), emphasizes the propriety and power of humor in the pulpit, and its ability to hold audience attention and unite congregations.[15]

In his 1988 book *Preaching for Growth*, Ronald J. Allen includes a discussion titled "Humor Can Serve the Gospel." While brief, it clearly sets out positive functions of humor: hold attention, diffuse the tension of a deadly serious topic, bring a moment of eschatological freedom as the joy of humor breaks into our somber present lives, lower defenses to aid congregational receptivity, and expose our foibles. He warns that care must be taken that our humor is well intentioned and doesn't erode the dignity of any listener. It's also crucial, he points out, that we are clear about why we are using humor so that it directs listeners' attention toward the theme rather than distract from it.[16]

Joseph Webb's practical, clearly written *Comedy and Preaching* (1999) describes a genre he calls "The Comic Sermon," a recipe whose fundamental ingredient is the hope of our comic faith, which, in Webb's view, shapes or ought to shape the persona of the preacher, the approach to the biblical text, the sequencing of the sermon, and its delivery.[17]

Rev. Susan Sparks, Baptist pastor and stand-up comedian, has written two books on preaching and humor: *Laugh Your Way to Grace: Reclaiming the Spiritual Power of Humor* (2010) and *Preaching Punchlines: The Ten Commandments of Comedy* (2019). Both books are peppered with practical insights into claiming one's creativity in the pulpit and using humor as a way of addressing difficult situations and building relationships with the congregation.

Episcopal priests Ian S. Markham and Samantha R. E. Gottlich, authors of *Lectionary Levity: The Use of Humor in Preaching* (2017), discuss the power of humor and Jesus' use of it, followed by advice on how to use a joke in a sermon. They then go through the lectionary's Gospel lessons, offering a theme for each week and an accompanying humorous story. The premise of their book is this:

> Humor has real power. When people laugh, they relax. They become more likely to listen and more receptive to what will follow. . . . Our model for using humor in communication is our Lord himself. Jesus had a wonderful sense of humor.[18]

Charles Campbell, in his *The Word on the Street: Performing the Scriptures in the Urban Context* (2000), co-authored with Stanley P. Saunders, suggests the model of the court jester for the preacher, lampooning the principalities and powers. He suggests that using a comic and burlesque style in preaching can be a powerful way to name and expose the powers. Says Campbell, "Rather than somber, self-important sermons dealing with such matters as capitalism or individualism, preaching . . . may offer startlingly comic or burlesque depictions of the powers, lampooning the absurdity of their claims."[19]

Johan H. Cilliers and Charles Campbell collaborated in the 2012 volume *Preaching Fools: The Gospel as a Rhetoric of Folly*. It explores the archetype of the fool as manifested in court jesters, clowns, and foolish ones across many religions and cultures. They challenge preachers to reclaim our identity as fools for Christ and our vocation as the proclamation of paradoxically foolish good news.[20]

More recently Campbell, in his *The Scandal of the Gospel: Preaching and the Grotesque* (2021), has further explored the element of grotesque humor inherent in the preaching of the gospel that he has dealt with in his earlier work. The term "grotesque" comes from an Italian phrase meaning "work (or painting) found in a grotto" (grotto-esque). The *Alexamenos graffito* (ca. 238–244) is a piece of Roman graffiti scratched in the plaster of a wall of a guardroom on Palatine Hill near the Circus Maximus in Rome. It was discovered in 1857. The image shows a figure with an ass's head and a human body hanging from a cross. In front of the figure stands a young man (presumably Alexamenos) raising a hand as if in prayer. Across the picture is written in broad strokes: *Alexamenos worships his God.*[21]

This graffiti depicting the crucified human with the head of a donkey epitomizes the grotesque. It is what seems peculiar, odd, absurd, macabre, and shocking to us. It embodies destabilizing pairings of opposites. It is contradictory and incongruous. It is weak power, foolish wisdom, and a Crucified Messiah. It is paradox on steroids. For Campbell, preaching this grotesque gospel is an act of folly, in which the preacher becomes a fool for Christ.

A recent addition to the bibliography of homiletics and humor is Karl and Rolf Jacobson's *Divine Laughter: Preaching and the Serious Business of Humor* (Minneapolis: Fortress Press, 2022), which explores biblical humor both as a means of cultural critique and an expression of a joyful homiletic.[22]

THE PREACHER'S CALLING TO BE A COMIC SPIRIT

It's time to zoom in from this panoramic survey to the impact the comic spirit/vision can have on your calling to preach. It's time to ask you a rather personal question: to what extent, Preacher, in your calling to preach, have you internalized a comic spirit?

We decided to call this chapter "The Preacher as Comic Spirit," playing on the double meaning of the term capable of indicating either an attitude or a person who possesses that attitude. We wouldn't recommend that you step into the pulpit your first week in a new church and announce dramatically, "I have come to be your comic spirit!" But if you have internalized the comic spirit into your calling, you won't have to announce it. Over the weeks and months and maybe even years (!) you are with them, your congregation will experience you as humble, open-minded, joyful, and relational, both through your sermons and your interchanges with them beyond the pulpit.

John Morreall in his book *Comedy, Tragedy, and Religion* distinguishes between tragic and comic protagonists, their view of themselves and life. He characterizes tragic spirits as more rigid in their thinking, viewing challenges as dilemmas rather than as opportunities for dialogue, factoring out ambiguity in favor of either-or interpretations. They expect an ideal world and are not willing to acknowledge or accept imperfections and foibles in others or themselves.

Comic spirits, by contrast, are more open, accepting of ambiguity, and willing to laugh at themselves and with others in the course of unpredictable daily events.[23]

Morreall's listing of qualities of comic and tragic protagonists inspired your authors to devise a little game we call "You may be a tragic or comic protagonist if" . . . and to highlight the impact each has on our use of humor in fulfilling our call to preach.

You May Be a Tragic Spirit If . . .

Fight any instinct to be humorless, because humorlessness is the worst of all absurdities.
—Jean Cocteau, French poet, playwright, novelist, designer, filmmaker, and critic (1889–1963)

In Morreall's view, you may lean toward viewing yourself as a tragic protagonist if . . .

— You have low tolerance for ambiguity.
— You are characterized by mental rigidity that affects your emotions and decisions. Tragic heroes, driven by single emotions, tend to be extremists. It's all or nothing to reach their goal. Ahab will kill Moby Dick or die trying. Hamlet will prove the king's guilt and try to execute perfect justice, no matter what it costs him and those around him.[24] Walter Kerr calls this "the tragedy of the locked will." The downfall of a tragic protagonist is made inevitable as much by their locked wills as by any external force.[25]
— You yearn for simple, unambiguous categories and conceptual order.

—You prefer clean abstracts like truth, justice, and duty to messy concrete realities like people, things, and situations.

—You crave an ideal, perfect world.

THE PREACHER AS TRAGIC SPIRIT: HOMILETICAL IMPACT

The Bible definitely is infallible. How else would it have survived so many years of bad preaching?
  —Leonard Ravenhill, English Christian evangelist
  and author (1907–1994)

The tragic perspective would lead toward preaching that oversimplifies complex realities in life and the Bible and demands obedience to the preacher's perspective rather than inviting dialogue with the congregation. It would favor sermonic forms that front-load the sermon with its conclusion, rather than inviting listeners on an unfolding journey of insight.

The tragic-spirited preacher would not be likely to admit weakness or use appropriately self-deprecatory humor. Over time this would run the risk of distancing the preacher from the congregation and their being perceived as above the message.

The tragic-spirited preacher would have difficulty preaching effectively on highly charged, conflictual topics on which there are differing views in the congregation. Among the rhetorical strategies Alyce recommends the following to students in her course on preaching on controversial issues: begin with humor, acknowledge your own struggle with the issue, acknowledge legitimate concerns of those who disagree with you, and end by inviting dialogue. The tragic-spirited preacher would begin with a bald statement of his own conviction, bypass humor, struggle with acknowledging other views, and end with "My way or the highway."

THE PREACHER AS COMIC SPIRIT: CALLED TO HUMILITY (AND RESPECT FOR AMBIGUITY)!

I realize that humor isn't for everyone. It's only for people who want to have fun, enjoy life, and feel alive.
  —Anne Wilson Schael, clinical psychologist and author[26]

We've looked at the impact of a tragic perspective on preacher and preach-ing. What about that of a comic perspective? Morreall contrasts the traits of the tragic spirit with the following characteristics of the comic spirit.

You May Be a Comic Spirit If . . .

You may lean more toward seeing yourself through a comic frame if . . .

— You are not wedded to seeing the world as ideal.
— You are a pragmatist and expect life and people to hold the im-perfect and the unexpected. Rather than being an idealist in the tragic sense, you are a comic pragmatist.
— Your emotions are not invested in your own life and life around you conforming to your ideal expectations.
— You are able to step back from how you wish things were to look at how they are.
— You think rather than feel your way through a problem, engaging your imagination and ingenuity rather than your emotions.
— You keep an unemotional clearheadedness even in extreme situa-tions. This emotional disengagement gives comic characters per-spective and objectivity in handling problems, allowing them to laugh amid misfortune—something tragic heroes never do.[27] The comic spirit combines respect for ambiguity with the ability to step away from emotional investment into the realm of clearheaded analysis. Add one more quality to the recipe: humility.
— You realize that you yourself, like life, are not perfect—and that, like all comic protagonists, you embody a mix of virtue and flaws, at times swinging like a pendulum between petty and profound.
— You recognize that you yourself have quirks, foibles, vices, and limitations that you are willing to acknowledge and, at times, laugh at. Therefore, you are better able to accept and forgive those traits in others.

Theologian Brian Edgar, in his book *Laughter and the Grace of God,* identifies as a characteristic of someone with a comic spirit that they are able to understand and forgive the foibles and frailties of others.[28]

When faced with the awe-inspiring task of preaching, humor and humility are both needed so that we take the task seriously but not ourselves. Writes Thomas G. Long in *The Witness of Preaching,*

No discerning person can stand . . . in front of the community of
Christ without a deep sense of awe and responsibility. It is also
true that no one should stand in this place without a deep sense
of humility and a healthy sense of humor. We come to the place
of preaching . . . from the congregation, and we share their faith,
but we also share their failings. We have no more right to be in the
pulpit than anyone else in the congregation; indeed, we have no
"right" to be there at all. As fully as anyone present, we have our
doubts and our patterns of disobedience about the very gospel we
are to proclaim. It is good to be there in the pulpit, but we are not
there because we are good . . . that we, of all people, could stand
before them to preach the gospel in Christ's name is humbling and,
in its own way, humorous.

Preaching, humility, and humor belong together. Concludes Long,
"Never lose a sense of humor about yourself."[29]

In Brian Edgar's view a mature and charitable sense of humor is an
expression of humility about oneself and the world. It is an expression
of faith in God and the joy of resurrection.[30]

THE PREACHER AS COMIC SPIRIT:
CALLED TO HUMILITY (AND RESPECT
FOR AMBIGUITY): HOMILETICAL IMPACT

If you don't think God has a sense of humor, look in the mirror.
    —Anonymous

The preacher as comic spirit's respect for ambiguity shows up in her
avoidance of proof-texting, her willingness to take the trouble to interpret texts in their broader canonical contexts, and her acknowledgment
that texts don't boil down to one single meaning. It also shapes her
choice of sermonic forms. The preacher as comic spirit experiments
with inductive sermonic forms that reserve the conclusion to the end
of the sermon, or end with a story they don't explain to death, or offer
the congregation a challenge or question that leaves the response up to
listeners.

The comic spirit's approach to preaching controversial issues would
be more effective than the tragic. While holding convictions, and not
diluting the challenge of the gospel, the preacher as comic spirit can

step back from emotional investment in an issue to set it in a biblical, theological context rather than the sole context of her own emotions. She thus refrains from following the tragic spirit's path of oversimplifying issues and personalizing any opposition to their position.

Preachers as comic spirits can do two things that tragic spirits cannot: one we discuss further in the next section: find joy and laughter in the midst of the most difficult circumstances. The other is to laugh at themselves.

Tragic-spirited preachers don't laugh at themselves and don't use self-deprecatory humor in sermons—not because there are not legitimate reasons to use caution, but because they perceive nothing amusing or ridiculous about themselves. We discussed in chapter 5 the effectiveness of appropriate, judicious use of self-deprecatory humor to help us laugh together at our own foibles and to humanize the preacher in the eyes of the congregation. The comic-spirited preacher understands this and has also learned the rules about the boundaries within which they should use self-deprecatory humor. Don't ever tell a story that involves the congregation picturing you naked. That's the main thing. Or a story that undermines your credibility and your leadership. But really, the naked rule is the most important one to remember.

To Ponder

—How do see yourself? Through more of a comic or tragic frame? As a comic or a tragic protagonist?
—Has your self-conception changed through your years of ministry?
—What connection do you see between the respect for ambiguity in life and humility?

THE PREACHER AS COMIC SPIRIT: CALLED TO JOY!

"When you're deadly serious, you're seriously dead. A better goal for believers is to be joyfully alive."
—Jesuit priest and author James Martin, SJ

The book of Revelation asserts that God will one day "wipe away every tear from their eyes. / Death will be no more. . . . See, I am making all things new" (Rev. 21:4–5). We (your authors) don't read that as saying that, in the meantime, there is nothing but tears, no room for joy and humor.

The medieval monastics we encountered in chapter 8 painted a droll picture of this life as a vale of tears in which joy and laughter must wait until the life to come and that to laugh in this life is to fail to take heaven seriously as the only appropriate venue for laughter. It conjures up visions of flavorless meals, cold cells, and horsehair sheets! In a world circumscribed by ecclesial seriousness and sobriety, the view was that laughter makes a mockery of heaven. Why? Because laughter suggests that heaven can be lived in the here and now. The church's question was, "How can you [we] laugh at a time like this?"

The preacher as comic spirit operates on the premise that a time like this is precisely the time for the inclusion of joy, humor, and laughter in their sermons. Such elements have an already, but not yet, eschatological quality. Their inclusion offers a foretaste, an anticipation of the joy to come in the next life folded back into the present sermonic moment.[31] The preacher operating with a comic spirit is not one who is playing everything for easy laughs but is, much more seriously, the one who trusts God's promises for the future and can put present priorities and problems in the context of the comic vision.[32]

Our exhibiting this joy doesn't have to be extreme, as in the account of St. Ignatius of Antioch joyful and laughing when being led to the lions, but we can allow the gift and power of this joy to overshadow lesser daily concerns. The comic spirit or vision insists that, while the present era is a mix of joy and sorrow, suffering and pleasure, defeat and triumph, the kingdom of God is present, not just future. Opportunities for humor and laughter are all around us. They deserve to be noticed and included in our sermons![33]

THE PREACHER AS COMIC SPIRIT: CALLED TO JOY! HOMILETICAL IMPACT

Better to light one candle than to curse the darkness.
　　—Chinese proverb

Dr. Marvin McMickle, in his classic text *Shaping the Claim*, reminds us that "preaching has the capacity to stir up a wide range of legitimate emotions within the listeners without attempting to draw people into manipulated and sometimes orchestrated acts of emotionalism. Sermons should be able to stir up the emotion of joy so that people can literally rejoice in the goodness of God and in the joy of their own salvation. The gospel is about 'good news,' and the best response to good news is joy."[34]

We are convinced that humor can play a role in stirring joy in listeners. In chapters 11 and 12 we explore the preacher's knack for noticing humor in her inner life, surroundings, and biblical texts. In chapter 13 we explore how to incorporate observational humor into our sermons both to point out common foibles and strengthen our faith and to resolve to persevere in tough times.

When challenged to come up with examples that point either to the sunny, positive side of human existence or its shadowy, negative aspects, too many of us will have an easier time coming up with the latter. Preachers struggle with the challenge of wanting to acknowledge the suffering and injustice of our human condition without allowing it to overpower the good news in any given sermon.[35] So many preachers, even after years in the pulpit, still tend to deliver sermons whose illustrative energy, vividness, and memorability is weighted toward the shadow side rather than the light. A good question to ask yourself in preparing a sermon is, what is the most memorable part of this sermon? Make sure it is the good news and not the bad. Make sure you acknowledge the bad but meet it with memorable, vivid, emotionally charged good news. Remember that humor can help with both.

The preacher as comic spirit knows she is not in the arena, surrounded by the lions of evil and injustice armed with human strength alone. God's Spirit is present. And that means, so is humor. The preacher who prays for divine assistance should not neglect also to call on humor waiting in an unlocked cage in the catacombs. Then take heart, as humor bounds onto the field, ready to demonstrate its full powers to expose the evil and defend the light.

Too dramatic a metaphor? We don't think so!

To Ponder

—What role does faith in a future joy play in your relationship with God now? In your sermon preparation and delivery?

—What connection do you see between humor and joy?

—Many preachers report that it is easier for them to find negative than positive examples in their preaching; have you found that to be true?

THE PREACHER AS COMIC SPIRIT:
CALLED TO COMMUNITY!

Laughter connects you with people. It's almost impossible to maintain any kind of distance or any sense of social hierarchy when you're
just howling with laughter. Laughter is a force for democracy.
—John Cleese[36]

Barbara Brown Taylor in her book *The Preaching Life* compares watching the preacher climb into the pulpit to watching a tightrope walker
climb onto a platform as the drum rolls. This metaphor is a vivid
expression of the risk and vulnerability that the act of preaching
entails.[37] Taylor uses it to make the point that preaching, given the
risk involved, calls for prior prayer for divine guidance and wisdom.
For the use to which Taylor puts it, the tightrope walker is an apt
metaphor for preaching.

Our study of humor in preaching emphasizes the communal context for preaching in which the congregation participates with the
preacher in the vulnerability and the risk taking as more of a trail
guide or pilgrim than a solitary tightrope performer.[38] This is in keeping with the difference we have seen between the cast of characters
in a tragic frame and those in a comic frame. In a tragedy, the focus
is one noble, often highly born hero who sacrifices everything for an
ideal goal. The spotlight is on the hero. By contrast, comedies feature
a motley cast of characters. There may be one protagonist, but it is a
group adventure.

This contrast challenges preachers to identify their perspective.
Lone noble figure or fellow traveler with a group of flawed (but fun!)
human beings? For much of homiletical history, the preacher has been
seen as the solitary truth teller, offering unassailable truths to congregations conceived of as recipients of their ideas. Over the past fifty
or so years there has been a sea change in the conception of preacher,
sermon, and congregation. Beginning in the 1970s with a movement
that came to be called the New Homiletic, preaching began to shift
from the monological delivery of prescriptive propositions about God
and life to a dialogical invitation into (or participation in) an experience of the difference the good news makes in one's life. It came
to be known as a *turn toward the hearer*. For the preacher, this shift
called for a re-envisioning of the congregation, no longer as recipients

of the preacher's ideas, but as participants in an experience of the good news.[39]

In chapter 3 we mentioned Fred Craddock, whose seminal book *As One without Authority* launched this turn toward the hearer, with his suggestions that, rather than announcing the sermon's theme at the outset and proceeding deductively along a conceptual outline of points, the preacher invites listeners into sermons with plots that moved inductively from the challenges of the human condition to the difference that God's character and actions can make in our lives.[40]

Several factors contributed to this growing recognition of the active role of sermon listeners. One was the emphasis on congregational exegesis as an integral part of biblical exegesis for preaching.[41] Another was a growing call for the experiences of marginalized groups to be honored and acknowledged in our understanding of preaching and the role of the congregation. African American preaching traditions, introduced into mainstream white Protestant preaching by Henry Mitchell's *Black Preaching* (1970), advocated active involvement in biblical narratives and were characterized by audible responses during sermon delivery. All these factors have served to underscore the participation of congregations during the event of preaching.

Beyond homiletical circles, cultural shifts have been pushing preachers to a more egalitarian view of their role as one shared with their hearers. One would have to have just crawled out from under a rock not to have noticed, that, over the past several decades, there has been a cultural shift in the way many people, probably preachers included, make meaning. No longer do many people define themselves as truth receivers from commonly recognized authority figures and institutions. More and more, many of us view ourselves as meaning makers for our own lives, willing to receive proposals from various sources, but reserving the right to decide which ones we privilege.

Increasingly operative is an acknowledgment that truth claims have a provisional quality. That is, they inevitably reflect the perspective (social location, assumptions, prejudices) of the claimant. The preacher preaches with authentic conviction but recognizes the congregation not just as recipients of that conviction but as collaborators and authenticators. A number of scholars, in their emphasis on congregational participation, have created what has come to be called a collaborative-conversational homiletic.[42] Humor, well-motivated and skillfully used, invites creative participation and builds community.

THE PREACHER AS COMIC SPIRIT: CALLED TO COMMUNITY! HOMILETICAL IMPACT

If you want to run fast, run alone. If you want to run far, run together.
   —African proverb

This shift toward preaching as conversational dialogue and the congregation as active participants is far more in keeping with comedy than tragedy and should come as welcome news to those who have been viewing themselves as lone, noble figures on whose shoulders falls the burden of redeeming the congregation. When we make the shift from seeing ourselves as comic spirits called to community rather than solo artists, changes in our homiletical practices will occur.

We focus some of our congregational exegesis on the congregation's humor history and personality. What are the shared humorous "insider stories" of our congregation? We can include those stories into our sermons, where, depending on the content, they can unify the congregation's sense of identity or lighten their spirits in grim times. One of the amusing insider stories at Southern Methodist University where Owen and Alyce both teach is of the year the tree in front of Perkins Chapel died, just in time to make it a bad metaphor for graduation. So SMU buildings and grounds came out and spray-painted it an unnaturally bright shade of green. And after they dug it up and planted something live, they made keychains with the painted green leaves on them. We each still have one!

What amusing stories are part of your congregation's history? What comedies do they watch? Who are considered by others to be humorous storytellers in the congregation? What social groups meet to share often humorous reminiscences and stories? In one church Alyce served there was a group called the ROMEOs which stood for Retired Old Men Eating Out. You can bet there were some humorous stories there!

Preachers who answer the call to be comic spirits will, from time to time, review our illustrative material, stories, scenes, and anecdotes to make sure they are not all about individuals, but rather include humorous stories of groups in need of or embodying the good news, its challenge as well as its sustenance. We may form sermon study groups, groups of laypeople who gather to discuss the text for the coming Sunday. We may initiate a pastor's study group with the same intention. In those groups, participants will be instructed that a large part of their mission is to search and rescue humor in their daily thoughts and encounters. There is no reason that the strategies for noticing humor in inscape, landscape, and textscape we present in chapters 11 and 12 couldn't be used in lay study groups as well as by preachers.

While being called to preach sets us apart, it never sets us above. We travel the path with our people, as co-adventurers, noticing humor whether it is on the sidelines of their sporting events or at their bedside in the hospital. Humor's ability to prevent our taking ourselves too seriously and to acknowledge our human limitations is an invaluable strategy in such preaching.

And what a relief to come down from the tightrope onto level ground!

Father James Martin, in *Between Heaven and Mirth,* says that in all his years of perusing statues of saints in churches around the world, he has seen none smiling. Sometimes Mary and the angels smile, but not the saints. They are depicted with their hands folded, eyes downcast with a morose expression on their faces.[43]

Like Father Martin, we see in these somber depictions not just an aesthetic inaccuracy but a theological one. It doesn't fit the ministries of many of the saints who had joy in their hearts and smiles on their faces. It doesn't fit with our understanding of the calling of the preacher both to have and to be a comic spirit.

Denominations feature a variety of norms for appropriate pulpit attire, from elaborate layered vestments to more simple preaching robes with stoles that match the liturgical season to skinny jeans and button-downs. Whatever your tradition, we leave you with this quote, not from a theologian, but wisdom nevertheless. It is the title line of a song from the Broadway musical *Annie,* written by Charles Strouse and Martin Charnin: "You're Never Fully Dressed without a Smile."

Stone statuary can't take a deep breath, scan the far horizon to discern the comic vision, and remember, when the occasion calls for it, to smile. But we preachers can—because we are called to be comic spirits!

To Ponder

—Do you regard preaching as a solo effort?
—How do you understand your congregation's role in your preaching ministry? As spectators or participants? In the preaching event itself?
—How do you regard your role as preacher? Set apart? Set above?

NOTES

1. Horace Walpole, *The Castle of Otranto* (Standard Ebooks, 2017).

2. The dialogical quality of African American preaching lent itself to the experience of humor between preacher and congregation. Martin Luther King, for example, made the phrase "If I had sneezed" a humorous refrain to describe the fragility of life. Its origins were a newspaper article after an attempt on his life early in his career that stated that if Dr. King had sneezed before he arrived at the hospital he would have died. See William H. Willimon, "Humor," in *Concise Encyclopedia of Preaching*, ed. Willimon and Richard Lischer (Louisville, KY: Westminster John Knox Press, 1995), 264.

3. Says Lewis, "We must picture Hell as a state where everyone is perpetually concerned about his own dignity and advancement, where everyone has a grievance, and where everyone lives the deadly serious passions of envy, self-importance and resentment" (C. S. Lewis, *The Screwtape Letters*, rev. ed. [New York: Macmillan, 1982], ix).

4. Says Rahner, "Laughter is an acknowledgement that you are a human being, an acknowledgement that is itself the beginning of an acknowledgement of God." Quoted in James Martin, SJ, *Between Heaven and Mirth: Why Joy, Humor, and Laughter Are at the Heart of the Spiritual Life* (New York: Harper-One, 2011), 200.

5. Reinhold Niebuhr, *Discerning the Signs of the Times: Sermons for Tomorrow Today* (New York: Charles Scribner's Sons, 1946), 130–31. For a nuanced discussion of Niebuhr's understanding of the relation of laughter to faith, see Reinhold Niebuhr, "Humour and Faith," in *Holy Laughter: Essays on Religion in the Comic Perspective*, comp. Conrad Hyers (New York: Seabury Press, 1969), 134–49.

6. Barth once observed (in a comment clearly meant to be funny) that a serious problem with Calvin is that he seems to have been unable to laugh! Barth viewed humor as liberation, an expression of an acceptance of our limitations in the light of our eschatological future. See Stanley Hauerwas, *The Work of Theology* (Grand Rapids: Wm. B. Eerdmans, 2015), 245–46.

7. J. Cheryl Exum and J. William Whedbee, "Isaac, Samson, and Saul: Reflections on the Comic and Tragic Visions," in *On Humour and the Comic in the Hebrew Bible,* ed. Athalya Brenner-Idan and Yehuda T. Radday (London: A&C Black, 1990), 119.

8. Darden has been senior editor of the *Wittenburg Door* for twenty years and a Baylor University journalism professor. His *Jesus Laughed: The Redemptive Power of Humor* (Nashville: Abingdon Press, 2008) offers a historical, biblical, philological, and psychological treatise intended to reclaim holy laughter for the church.

9. Alice Sheppard, "Continuity and Change: The Cultural Context of Women's Humor," paper presented at the eleventh annual meeting of the National Women's Studies Association, Towson, Maryland, June 1989.

10. Athalya Brenner-Idan, *Are We Amused? Humour about Women in the Biblical World* (London: T&T Clark, 2003), contains essays by a number of women biblical scholars, among them Mary Shields, Kathleen M. O'Connor, Toni Craven, Kathy Williams, Athalya Brenner, Gale Yee, Amy-Jill Levine, and Esther Fuchs.

11. K. M. Sands, "Ifs, Ands, and Butts: Theological Reflections on Humor," *Journal of the American Academy of Religion* 64, no. 3 (January 1, 1996): 499–523, https://doi.org/10.1093/jaarel/lxiv.3.499. Her book *Escape from Paradise: Evil and Tragedy in Feminist Theology* (Minneapolis: Fortress, 1994) would caution too glib an embrace of a comic spirit without recognition of the wounds that tragedy can inflict, especially on women's lives.

12. Mary Daly and Jane Caputi, *Websters' First New Intergalactic Wickedary of the English Language* (San Francisco: HarperSanFrancisco, 1994), 142–43.

13. John C. Holbert and Alyce M. McKenzie, *What Not to Say: Avoiding the Common Mistakes That Can Sink Your Sermon* (Louisville, KY: Westminster John Knox Press, 2011), chap. 3.

14. David G. Buttrick, *Homiletic: Moves and Structures* (Minneapolis: Fortress, 1987), 95–96. Says Buttrick, "While there may be passages from scripture that are hilarious (in some ways, profoundly, Christian faith *is* a laughing matter!), the gospel is ultimately serious, for it speaks of a crucified Christ to the deepest levels of human self-understanding. Humor at the start of a sermon can set a tone of down-home triviality which, predictably, people will like, but from which few sermons can recover."

15. John W. Drakeford, *Humor in Preaching* (Grand Rapids: Zondervan, 1986), 39.

16. Ronald J. Allen, *Preaching for Growth* (St. Louis: Chalice Press, 1988), 43–44.

17. Joseph M. Webb, *Comedy and Preaching* (St. Louis: Chalice Press, 1998).

18. Ian S. Markham and Samantha R. E. Gottlich, *Lectionary Levity: The Use of Humor in Preaching* (New York: Church Publishing, 2017).

19. Stanley P. Saunders and Charles L. Campbell, *The Word on the Street: Performing the Scriptures in the Urban Context* (Grand Rapids: Wm. B. Eerdmans, 2000), 77.

20. Johan H. Cilliers and Charles L. Campbell, *Preaching Fools: The Gospel as a Rhetoric of Folly* (Waco, TX: Baylor University Press, 2020).

21. Charles L. Campbell, *The Scandal of the Gospel: Preaching and the Grotesque* (Louisville, KY: Westminster John Knox Press, 2021), 7.

22. Another work is Jake Myers's *Stand-Up Preaching: Homiletical Insights from Contemporary Comedians* (Eugene, OR: Wipf and Stock, 2022).

23. John Morreall, *Comedy, Tragedy, and Religion* (Albany: State University of New York Press, 1999), 41–48.

24. Morreall, *Comedy, Tragedy, and Religion*, 26.

25. Walter Kerr, *Tragedy and Comedy* (New York: Simon and Schuster, 1967), 139. Henri Bergson based his whole theory of comedy on its being a counter

force for characters with idée fixes, what he called "mechanical inelasticity" (see Morreall, *Comedy, Tragedy, and Religion,* 28).

26. K. Sathyanarayana, *The Power of Humor at the Workplace* (New Delhi: SAGE Publications India, 2007), 74.

27. Morreall, *Comedy, Tragedy, and Religion,* 26–27.

28. Brian Edgar, *Laughter and the Grace of God: Restoring Laughter to Its Central Role in Christian Spiritualty and Theology* (Eugene, OR: Cascade Books, 2019), 16.

29. Thomas G. Long, *The Witness of Preaching,* 3rd ed. (Louisville, KY: Westminster John Knox Press, 2016), 9.

30. Edgar enumerates that someone with a mature sense of humor is able to

> Observe the unintended irony involved in certain political statements
> Be alert to satire
> Be able to find joy and laughter in the midst of the most difficult circumstances
> Be amused by the most simple daily situations in life
> Be provoked to action by the incongruity—and injustice—of certain events
> Be better able to understand and forgive the foibles and frailties of others.
> Draw closer to others through appreciation of shared humor
>   —*Laughter and the Grace of God,* 16

31. M. Conrad Hyers, *And God Created Laughter: The Bible as Divine Comedy* (Atlanta: John Knox Press, 1987), 4.

32. Brian Edgar, *Laughter and the Grace of God: Restoring Laughter to Its Central Role in Christian Faith and Theology* (Eugene, OR: Cascade Books, 2019), 10.

33. Brian Edgar, *The God Who Plays: A Playful Approach to Theology and Spirituality* (Eugene, OR: Wipf and Stock, 2017), 31.

34. Marvin A. McMickle, *Shaping the Claim,* Elements of Preaching (Minneapolis: Fortress Press, 2008), 48.

35. For a discussion of acknowledging the inescapable character of suffering and sin in preaching while proclaiming the good news, see O. Wesley Allen Jr., "A Cumulative Approach to Preaching on the Human Condition," in *Preaching and the Human Condition: Loving God, Self and Others* (Nashville: Abingdon Press, 2016), 9–11.

36. From the BBC miniseries *The Human Face,* hosted by John Cleese, 2001.

37. Barbara Brown Taylor, *The Preaching Life* (Lanham, MD: Rowman and Littlefield, 1993), 76.

38. Kenyatta R. Gilbert, *The Journey and Promise of African American Preaching* (Minneapolis: Fortress Press, 2011), 14. Homiletician Kenyatta Gilbert highlights the communal nature of preaching in African American traditions that can be instructive for all preachers. He commends the notion of the trivocal voice for the preacher: prophetic, priestly, and sagely. The prophetic voice challenges the congregation with God's demands; the priestly voice mediates divine grace through worship and prayer; the sagely voice, the one Gilbert regards as most overlooked in African American preaching traditions, "is a peculiarly communal voice"

combining biblical wisdom with the congregation's own repository of tradition and vision. The sagely voice, says Gilbert, corresponds with the voice and activity of the African *jaili*. In West African lore, the *jaili* (poet) used praise singing and storytelling and functioned as the repository of the community's oral tradition.

39. O. Wesley Allen Jr. and Carrie La Ferle, *Preaching and the Thirty-Second Commercial: Lessons from Advertising from the Pulpit* (Louisville, KY: Westminster John Knox Press, 2021), show that this homiletical shift was part of a larger cultural shift in the understanding of communication that preaching and advertising have in common.

40. See O. Wesley Allen Jr.'s introduction to *The Renewed Homiletic* (Minneapolis: Fortress Press, 2010), "The Pillars of the New Homiletic," which sets forth the key components and actors in the movement.

41. Nora Tubbs Tisdale, *Preaching as Local Theology and Folk Art* (Minneapolis: Augsburg Fortress, 1997).

42. For a description of some of the key figures in this movement, see Allen and La Ferle, *Preaching and the Thirty-Second Commercial*, 21–23. They include John McClure, Lucy Rose, O. Wesley Allen, and Ronald J. Allen. For a fuller exploration of the implications of a conversational approach, see O. Wesley Allen Jr. and Ronald J. Allen, *The Sermon without End: A Conversational Approach to Preaching* (Nashville: Abingdon Press, 2015).

43. Martin, *Between Heaven and Mirth*, 71.

11

The Preacher's Knack for Noticing Humor in Inscape and Landscape

> Humor is everywhere, in that there is irony in just about everything a human does.
> —American mechanical engineer, science communicator, and television presenter Bill Nye[1]

By now readers should have a sense of what the comic spirit's gift of humor is (chaps. 1–3), an understanding of how it works (chap. 6), and a wealth of strategies for how to put it to work in sermons (chap. 5). But where does one find humorous material to include in their sermons?

In this chapter we offer habits for preachers to develop to help them overcome cognitive overload that leads to a lack of noticing humor and instead develop a Knack for Noticing (KFN) humor in our inner world (inscape) and our surroundings (landscape). We explore a crucial third arena, the biblical textscape, in chapter 12. The three habits to develop for noticing humor are soft eyes, comic notes, and targeted questions.

THE KNACK FOR NOTICING

In her book *Novel Preaching,* Alyce introduced the concept of KFN. It was inspired by a conversation with C. W. Smith, prolific novelist and then head of the English Department at Southern Methodist University.[2] In response to Alyce's question "What can preachers learn from novelists?" Smith said, "As a teacher of creative writing to eighteen-year-olds, much of my time is spent in trying to get students to notice what they see. And then, the next step is to get them to trust that there may be some significance in their observations."[3]

Alyce encourages preachers to develop their powers of observation, their knack for noticing, in three arenas: their inner lives (inscape); their congregational, community, and cultural contexts (landscape); and the biblical text(s) they are in dialogue with for their sermons (textscape).[4] Here we augment the discussion in *Novel Preaching* with specific attention to honing our powers of observation with regard to humor that might be useful in sermons.

LACK OF NOTICING: COGNITIVE OVERLOAD

In freeing our energies and imaginations to notice humor, preachers—who wear many hats and shoulder multiple responsibilities to church, family, and community—encounter a persistent obstacle: *cognitive overload*. Stressful situations suppress both the preacher's energy to notice and create humor and the congregation's ability to receive and process it. John Sweller, an educational psychologist, developed cognitive load theory (CLT), a theory that has relevance for both the preacher's creativity (or lack thereof) in noticing humor and the congregation's available energy to appreciate it.[5]

CLT suggests that our minds are information processing systems, and when working on a problem or performing a task, especially one that is new to us, we rely on our working memory, which is limited in both the amount of information it can hold and the time it can hold it. When stress is increased, especially in the context of performing a new task, we have less capacity to access our working memory, to think through a problem effectively. Here we are relating CLT to comedy, which, with the exception of slapstick, is a complex cognitive function.

In his Introduction to Communication Theory class, Owen uses a simple exercise to demonstrate CLT to his students. He asks for three volunteers, sends them out into the hall, and tells them to come in one at a time every minute; the order is their choice. He tells the rest of the class to join in the experimental task for fun.

—Student 1 comes in. Owen tells that student, "This experiment is a joke, the task is meaningless, and you will all get extra credit regardless how you perform in the task, which is to remember a few numbers in order." Owen also says, "Ignore what I tell other participants. It is all part of the experiment. Everyone gets extra credit at the end."

— Student 2 comes in. Owen tells that student, "This experiment is simple and as long as you can remember the first five numbers, which is less than a telephone number, you will get extra credit. If you can remember nine numbers then you get even more credit. Also ignore what I tell the next student; it does not apply to you."

— Student 3 comes in. Owen tells that student, "Both your fellow students have made bets and are really confident they can remember at least seven numbers in row, so seven is the minimum you have to beat to win. This is a competition. The one who performs the task best gets extra credit, and the student who performs worst gets points taken off their next test. So whatever you do, don't come in last!"

Owen then very quickly reels off thirty-five numbers and asks his teaching assistant to write them down in order as he says them but doesn't show them to the class. When he is finished listing numbers he asks the volunteers as well as the rest of the students to write down the numbers on a piece of paper in order as far as they can remember. He then asks that all hold onto their list, calls for applause for the three volunteers, and reveals that regardless of how they did they all will receive extra credit.

Then Owen teaches the class cognitive load theory and explains why the test was not fair, that he set them up to fail by increasing stress and asking them to rely on short-term memory. When he finishes the lesson, he says, "Let's see if the theory is correct." He writes all thirty-five numbers on the board from memory, and the teaching assistant confirms that they are correct. He then has the three volunteers read their lists of numbers. Student 3 (highest stress) rarely has more than the first four numbers correct and never seven or more. Student 2 sometimes has five but rarely nine or more. Student 1 is usually in the same range as Student 2. Finally, Owen asks the wider class if any of them did better and there are always three or four students in the class who did. Stress hinders cognitive processing and memory.

A student usually asks Owen how, given CLT and the stress of teaching, he was able to recall all thirty-five numbers. Owen responds, "Because it was my mum's London number, followed by my wife's cell, followed by mine." Everyone laughs. The ruse or joke at the end relieves the tensions. The whole thing is revealed as a setup!

This exercise clearly demonstrates how stress complicates the performance of new tasks. Conversely, when you are an expert with lots of experience with a certain activity, you are less likely to rely on working memory to complete the task.

In stressful times, which includes much of the pastor's life, there are added changes in our daily lives and routines. Preachers have additional responsibilities in managing their own and others' health, dealing with complex systems of relationships in the congregation, offering, as needed, pastoral care and conflict mediation, performing administrative tasks that are constantly past deadline, and developing and delivering a sermon on a new text and topic every week. These obligations, however important, add to the cognitive load. As cognitive load increases, people either hyperfocus on one task, limiting their ability to take in surrounding information, or they get so distracted they are less likely to complete an assigned task—like when Owen has to ask his wife, Catherine, "What was I going into the garage to get?"

A well-known study of cognitive load theory (CLT) dates back to the 1970s, the seminary experiment about the sermon on the Good Samaritan conducted by researchers John M. Darley and C. Daniel Batson.[6] It focused on a group of seminarians all new to the profession. Each was asked to prepare a sermon on the Good Samaritan. They began in one building, and then were told to go to another building to give the sermon. With one group—the high-hurry group—researchers told the subjects they were late for their task. To a second group—the medium-hurry group—they told subjects they had a few minutes or more, but they should head on over anyway. For the third group—the low-hurry group—they indicated there was no hurry, just to move at their own pace. On the way they encountered a man slumped over moaning in an alleyway, apparently either drunk or hurt; 40 percent offered some help to the victim among all three groups. In low-hurry situations, 63 percent helped; in medium-hurry, 45 percent; and in high-hurry, only 10 percent. There was no correlation between "religious types" and helping the man in pain.

There is some ironic humor that people going to preach on the Good Samaritan failed the commandment to "go and do likewise." While the study has been criticized for the psychological effect it had on the seminarians, the students learned that the more stress and perception of urgency they experienced in relation to a task, the less likely they were to notice and respond to those in need of charity. They judged themselves harshly, as failing to live up to the very message they were preaching, but the seminarians were set up to fail, just as much as Owen's students in the number game. What does this tell us?

—Be careful to build in prep time to reduce stress in our work in general, not just preparing and delivering sermons.

—In stressful periods, we might do well to aim for less cognitively complex sermons and humor.

—The knack for noticing, the very basis of observational and humor attentiveness, will be harder if not impossible during high-urgency or stressful times.

HUMOR, HUMOR EVERYWHERE!
THE WESTERN SUPERMAN EFFECT

The good news is that in spite of cognitive overload that gets in the way of our attending to humor, humor can be found almost everywhere, giving us more opportunity to notice it, even in times of stress. Once we activate the comic spirit's KFN, it is not so much that we have to go out and find humor as that we need to allow humor to find us! The busyness and results-driven nature of our daily lives that contributes to cognitive overload can cause us to factor out humor in conversations and encounters as distractions from the serious business of living.[7] Owen counters this preoccupation with what he calls "the Western Superman effect" to express the ubiquity of humor just waiting for us to discover it.[8]

What is the Western Superman effect? When Owen was very young, his family moved to London from New York. In school when he was around eight years old he had a report to do on a "seaside town" in Britain called "Western Superman." His parents, being new to the country as well, were reasonably convinced there was no such place and that he had misheard the name. But they did not have the geographic references to help Owen. Luckily, someone they knew said, "I don't think it is Western Superman [which Owen still thinks is a great name for a town!]. He must mean 'Weston-super-Mare.'" Weston-super-Mare is a seaside town on the Severn and Avon estuary into the British Channel. Back then, there was no internet, so Owen's parents could do little to help him beyond pointing to it on the map. His report suffered as he tried to find out all he could about the mysterious place. He doesn't remember the grade he received for his submission (or he has repressed the memory), but he remembers it wasn't great. What happened afterward was very strange indeed. Over the next three months or so, seemingly every day—in the paper, on the news, in conversations—strangely the name "Weston-super-Mare" kept coming up. The nice lady who ran the high-street bakery told Owen it was her home-town. Neither his parents nor Owen had heard of this place before, and now it was everywhere! How could this be? How did a school report suddenly make this place noteworthy?[9]

The answer is that once Owen's parents and Owen had a reference point, they noticed and flagged the town's name every time it came up in their daily lives. This explanation doesn't make the phenomenon less remarkable. They must have often encountered the strange name before but ignored it as irrelevant. Owen uses this story when discussing humor appreciation to help people look and think of the topic of humor as if it were this mythical place, Weston-super-Mare. Humor is all around you, but your cognitive antenna must be tuned to notice it.

So how might preachers open ourselves to humor in our world, actively paying attention to humor, in our thoughts, interactions, and in the everyday incongruities we notice? How can we activate our comic spirit in encountering the events and news of the day that surround us?

Developing a knack for noticing humor, in our inner thoughts (inscape) or our surroundings (landscape), means replacing the tragic frame's deadly seriousness that consigns all humor—whether acerbic wit, whimsical imagery, or lighthearted warmth—to a file marked "frivolous distractions" with a comic frame that frees us to allow Weston-super-Mare to come to our daily attention. We turn now to the three habits we suggest for developing a knack for noticing humor daily that are worthy of homiletical use: soft eyes, keeping comic notes, and asking targeted questions.

FROM LACK TO KNACK: SOFT EYES

The first such habit is a method of ethnographic observation that we refer to as having "soft eyes." The label comes from the television show *The Wire,* which tells the story of the Baltimore streets from the perspective of the people who live there. In a scene from episode 4 of season 4, Bunk, a veteran detective, instructs a new homicide detective, "You need soft eyes. . . . You got soft eyes, you can see the whole thing. You got hard eyes, you be staring at the same tree missing the whole forest." Having soft eyes means opening yourself up to take in the whole scene—what is there and not there—rather than immediately hyperfocusing, like when we squint, which results in hard eyes.

Owen uses the soft-eyes concept as a way to introduce ethnography observation to his students. He stresses the importance of soft eyes in initial encounters or observations as these are especially not the time to hyperfocus. Having soft eyes means embracing naiveté when first encountering something, looking at the whole of it as something to be discovered in contrast to immediately applying critical lenses to understanding it. This is analogous to preachers initially doing a naïve reading of a biblical text before moving on to critical exegetical methods for analyzing the text.

Having soft eyes also means going into a situation with questions instead of immediate assumptions and judgments. It means not assuming you know why something is there or not there or why people are saying or doing what they are saying and doing. Soft eyes represents curiosity before interpretation. We suggest that this approach goes beyond taking in the physical and social scene but the spiritual one as well. Soft eyes does not confront an inscape, landscape, or textscape with preconceived conclusions, but welcomes us to be open to them. Then we ask open questions like, "I wonder why . . . ?" And we confront our own predispositions by asking, "Why does that seem odd to me?" "Why is this not what I expected?"

Developing a knack for noticing humor means entering the fields within us (inscape) and around us (landscape) that are ripe with a harvest of humor—not ignoring the tragic but emboldened by the comic spirit's trademark openness, curiosity, and anticipation.

Alyce's homiletical colleague Luke Powery is the dean of Duke Chapel and associate professor of homiletics at Duke Divinity School. He is the author of *Dem Dry Bones: Preaching, Death and Hope,* whose topic is the need to face into the reality of death in order to preach life and hope, using the spirituals as inspiration for hope amid despair. The book began with soft eyes trained on a graveyard. He wrote much of the book from the Princeton Public Library, from which he had a view of the Princeton Cemetery of the Nassau Presbyterian Church, where well-known persons like Jonathan Edwards, as well as many whose names are not famous, are buried. Gazing out at the graves with spiritual soft eyes, he saw more than row upon row of the dead, proof that endings have the last word. He began to ask questions from his inner life and his tradition and surroundings: How do I feel about death? How do I feel about the resurrection over against these rows of gravemarkers? Why is the "candy" theology of prosperity preaching so popular, and so troubling, given the sufferings of so many African American communities? And given his musical background and tradition, the refrains of spirituals began to play in his mind. The need to acknowledge the reality of death as the context for the proclamation of the good news solidified as his purpose. Powery, through those library windows, saw death's sting and the grave's apparent victory.[10] Revelation 21:4 came to his mind: "Death will be no more / mourning and crying and pain will be no more." God's love is stronger than death.

Such were the impressions and thoughts to which soft eyes trained on a graveyard gave rise. Dr. Powery's soft-eyed approach led him to see from his window more than stubs of granite row on row, emblems of lives ended. It led him to reflections on his inner life, life around him, and the biblical faith he shares with others. He ends his book with what your authors regard as a wickedly humorous line. "Whenever a preacher enters the pulpit, he or she is preaching Death's funeral. . . . The next time you proclaim the glorious gory gospel, just tell death to 'go to hell!'"[11]

FROM LACK TO KNACK: COMIC NOTES

Homileticians often recommend that preachers record potentially preachable insights and observations in a notebook or on their smartphones. The KFN in one's inscape and landscape is key to our vocation as preachers. We need to take care to include the search for humor in this practice. We need to be on the lookout for comic themes and for examples of the various types of humor (superiority, relief, and incongruity). Once we get in the habit, we don't have to categorize and theorize to recognize humor, and categorizing can come later when we decide how and if to use it in a sermon.

Comedians do the same sort of thing. It is a necessity. Constantly finding humor in new places is their livelihood. Larry David, the cocreator and writer of *Seinfeld*, the *Larry David Show*, and *Curb Your Enthusiasm*, carries a notebook with him everywhere to record his "ideas" or comic notes. When David is in the process of writing and producing a show he actively seeks comic ideas that are appropriate to the characters and fit with the themes of that show. They seemingly come from everywhere. It is the Western Superman effect. In David's case, he uses his skewed comic frame as someone who is continually questioning and challenging social conventions as a lens through which to view the world and be open to humor in it.

Preacher and stand-up comedian Susan Sparks refers to this habit of recording humorous insights for later use as developing her "humor canon."[12] You never know when some amusing, satirical, absurd thought of yours, if recorded and remembered, will be just the thing for a set if you're a comedian or your sermon if you're a preacher. Your authors recommend giving your observations monikers to jog your memory when you come back to them later. Remember, you don't have to know how or even if you would use a comic note to squirrel it away!

Your Inscape as a Source of Comic Notes

For several years Alyce thought she had invented the term *inscape* and congratulated herself on her cleverness. But when she discovered who really coined the term, it took on a deeper meaning than she could have anticipated. Romantic poet and Jesuit priest Gerard Manley Hopkins (1844–1889) beat her to it by at least a century! Hopkins, a poet of the Victorian Era, used the term *inscape* to refer to the "unified complex of characteristics that give each thing its uniqueness and that differentiate it from other things." Hopkins's inscape was fundamentally religious. He believed that a glimpse of a thing's inscape shows us why God created it and what its unique purpose is.[13] This fits beautifully with what we said in chapter 3 about humor as part of what it means to be made in the image of God. In mining our unique inner lives (our inscapes) for humor with homiletical potential, we are seeking ways to share something of God that only we can share.

From the perspective of communication theory, attentiveness to one's inscape falls into the category of intrapersonal communication as distinguished from interpersonal communication. Intrapersonal communication refers to the process of message and information creating and exchanging *within* the individual.[14] Whereas interpersonal communication is verbal or nonverbal communication between at least two people, intrapersonal communication is more like an imaginary interaction or dialogue one has with oneself.[15]

We all have such intrapersonal communication, but there are some people who never laugh when they are alone. You are likely not one of them or you wouldn't be reading a book on preaching and humor. Your inscape is home to many whimsical, odd, absurd observations that meander or flit through your mind throughout your waking hours and that feature in strange, sometimes absurd dreams while you are sleeping. You have snarky, sardonic thoughts. Sometimes you discern lighthearted, good-natured humor and joy in everyday scenes. You do stupid things and laugh at yourself. You see other people doing stupid things and try not to laugh at them too noticeably. Your inscape is like a compost heap. Don't let all those coffee grounds and egg shells and banana peels go to waste. Write them down and keep them in your own form of comic notes: stir them all together, give them time, and they will fertilize your sermonic humor.

Remember that KFN includes the recognition that what you notice might have (indeed does have) significance. But as you are recording instances of inscape humor, keep in mind that you don't have to know how or even if you will use them in a later sermon to tag them and preserve them. Based on what we learned in chapter 6, you are now equipped to discern the type of humor (superiority, relief, or release) that your observations include. Based on chapter 7, you are also now equipped to discern comic and tragic themes your observations may include. And being a preacher, biblical texts will occur to you as well. But don't obsess about any of that. Just collect, don't judge. If you censor yourself for being too whimsical, silly, or snarky, you'll never save anything. Collecting something doesn't mean you'll use it. Here are few examples of inscape comic notes. In some cases we can't resist the temptation to brainstorm how a comic note might be used, but in others, we leave it up to you, the reader.

Exhausted Dogs

> Alyce took a lot of walks during COVID. Walks in the heat. Walks in the rain. Just walks. Not to walk her dog. She doesn't have a dog. Not related to fitness. She's not a step counter. Just related to getting out of the house. She was not alone. Many of her neighbors were out walking too. She would encounter them in the neighborhood or see them out her office window. Some were multiple walkers, logging several treks a day. With their dogs. And some of the dogs looked really, really tired. She made eye contact with them as she passed them on her walks and imagined being able to overhear what they would say to their humans. "OMG, again! I did not sign on for this! Don't even pretend that this is for my sake and not for yours! We both know the truth. You do realize that it's legal in the state of Texas for a human being to take a walk without their dog!"

This would be an example of incongruity humor since dogs can't talk.

The Best Intentions

As Alyce recently was attempting to take a bag bulging with plastic bags to the recycle bin at her local grocery store, a gust of wind happened along and blew a third of the contents of the bag out into the parking lot. The air was filled with swirling plastic grocery bags as, in the blink of an eye, recycling morphed into littering.

This would be incongruity since a good intention morphs into a destructive environmental action. It could also be relief humor that unifies us in our common, earnest attempts to be good people who do good stuff, and our common experience that sometimes it just backfires and all we can do is laugh together because, truly, "No good deed goes unpunished."

Church Dogmatics in a Pushcart

There is a well-known quotation from theologian Karl Barth, whose *Church Dogmatics* is considered by many to be one of the greatest theological achievements of the modern era. Alyce is convinced that the quotation began as an inner dialogue that took shape one day in the mind of the great, yet humble theologian. He hung onto it and eventually wrote it down:

The angels laugh at old Karl. They laugh at him because he tries to grasp the truth about God in a book of Dogmatics. They laugh at the fact that volume follows volume and each is thicker than the previous one. As they laugh, they say to one another, "Look! Here he comes now with his little pushcart full of volumes of the *Dogmatics!*" And they laugh about the men who write so much about Karl Barth instead of writing about the things he is trying to write about. Truly, the Angels laugh.[16]

The juxtaposition of theological greatness and self-deprecatory humor shows Barth capable of stepping outside himself and seeing his human efforts in broader, comic perspective.

Bring Your "A Game"

A couple of years ago a pastor invited Alyce to come to a retreat center and offer a two-day training in the basics of effective preaching. He concluded the conversation by saying, "We are going to pay you a healthy honorarium, so be sure to bring your A game." You'll be proud of your author that she did not share her intrapersonal communication with the pastor! But after she hung up, she crafted a few replies that she would have liked to share. Only a couple of them are fit to report here: "Gosh, thanks for that reminder. Otherwise I would have done like I usually do and not make any preparations at all." "How much is the honorarium? Is it enough to offset how insulting you just were?"

Alyce isn't sure how to categorize this humorous intrapersonal dialogue, but remembering it still makes her smile.

Your Landscape as a Source of Comic Notes

Preachers draw on their inscape for humorous observations with which hearers might identify in terms of their own inscapes. We also draw on our landscapes, our surroundings, to provide imagery and humor in relation to things the congregation observes and experiences in the world. We can learn how to do this by watching any late-night show. For example, during the height of the coronavirus pandemic, during the opening monologue on *The Late Show with Stephen Colbert*, Colbert commented on the news concerning shortages in stores and problems with the global supply chain.[17] By simply being topical and using wordplay, he allowed his audience to laugh at something that was potentially worrying them:

> Shipping containers are backlogged, which means trains can't unload goods, which mean trains and containers can't get loaded up with new goods that are waiting to be shipped. We can't switch to trucks because there are shortages of drivers.
> It is what is being called a "veritable hydra of bottlenecks" [headline shown]. The hydra of bottlenecks is also the bad guy of "Captain America 4: Winter of Shipping Logistics!" The solution is that we have to scale back and live a more sustainable lifestyle. A sustainable lifestyle? Noooooo! We're all going to die.

Preachers, like comedians, need to train themselves to be astute, alert observers, not only of their inward lives, but of their surroundings, noticing incongruities that can be humorous.

Preachers know that in order to connect with the diverse people in our congregations, we need to draw our sermonic imagery from a variety of story buckets. Stories in our sermons need to come from personal experiences, family lore, literature, movies, television, history, culture, and current events. The same is true of our humor sources. Across our preaching ministry, Sunday after Sunday, we need to draw from multiple humor buckets. This means that long before we are working on a particular sermon, we need to be collecting humor from these diverse buckets in our comic notes. Some of them are as follows:

"Honey, I Forgot to Duck!" (History)

There is a more or less historical account of when President Ronald Reagan was shot in 1981, rushed to the hospital, and prepared for surgery. He famously said to his wife, Nancy, "Honey, I forgot to duck," and then to his medical team, "I hope you're all Republicans."[18] This qualifies as a bit of relief humor from Reagan, a deft presidential humor user.

"Ridiculous" Solutions to Gun Violence (Contemporary Culture)

Comedians feel freer than preachers to call out hypocrisy. In fact, they see it as their job. In an episode of *Last Week Tonight with John Oliver* that aired Sunday, June 5, 2022, Oliver broached the subject of the mass shooting at Robb Elementary School in Uvalde, Texas, on May 24, 2022, in which nineteen children and two teachers were killed inside their classrooms. A viewer might flinch upon seeing the subject come up on the screen and think, "There is nothing funny about this, John. Stay in your lane."

But what Oliver did next was to address the topic of gun violence head-on and make it his lane. He said, "We all know what the problem is. It is guns. The availability of guns. That doesn't stop any number of people from attributing it to everything else under the sun." Then he showed clips of various church, community, and political leaders offering "solutions" to the problem of gun violence in schools.

One person suggested we needed more prayer and spirituality in schools. Another that we needed to set up a series of interlocking doors at every school entrance triggered by a trip wire. Another blamed parents for buying their children high-tech toys when they should be investing in bulletproof blankets that could be hung on classroom walls. These ridiculous suggestions really needed no comment. So with his trademark eyeroll Oliver moved on to a segment in which he skewered the chief executive officer of the National Rifle Association, whose annual rally had been held in Houston a few days after the shooting.[19] Oliver was using the comedic strategy of punching up, a form of superiority humor, in which those with less power use humor to poke fun at (or reveal the hypocrisy of) those with more.[20]

Best-Selling Ukrainian Stamp (Current Events)

> When the Russian warship *Moskva* ordered the Ukrainian border guards on Snake Island to surrender, the soldiers told the ship to go f**k itself. The moment of resistance was turned into a painting that has become a popular meme. On March 1, 2022, the Ukrainian postal service announced a competition to design a stamp based on the phrase. Boris Groh's painting of a Ukrainian soldier flipping the bird to a distant *Moskva* won after being put to a vote on Instagram and Facebook. The background, the yellow ground and blue ocean, evokes the Ukrainian flag.[21] A million of the stamps were entered into circulation by the Ukrainian postal service Ukrposhta on April 13, 2022. The next day, the *Moskva* sank after being struck by a Neptune antiship missile fired by Ukraine. The stamp is now a collector's item.

This is an example of punching up embraced by a whole society under attack by a superior force.

Dress Code for the Afterlife? (Human Interest Anecdote)

Several years ago, Alyce attended a storytelling workshop in Phoenix, Arizona. While there she signed up for a class taught by Connie Regan-Blake, a famed southern storyteller who liberally employs humor in her craft.[22] Connie told a story called "A Memory of My Mother" that Alyce noticed and remembered for possible future sermonic use. This is Alyce's recollection and does not claim to be a verbatim capturing of the original telling.

> Connie was in Florida to lead a workshop and added a day to her trip to visit with her mother, who lived near the workshop location. Her mother, while aging, was in relatively good health. Connie put thought into how they would spend their day together. Maybe a movie? Possibly pedicures? When she arrived at her mother's condo, she was hardly in the door before her mother informed her, "I want you to come with me to pick out my casket. I've been to a couple of friends' funerals lately, and I want everything planned out for mine."

> She took Connie by the elbow and led her down the hall. "First, I want you to help me pick out my outfit. I want the lining of my casket to match my outfit." In the back bedroom there were three outfits already laid out on the bed. Her mother held up a navy pants suit. "This fits well but may be too casual," she said. She held up a full-length aqua-colored formal evening gown. "This is a very becoming color, but I am afraid it may be too formal." Finally, she held up a pink blazer and skirt: "This is very well tailored, but the fabric is heavy, and I worry that it may be too hot."

We don't have to know how we will use a story like this to hang onto it until a biblical text it complements comes along.

FROM LACK TO KNACK: TARGETED QUESTIONS

Earlier we mentioned Larry David in association with his practice of collecting comic notes. Because of his quirkiness and his success, he is often interviewed on his creative process. David discusses how he takes his comic notes and turns them into comedy. He says that an important part of this process involves constantly asking what comics call *targeted questions*—things like "Why should I?" or "I wonder why that is." "How come people don't notice how weird it is that . . . ?" "Is it, though?" or "Let's wait and see." He has built a skeptical frame around the mundane events and conventions in his own life. By noticing them he builds material for his shows.[23] He describes his process in this way: "When I am writing a show, everything is an idea; it doesn't matter how bad it is, I am writing it down."[24] David uses this freewheeling process because even what seems like a bad idea may later spark a good one.

He provides an example that became the basis for a fan-favorite scene in *Curb Your Enthusiasm* in which an after-dinner conflict with a friend's wife turns into fight with his own wife and then spirals out of control for the rest of the episode.[25] The origin for the scene came from real life. As David told the story, "I went out to dinner with a friend and his wife. After dinner [for which his friend had picked up the tab] I said to him, 'Thank you very much for the dinner.' My friend's wife said to me, 'Well, aren't you going to thank me as well?' So I replied, 'Of course, thank you,' and I am not a sociopath." David goes on to explain his process. In his comic notes, he jots down, "Don't thank her for dinner." Later he played the scene and wrote out an imaginary interaction based on the targeted question, "Why should I?" David is famous for saying his comedy involves what other people are thinking but no one says.[26] And where there is social tension and conflict and an odd version of the "truth," there is comedy. So then David drafts a scene of an imagined interaction as an exaggerated and awkward conflict that took inspiration from a real experience. In the scene he was more extreme as his friend's wife became irate at him, and Larry's entire evening blew up and by the end of the show karma caught up with him, as it always does.

Comedians use their targeted questions as the lens through which they perceive humor in the encounters, absurdities, and mishaps of daily life. In keeping with their offbeat, humorous perspective, they are always on the hunt for humor (superiority, incongruity, and relief) and for comic themes. We are calling our preacherly version of that playfulness the comic spirit. We exercise the comic spirit in the context of the comic vision of God's ultimate victory of life over death.

Preachers do well to always be on the hunt for humor (whether superiority, relief, or incongruity) and comic themes as well, in fulfilling our vocation to show how the comic vision folds into the present lives of our congregation. Our targeted question is "How can the humor I perceive in this situation, conversation, article, and so on convey the good news to my life and my people's lives now?" Then, guided by the specific themes and genre of the text and the specific needs and challenges of our congregation, our questions in our sermon preparation process become more and more targeted. In the next chapter we focus more closely on asking targeted questions in relation to the biblical texts on which we are preaching.

In the meantime, let's look at one of the landscape comic notes we have collected and, using targeted questions, reflect on how we might use it homiletically. Let's take the example about Connie's mother. A targeted question would be, what type(s) of humor do we discern here? The story has comic elements of incongruity as a movie or a pedicure morph into casket shopping. And why would we need to worry about formality and fabric weight in the next life? It also could be used as relief humor—to relieve the tension we all feel at uncertainty about the future life. There are comic themes: it portrays a protagonist who has foibles. It would turn tragic, ending in division and relationship damage if the daughter had flat-out refused to fall in with her mother's plans for the day or laughed at her or belittled her in any way—which of course she did not do. After all, she came into the encounter with a comic spirit and soft eyes! So the scene ends with a mother-daughter bonding experience, undergirded by compassion, even if it was casket shopping rather than lunch and a movie.

Then comes the more targeted homiletical question: how can the humor we discern in this text be used to offer good news to our congregation? As mentioned, it could be used to unite us in our shared human condition—our common lack of knowledge about the next life and our anxiety and desire for fuller knowledge. Through the story of Connie and her mother, we can step back from it, see ourselves in her, and share a smile, knowing that we are not alone in our anxiety about what is to come. It also invites a preacher to offer what we *are* told about the afterlife as a counterpoint to anxiety and the need for certainty. Two of the many texts that might occur to our preacherly brains are 1 Corinthians 13:12–13[27] and Colossians 3:12, 14.[28] The good news is that, whatever Connie's mother chooses to wear, the most important part of the future occasion for which she is preparing is the host—and we know that host to be welcoming and merciful, no matter what we are wearing!

To Ponder

—Have you ever experienced the Western Superman effect? Describe.
—Have you ever experienced cognitive overload? What was its effect on your comic creativity?
—Why are preachers advised not to bypass the inscape and landscape exploration and head straight to the commentaries to save time?

NOTES

1. Joseph Demakis, *The Ultimate Book of Quotations* (Charleston, SC: CreateSpace, 2012), 194.

2. Professor Smith is currently Professor Emeritus of English at Southern Methodist University, Dallas, Texas.

3. Alyce M. McKenzie, *Novel Preaching: Tips from Top Writers on Crafting Creative Sermons* (Louisville, KY: Westminster John Knox Press, 2010), 15.

4. McKenzie, *Novel Preaching*, 16–17.

5. John Sweller, "Cognitive Load Theory," in *Psychology of Learning and Motivation*, vol. 55, ed. Jose Mestre and Brian Ross (Cambridge, MA: Academic Press, 2018), 37–76.

6. John M. Darley and C. Daniel Batson, "'From Jerusalem to Jericho': A Study of Situational and Dispositional Variables in Helping Behavior," *Journal of Personality and Social Psychology* 27, no. 1 (1973): 100–108, 100, https://doi.org /10.1037/h0034449; also see C. Daniel Batson et al., "Failure to Help When in a Hurry: Callousness or Conflict?," *Personality and Social Psychology Bulletin* 4, no. 1 (January 1978): 97–101, https://doi.org/10.1177/014616727800400120.

7. This is known as *selective attention,* which refers to the processes that allow an individual to select and focus on particular input for further processing while simultaneously suppressing what they regard as irrelevant or distracting information. See W. A. Johnston and V. J. Dark, "Selective Attention," *Annual Review of Psychology* 37, no. 1 (January 1986): 43–75, https://doi.org/10.1146/annurev.ps .37.020186.000355.

8. The Western Superman effect is a personal and comical way of introducing the Baader-Meinhof effect commonly known as "frequency illusion," a form of selective attention.

9. "Weston" is derived for the Anglo Saxon for "settlement." "Super-Mare" is Latin for "above the sea." The town name is literally "Settlement above the sea." Like many towns in England the name is an amalgamation of different people and languages that make up the country.

10. Luke A. Powery, *Dem Dry Bones: Preaching, Death and Hope* (Minneapolis: Fortress Press, 2012), 134.

11. Powery, *Dem Dry Bones,* 134.

12. Susan Sparks, *Preaching Punch Lines: The Ten Commandments of Stand-Up Comedy* (Macon, GA: Smyth and Helwys, 2019), 52–53.

13. Glenn Everett, "Hopkins on 'Inscape' and 'Instress,'" Victorian Web, 1988, https://victorianweb.org/authors/hopkins/hopkins1.html.

14. Donna R. Vocate, *Intrapersonal Communication: Different Voices, Different Minds* 1st ed/ (New York: Routledge, 1994).

15. James M. Honeycutt and Reneé Brown, "Did You Hear the One About?: Typological and Spousal Differences in the Planning of Jokes and Sense of Humor in Marriage," *Communication Quarterly* 46, no. 3 (June 1998): 342–52, https://doi.org/10.1080/01463379809370106.

16. Johannes A. Lombard, *Antwort* (Zollikon-Zurich: Evangelischer Verlag AG, 1956), 895.

17. See "Stephen Colbert Presents: The Best Moments from 25 Years of Fox News," *The Late Show with Stephen Colbert,* October 8, 2022, YouTube, https:// www.youtube.com/watch?v=h5YIN5Khbx4.

18. On March 30, 1981, John Hinckley Jr. shot President Ronald Reagan in the left lung; the .22-caliber bullet just missed his heart. In an impressive feat for a seventy-year-old man with a collapsed lung, he walked into George Washington University Hospital under his own power. See History.com Editors, "President Reagan Shot," *HISTORY,* November 24, 2009, https://www.history.com/this -day-in-history/president-reagan-shot.

19. John Oliver, "Ridiculous 'Solutions' to Gun Violence," *Last Week Tonight with John Oliver*, June 5, 2022.

20. Emma Bowman, "A New Stamp Honors the Ukrainian Soldiers Who Profanely Told Off a Russian Warship," *NPR*, March 13, 2022, https://www.npr.org/2022/03/13/1086371078/ukraine-russian-warship-postage-stamp.

21. Matthew Gault, "Ukraine Issued 'Go F--- Yourself' Stamps. Prices Are Skyrocketing on EBay," Vice, April 20, 2022, https://www.vice.com/en/article/qjb9y7/ukraine-issued-go-fuck-yourself-stamps-prices-are-skyrocketing-on-ebay.

22. StoryWindow Productions, "About Connie Regan-Blake—Storyteller Connie," StoryWindow, December 19, 2016, https://storywindow.com/about/.

23. Times Talks, "Interview with Larry David Hosted by Charles McGrath," *New York Times*, March 10, 2015, YouTube, https://www.youtube.com/watch?v=v2Payk0OSlw.

24. Larry David in interviews often discusses his writing process. He explains how he, like many comedians, has an everyday pad that he uses to write down his thoughts. He indicates that he then talks them through (plays them interpersonally as imagined interactions) and then transfers the best to his "idea pad" and maybe his show.

25. "Paying for Dinner," *Curb Your Enthusiasm*, season 3, episode 5, September 15, 2002, YouTube, https://www.youtube.com/watch?v=2RbNpzasvqw.

26. "Larry David Meets Ricky Gervais," episode 1, Channel 4, January 5, 2006.

27. "Now we see in a mirror, dimly, but then we will see face to face. Now I know only in part; then I will know fully, even as I have been fully known. And now faith, hope, and love abide, these three; and the greatest of these is love."

28. "As God's chosen ones, holy and beloved, clothe yourselves with compassion, kindness, humility, meekness, and patience. . . . Above all, clothe yourselves with love, which binds everything together in perfect harmony."

12

Humor-neutics 101

Developing Your Knack for Noticing Biblical Humor

Can't we see the tongue in Jesus' cheek? Or even the cheek in Jesus' tongue!
    —Writer and retreat leader Margaret Silf[1]

Alyce did her PhD work at Princeton Seminary on biblical hermeneutics related to proverbial wisdom. Her two youngest children—Matthew, then four, and Rebecca, then eight—after overhearing her side of several phone conversations with her doctoral adviser Dr. Thomas Long asked, "Does Herman Noodics live in our neighborhood?" Only then did she realize with how much familiarity and affection she must have spoken of him! This chapter deals with another neighbor in the world of biblical interpretation for preaching: humor-neutics. This is a term so clever that Alyce is jealous she didn't think of before New Testament scholar Terri Bednarz coined it, serving as the title of her 1999 dissertation on humor in the Synoptic Gospels![2]

We are using humor-neutics in both a general and a specific way. In general, *humor-neutics* refers to preachers training themselves to notice humor in Scripture. Specifically it refers to our humor-inclusive process of exegeting individual texts for preaching. When we view the Bible as devoid of humor, we envision our homiletical task as a desperate wracking of our brains and searching the Web for humorous material to liven up the decrepit old book. How much better to acknowledge that humor pervades the Bible and use our knack for noticing it as part of our exegetical process for preaching![3]

LACK OF NOTICING

The Syndrome of Reverence

It has been, until relatively recently, considered blasphemous to impute humor to the Holy Writ. Biblical scholar Francis Landy, in an essay titled "Humour as a Tool for Biblical Exegesis," attributes this to the "syndrome of reverence," which he names as idolatry, a forgetting that real people wrote the Bible out of their common experiences. Landy states, "The solemn ritual of reading the Bible excluded humour as a valid way of worshipping God, and has created an impression of a stiff and serious document that never relaxes into a smile, so that many sensitive readers have closed their minds to its comic possibilities."[4]

For many people, as biblical scholar William Whedbee points out, "The coupling of comedy and the Bible is a contradiction in terms. Centuries of liturgical and theological use of the Bible have largely excluded a vital role for comedy and humor in biblical literature and religion."[5] Those who have bought into this popular depiction of Scripture equate discerning humor in the Bible with trivializing its truths. The assumption is that to discern humor or comic forms in the Bible is to make fun of it or diminish its value. On the contrary, the Bible makes fun of us! The Bible pokes fun at human pride and pretention, selfishness and greed, and the myriad other sins to which flesh and spirit are heir. Jesus freely used humor, irony, and satire to that end. "His descriptions of the hypocrisies of the Pharisees use overtly humorous images: the blind leading the blind; straining out a gnat then swallowing a camel; meticulously cleaning the outside of a cup while leaving the inside filthy; and maintaining white-washed tombs that are outwardly beautiful but inwardly full of dead bones."[6] The premise of the present volume is that, as an attribute of God and a gift to humankind's *imago Dei,* humor pervades the Bible: humor is an integral part both of the Hebrew Scriptures and the New Testament, and a comic vision ultimately encompasses them both.[7]

Holiness = Humorlessness

The assumption is that the God of the Bible is wholly humorless and infinite in gravity. Therefore, the greater the holiness, the less the humor and laughter. Holiness equals humorlessness. According to this understanding, says Conrad Hyers, "It [humor] belongs in the streets but not the sanctuary, in the church kitchen but not in the church service. This understanding, however, serves better as a definition of sanctimoniousness (than holiness) and as a pretext for fanaticism."[8] Amy-Jill Levine theorizes that the early church fathers were, in general, more focused on combating heresy, which was seen as no laughing matter. They put the kibosh on the genre of humor as inappropriate to their times and the suppression stuck for centuries.[9]

Fear of Imposing Greek and Roman Categories on the Hebrew Scriptures

Yet another contributor to biblical scholars' neglect of humor in the Bible is their justifiable caution about applying categories like tragedy and comedy, which have Greek and Roman origins, to biblical texts. Over the past generation of biblical scholarship, scholars have recognized that the Greek and Roman dramatists don't hold exclusive rights to essential components of plot, incongruity, and characterization. Nowadays scholars are coming to see that comic presentation was much more widespread in the ancient Near East than once believed.[10] To perceive comic form in biblical texts, then, can be to discern what is present rather than to impose categories from a later time and culture.[11]

Minding the Gap!

When riding trains in Britain, as you step from platform to train, a cultured voice over the intercom reminds you, "Mind the gap." This is good advice for interpreting any text for preaching. But it is especially true when inferring humor. There is an inevitable gap between textual intentionality and reader reception. Hebrew Scripture scholars A. Brenner and Y. T. Radday point out the challenges of discerning humor in ancient texts. "Reading texts which are not self-defined by some intrinsic means as 'humorous' or 'comic' (which biblical texts are not) is more controversial than evaluating a self-declared 'humorous' oral or written presentation."[12]

In a chapter of his book *Between Heaven and Mirth* titled "Why So Gloomy? A Brief but 100 Percent Accurate Historical Examination of Religious Seriousness," Father James Martin explores why, when scholars acknowledge that parts of the Hebrew Scriptures are intentionally funny, our assumption is that Jesus of Nazareth had no sense of humor.[13]

Aided by the insights of several New Testament scholars and theologians, Martin attributes this assumption to the culture-bound nature of humor. Biblical scholar Amy Jill Levine, whose expertise is the Jewish background of Jesus and the ways the church has often misunderstood it, suspects that what was funny to original audiences during Jesus' time may not seem funny to us at all. She posits that first-century audiences would have been amused by the exaggeration, for example, that a mustard seed sprouted into a big bush for nesting birds. Other scholars suggest that people would have laughed at the absurd scenarios of logs and splinters and the ridiculously exaggerated characters and situations of Jesus' parables. That someone would light a lamp and put it under a basket, build a house on sand, or that a parent would give a child stones instead of bread are all absurd![14]

While your authors recommend engaging texts with respectful scholarly care, we must reckon with the risk that the contemporary interpreter will discern humor where the ancient text offers no grounds for it or fail to recognize it where it does. However, we do not see this as reason to jettison the possibility of humor. Isn't there always a gap between intention and reception in humor? Alyce sometimes finds things amusing that others, undoubtedly more noble and pure minded, do not. She has learned to maintain a poker face or, in desperate situations, to feign a coughing fit. Sometimes when she is preaching she says something she didn't intend to be funny and is disconcerted when people laugh uproariously. Other times, her comedic efforts are met with crossed arms and stony faces. Humor is partly in the eye of the beholder. Biblical scholars, proceeding with appropriate scholarly care, are increasingly answering humor's invitation to take the risk!

In the rest of this chapter we offer some general humor-neutical guidelines that scholars use for noticing and recognizing humor in Scripture. We then direct you toward scholarly treatments of biblical humor, should you want to pursue them more deeply.

Finally, we focus on humor-neutics in its specific sense—employing humor as a part of your biblical exegesis process for preaching. This means applying the approach used in chapter 11 for noticing humor in our inscape and landscape to our textscape: soft eyes, targeted questions, and comic notes.

THE WESTERN SUPERMAN (WESTON-SUPER-MARE) EFFECT: HUMOR IN THE BIBLE!

Owen's Western Superman effect applied to our knack for noticing biblical humor means that we now have permission to find it or let it find us throughout Scripture. Biblical scholar William Whedbee, in discerning "comic sense and sensibility" in the Bible, counsels us to look for three intertwined features that recur in comedy throughout the ages: plotlines, characterization of protagonists, and purpose or function.

Plot Reversals

We discussed the plotline of the comic frame in chapter 7. The typical plotline of comedy begins with a view of a largely harmonious, integrated society. This equilibrium is challenged and tested as the action unfolds. Comedy swings upward at the end and restores the hero to her or his rightful place in society; tragedy typically ends with a fallen hero in a situation of disintegration, alienation, and death. Comedy ends in Carnival, a celebration of human hope and community; tragedy ends in catastrophe. Biblical scholars have discerned a comic plotline in Exodus 1–15, the book of Ruth, and the comic visions of Genesis, Exodus, Esther, Jonah, and Job.[15]

Comic plots often involve a reversal of status between exalted and lowly, a puncturing of pomposity and a positive outcome for the unlikely protagonists. The Bible is filled with comic reversals that show the socially despised in a positive light and cast the socially esteemed into the shadows. Conrad Hyers calls this a "spiritual democratization."[16]

The comic theme of reversal threads through the whole Bible in the motif of divine foolishness overturning human wisdom and of divine weakness overcoming human strength. Such themes form the plotlines of a good many biblical stories, from Genesis through the Gospels and Acts, culminating in the ultimate comic denouement: the overcoming of death by life in the resurrection. Humor-neutics keeps an eye out for reversals.

Unlikely People

A second feature of the comic frame is the choice of people who are lifted up as unlikely protagonists and shown in a positive light. Paul, in reminding the Corinthians of their own lowly origins, could be describing many of the heroes and heroines of the Bible: their lack of distinction is what qualifies them for divine service. Rather than choosing the powerful and those of noble birth, God chooses what is foolish and weak in the world to shame the wise and the strong (1 Cor. 1:26–29)— hence God's choice of the Israelites, a people trapped in slavery. This is followed by the choice of Moses, son of slaves, outwitting Pharaoh with the help of God; David the young shepherd boy felling the Philistine giant Goliath; a poor young peasant woman chosen to bear the Savior of the world; Jesus choosing twelve fishermen to be his initial disciples; and a woman being the first preacher of the good news of the resurrection. In many scriptural stories and scenes, an unnamed person, often a woman, plays a central role in the comic action. Examples abound, but here are a few examples: the servant girl in the story of Naaman (2 Kgs. 5:2–3), the servant girl who rats out Peter (Mark 14:66–67 and parallels), the unnamed woman who anoints Jesus beforehand for burial (Mark 14:3–9), and Pilate's wife (Matt. 27:19).

Note that the Gospels make a special effort to authenticate Jesus' messianic identity by placing him in the royal line of David through his father, Joseph. But no effort at all is made to dress up the obscurity and lowly estate of his birth. If anything, these elements are highlighted as part of the inner plot and meaning of his nativity.[17] Jesus himself has the qualities of a comic figure, given his lowly origins.

Humor-neutics keeps a keen watch for the person with no name, the person with the lowliest status in a biblical scene, with eyes on the irony that that person often exercises the most important role in the action.

Bubble-Bursting Purpose

In seeking to discern humor in the Bible, a third key feature, after plots and people, is purpose. Humor's purpose and impact can vary, as we have seen earlier in this study. Humor can build community identity, subvert the status quo (or sometimes preserve it), and strengthen individual and group resolve.[18]

But running through much of the Bible is a key thematic purpose of comic expression: bursting the bubble of pride of the arrogant and exalting the humble. This dynamic is expressed in the Magnificat, Mary's Song, "[God] has brought down the powerful from their thrones, / and lifted up the lowly" (Luke 1:52).

While the Bible uses a variety of forms and functions of humor, they share a common purpose:

A common concern in comedy and the Bible is human pride and pretention. Both deal with the arrogance of power and status and the follies of selfishness and self-importance. Jesus' terse comment that "whoever exalts himself will be humbled, and whoever humbles himself will be exalted" (Matt 23:12) is not only a fundamental biblical theme, but a fundamental theme in the history of comedy.[19]

This dynamic is at play in the account of the woman brought to Jesus who had been caught in adultery (John 8:1–11). To trap Jesus, the Pharisees wanted him to pass judgment on her according to the law of Moses. As Jesus sees all (he has soft eyes!), he sidesteps the test, writes on the ground, and says, "Let anyone among you who is without sin be the first to throw a stone at her" (John 8:8). Slowly the accusers slip away. What Jesus wrote on the ground, we will never know, but the comic theme of the humiliation or being brought low of the arrogant and the self-righteous is clear. The scene has a comic ending: there is not punishment and isolation, but acceptance of the sinner back into the new possibilities of a positive future and the instruction to sin no more.

This pretension-pricking dynamic is front and center in Jesus' teachings—his short, proverbial sayings and his parables. Reversal and surprise, integral to the plots of many parables, are key to achieving the purpose of unsettling listeners, subverting the status quo, and pointing to an inbreaking reality, the reign of God. This inbreaking partakes of the creative disruption dynamic we have encountered in relation to humor. Whether one discerned (and perhaps discerns!) humor in them depends on where one fell (falls) in the social hierarchy. Obviously, not everyone found Jesus amusing. Quite the opposite!

We imagine that someone on the lower rungs of the ladder, hearing the parable of the Pharisee and the Publican or the Rich Man and Lazarus, would have found humor in the positive depiction of social outcasts and their exaltation rather than their humiliation, a foolish shepherd seeking one lost sheep (Luke 15:4–6), a feast attended by the homeless poor (Matt. 22:1–14), and a widow pestering a judge until she wears him down and justice is served (Luke 18:2–5).

Humor-neutics tags the parables as a potential field ripe for a humor harvest in our preaching. More broadly, it notices other biblical instances of pride going before a fall, of the powerful thwarted, their pomposity pricked.

THE WESTERN SUPERMAN EFFECT:
RECENT SCHOLARSHIP

Biblical scholars, in their identification of humor in the Bible since the late 1980s, have increasingly illustrated the Western Superman effect, finding humor in the plots, people, and purposes of many biblical texts. For readers who are interested in exploring humor with regard to particular genres or texts, here are some helpful resources. The chronology of their publication charts the growing interest in humor over the past several decades.

Folklorist Susan Niditch writing in 1987 discerned the comic pattern of the underdog or trickster that appears in folklore across many cultures, including the biblical tales of Jacob, Joseph, and Esther.[20]

In 1990, when many biblical scholars were still wondering if there was such a thing as humor in the Bible, Hebrew Bible scholars Yehuda Radday and Athalya Brenner served as editors of a groundbreaking anthology *On Humour and the Comic in the Hebrew Bible*. It featured essays by biblical scholars on the presence of humor, among other places, in the stories of Isaac, Samson, and Saul; the encounter between David, Nabal, and Abigail in 1 Samuel 25; and the prophetic books of Jonah, Job, and Esther. While acknowledging the complexities of discerning humor in an ancient text, the volume demonstrated how careful scholarship that is attentive to context can reveal humor in biblical texts.[21]

In 1998 William Whedbee published *The Bible and the Comic Vision* in which he offered an in-depth analysis of humor in diverse biblical texts: Genesis, Exodus, Esther, Jonah, Job, and Song of Songs. In the book he seeks to show how the Bible uses a comic vision to counter death and despair with life and hope. Whedbee asserts that the creation narratives are characterized by the central themes of comedy: creation of order out of chaos, the triumph of light over darkness, and the affirmation of the essential goodness of creation. He regards Israel's fathers and mothers as comic figures (Gen. 12–50); Exodus and Esther as comedies of deliverance; Jonah as joke; Job as a comedy of creation, chaos, and carnival; and the Song of Solomon as paradox and parody.[22]

Over ten years after her collaboration with Yehuda Radday in *On Humour and the Comic in the Hebrew Bible,* in 2003 Athalya Brenner edited another volume of essays on biblical humor, this time one that expressed a feminist critique of biblical humor. Titled *Are We Amused? Humour about Women in the Biblical Worlds,* it features essays by feminist scholars who reenvisioned several biblical women, some of whom have been labeled as "sinners," as comic protagonists working out their own salvation through ingenious and humorous actions in otherwise tragic situations of loss and abuse. They include the several women in Matthew's genealogy: Tamar, Rahab, Ruth, and the "wife of Uriah" (Bathsheba), as well as Esther.[23]

In 2012 feminist biblical scholar Melissa A. Jackson published *Comedy and Feminist Interpretation of the Hebrew Bible: A Subversive Collaboration*. She discerns comic plots, characterizations, and purposes in women in the Hebrew Bible. They include trickster matriarchs: Lot's daughter, Rebekah, Leah, Rachel, and Tamar; the Five Women of Moses' infancy: Shiphrah and Puah, Moses' mother and sister, and Pharaoh's daughter; Rahab (Josh. 2); Deborah and Jael (Judg. 4); Delilah; David's wives; Jezebel; Ruth; and Esther. Quite a lineup! While these comic portraits of biblical women include some cautionary tales, they also serve to subvert oppressive social norms and gender roles, and to inspire perseverance for survival.[24]

Efforts to discern humor in the New Testament have paralleled similar work on the Hebrew Bible. In 1997 Douglas Adams, then professor of Christianity and the arts at Pacific School of Religion in Berkeley, California, published *The Prostitute in the Family Tree: Discovering Humor and Irony in the Bible*. In it he explored the humorous potential of the dialogues of the Hebrew Scriptures as well as the humor and satire in Jesus' parables.

Terri Bednarz, from whom we have borrowed the term "humor-neutics," in 2015 published *Humor in the Gospels: A Sourcebook for the Study of Humor in the New Testament, 1863–2014*. In it she traces the history of several quests for Gospel humor going back to the late 1700s when scholars began to come to terms with Jesus' humanity. Rather than maintaining a superhuman idealized portrait of him, they gradually began shifting from "gentle Jesus meek and mild" to recognizing his use of fiery prophetic wit.[25]

Bednarz's compendium of humor research related to Gospel literature covers such topics as "The Seriousness of Humor in the Teachings of Jesus," "The Comic and Playful in the Teachings of Jesus," "The Cynic and the Rogue," and "The Comic Savant." These depictions of Jesus have in common a delegitimizing of the authority and status claimed by Jesus' opponents. Charting advances in literary, contextual, and rhetorical approaches to recognizing humor in the Gospels, Bednarz offers the most comprehensive resource on Gospel humor to date.

HUMOR-NEUTICS 101 FROM LACK TO KNACK:
SOFT-EYES BIBLICAL EXEGESIS

Having looked at humor-neutics as general guidelines for noticing biblical humor, we turn to its more specific application to exegeting individual texts (textscape), using the three-part approach from chapter 11: soft eyes, targeted questions, and comic notes.

Homiletical advice from previous generations was to go to the commentaries first and find out what the experts said the text meant. Chances were good they would find little humor to harvest there. More recent approaches to biblical exegesis for preaching emphasize starting in front of the text with the experiences and unique perspective of the preacher (inscape) and the needs of the congregation in cultural context (landscape). This take asserts that biblical exegesis needs to involve personal and congregational exegesis—insights gleaned from close observation of the preacher's inner life and congregational/communal context. It acknowledges that texts are not reducible to a single conceptual point, bypassing the sensory world of the text, its imagery, genre, literary context, and backstory.

Comics look at inner and outer life through the meta question, how do I find humor here? They approach life with soft eyes, then narrow their perspective into targeted questions that reflect their quirky, usually skeptical worldview that asks why things are the way they are and whether anyone else has noticed how messed up everything is. The preacher starts with the meta question, how is the good news of the gospel (often through a chosen or assigned biblical text) related to the lives of my congregation today? She comes to a biblical text with soft eyes that help her discern a full description of the biblical text in context and enter into its existential, literary, theological, historical, and cultural worlds. She asks soft-eyes questions and resists imposing forgone conclusions in favor of open-minded curiosity. All these soft-eyed questions are asked within the purview of the preacher's meta question. How does this text relate to my and my congregation's life here and now?

Alyce for several years has taught "McKenzie's Ten Steps of Biblical Exegesis for Preaching." This methodology has strong similarities to Owen's soft-eyes method of ethnographic observation described in chapter 11. The approach is the same: The preacher approaches the biblical text(s) with keen observation of skills (knack for noticing), but also with openness and questions rather than forgone conclusions, assumptions, and judgments. The process begins in front of the text with existential questions, moves into the text asking literary questions, then theological questions, and finally, questions of historical/cultural context behind the text.

Only as she nears the end of the process does the preacher go to biblical resources to compare and contrast her insights with theirs. The goal is to move toward a single sermonic claim that expresses an aspect of the human condition revealed in the text as it is impacted by an aspect of the character and actions of God to be found there.[26]

Here are some of the types of questions Alyce suggests that preachers pose to a text in this soft-eyes exegetical process. They fit Owen's criteria of coming to an ethnographic immersive experience seeking a full description, asking all kinds of questions rather than making all kinds of assumptions, and bringing curiosity rather than judgment to the exercise.

Soft-Eyed Existential Questions

Soft-eyed biblical exegesis begins in front of the text with what philosopher of language Paul Ricoeur would call a "naïve reading." The preacher reads the text, allowing emotions, thoughts, and images to surface freely. She is attentive to emotions the text sparks in her, her emotions about the text, and images from the text that connect with congregational life, experiences, memories, stories, questions, and intuitions about where the sermon might go. The preacher silences their inner censor and project manager, jotting down key words and images, not evaluating at this stage but accumulating. This sounds a lot like the comic's comic notes collecting.

Later in the process, after reading the text for basic understanding, setting it in the context of the biblical book in which it appears, noting differences among several translations, and brainstorming canonical connections, the preacher asks a series of questions for which he/she has no predetermined answers. Openness is key in this process. Soft eyes!

The process moves into the literary world of the text, asking soft-eyed questions about matters of scene, character identification, conflict, plot, and imagery. Whatever the genre of the text, narrative or otherwise, the preacher remembers that there is always a story behind the text. The preacher keeps a running list of insights and further questions, still refraining from checking things out in the commentaries. The next step is to ask theological questions about the images of the human condition and the divine character that the text projects. The final step is to gather what one can about the historical/social context of the original intended audience of the biblical text.

Soft-Eyed Literary Questions

Striking details:

> Does something pique your curiosity or not seem to fit? It could be an aspect of the text's structure or style, or the use of distinctive words or phrases.

Image:

> Does an image(s) speak to you from the text?

Character identification:

> If the text is a narrative, ask yourself, "How would it feel to be each of the characters?" List adjectives and brief phrases. With whom do you identify most closely? How about your congregation? Remember that even in nonnarrative texts, there are always characters and a story behind the text.

Conflict:

> What is the main conflict here? What caused it? Conflict can occur both in and behind a biblical text.

Power:

> Who has power and who doesn't?

Congregational connection (including you, the preacher):

> How does my social location, background, and self-identity affect my approach to this text: my life experiences, socioeconomic level, educational level, sexual orientation, ethnicity, etc.?

> What about your congregation?

> What would challenge or comfort individuals in your congregation? Your congregation as a whole? You the preacher? Is there anything in your context that would make this passage difficult to preach? Or that could cause harm to someone if it is preached? What is the good news?

Freewheeling imagination:

Here are some questions to ponder and sentences to complete to spark your imagination:

What I don't like about the text: (Something that unsettled you? A troublesome outcome? A view of God or humankind that was disturbing?)

What I really like about the text: A positive outcome? A healing view of God? A character whom I can admire?

The voice(s) that seems absent from this text is. . . .

What do you hear, smell, taste, and/or see in the text?

Ask: What if Peter had walked on the water all the way to Jesus? What if God had answered Jesus' prayer in Gethsemane?

Ask: Why are there four different accounts of the resurrection? Why did only one leper come back to thank Jesus?

Soft-Eyed Theological Questions

What images or concepts does the text present to express God's character and actions?

What images or concepts does the text present to express the human condition?

What images or concepts does the text present to express human transformation?

Note that these soft-eyed questions require the preacher to reflect on all three arenas we are encouraging you to explore for signs of humor: your inner life (inscape); your outer, congregational context (landscape); and the biblical text (textscape) in their interrelationship

HUMOR-NEUTICS: THREE TARGETED QUESTIONS TO ASK A BIBLICAL TEXT

Now that we have asked the soft-eyed questions, it's time to sharpen our focus and ask some targeted questions. We keep in mind that our purpose is to discern humor in a text that could help us connect its good news to our congregation by both challenging and comforting. With that purpose before us, humor-neutics involves three targeted questions that can become the genesis of comic notes as you creatively interact with the biblical text.

1. What comic or tragic themes do you discern in this text?
2. What forms of humor—superiority, relief, incongruity, or some combination—do you discern?
3. How could you be playful with the text?

By now you are equipped to ask questions regarding comic and tragic themes and to identify types of humor. As for #3, here are some suggestions of what we mean by taking a playful approach to a text, which is more of an art than a rule-bound science.

Remember the comics' targeted questions for discerning humor in life around them: things like "Why are things this way?" "Why am I the only one who sees how messed up this is?" "Do I really have to?" "Who says so?"

Use the following freewheeling, creative approaches to connect your inscape and landscape, your inner thoughts, issues, and surroundings with humorous possibilities in the biblical text.

—Identify with someone acting badly in the text to show how we share in their flaw.
—Brainstorm a different ending—a comic ending to a potentially tragic situation, or a tragic ending if the protagonist doesn't change.
—Embellish a potential conversation with a character or imagine a soliloquy you overhear.
—Bring the text into today or put yourself back into the text.
—Complain about what you don't like about the text.
—Ask, why not?
—Identify the voice that seems absent from the text and give that person some lines!
—Is there any humor in the sensory world of the text? What do you hear, smell, taste, or see in the text?
—Ask, what if? What if Peter had walked on the water all the way to Jesus? What if God had answered Jesus' prayer in Gethsemane?
—Ask, why? Why are there four different accounts of the resurrection? Why did only one leper come back to thank Jesus?

Here are a couple of examples of comic notes based on being playful with a text.

Taking a Playful Approach:
Identify with an Unappealing Character

Example #1—"The Devil Debriefs": Sermon based on Jesus' temptation by Satan in Matthew 4:1–11.

Satan gets shown up in this little episode. The Tempter trips up. Lucifer loses out. The devil gets duped. The Adversary gets something I can't mention in polite company handed to him on a platter. Whatever label you want to slap on this debacle, I imagine that the devil went back to his lair and engaged in a serious self-deprecation session followed by some determined debriefing. Here is how I imagine it went:

> Well, that was certainly humiliating. Thank God no one else was present to witness that debacle. I can't believe I made such a newbie mistake! I way overplayed my hand. I had to go all special effects and high drama: I could have kept it simple; I could have just said, "Jesus, turn these three pebbles into donut holes"; or "Jesus, step off this curb and you will not twist your ankle"; or "Come with me to the highest building in Plano, Texas, and I will give you all of Plano if you will worship me." But no, I had to go all dramatic and set off his alarm bells. I can't believe I made such a newbie mistake![27]

Taking a Playful Approach to the Text:
Bring the Text into Today

Example #2—"Getting What's Coming to You": Sermon based on Jacob's struggle at Peniel (Gen. 32:22–32) was preached at a service a few years ago honoring graduating seniors and their families, faculty, and staff at Perkins School of Theology, Southern Methodist University, Dallas, Texas. It is based on the whimsical depiction of Jacob as a member of the graduating class.

"I'm trying to break this to you gently, but I may as well just come out with it. Incriminating footage has surfaced recently regarding your classmate Jacob. Because of it, he has been asked to take a leave of absence and will not be graduating with you tomorrow. I read to you from the Perkins Catalog page 24, 'Fitness for Ministry,' where it says this: 'the

Presence of Patterns of personal behavior tending to be seriously disabling to ministry can be grounds for the deferral of awarding a degree until such time as the disabling patterns are overcome.'"[28] The sermon goes on to catalog instances of these patterns in the "heel grabber's" life.

POSING HUMOR-NEUTICS' TARGETED
QUESTIONS TO A BIBLICAL TEXT

Owen and Alyce, as part of their collaboration in this project, held a workshop several months before publication to crowdsource their approach to preachers' knack for noticing biblical humor.

We divided the group of about forty people into four groups. We assigned each group one of four texts, intentionally choosing a parable, two New Testament narratives, and an Old Testament narrative:

—Luke 11:1–13: Jesus' instructions in prayer and the parable of the
  Friend at Midnight
—John 20:1–12: John's account of Easter morning
—John 21: Jesus' postresurrection serving of breakfast to the disciples on the beach
—2 Kings 5:1–19: The cleansing of Naaman

We projected the humor-neutics targeted questions on a big screen and told them they could talk about any of them that seemed relevant. Then we waited to see and hear what would happen.

Very quickly the conversation started up, and just as quickly, the laughter. The energy in the room was palpable. It was like a good party without the alcohol! I had never been to a Bible study where there was this much animation and laughter.

We asked participants to look for three things and to keep comic notes on their observations. We told them this was not a legalistic process. They could pick whichever of the three fit best and that a good way to proceed would be simply to start noting things that amused them without an initial need to categorize.

1. Structure: Comic or tragic? Some combination?
2. Which types of humor do you discern? Superiority, relief, incongruity, or some combination?
3. How could you be playful with this text?

We suggest you try this—either with these texts or others of your choosing—to begin practicing humor-neutics, enlisting the power of humor to convey in your sermons the good news, both its challenge and its comfort.

To prime the pump, we offer a few comic notes on each text and leave you to figure out how you want to be playful with them, how humor could be a conveyance of both the challenge and the comfort of the good news. Don't expect these biblical observations to be neatly categorized and expressed in full sentences. These are comic notes.

Luke 11:1–13

—The Lord's Prayer is, of course, normally interpreted with high holiness, and rightly so. But is it kind of amusing that the disciples don't want to be shown up by John's disciples who already have been taught how to pray? (11:1)

—There is definitely incongruity humor at work in the parable of the Annoying Friend at Midnight which follows Jesus' instructions on how to pray. No one in an ancient Near Eastern village would act as churlishly as the man awakened at midnight (though we might!). Hospitality was a point of honor.

—There is incongruity humor in the ridiculous picture of a parent giving a child a stone rather than a fish, or a scorpion rather than an egg. Definitely grin-worthy!

John 20:1–18

—Peter and the other disciple competed to see who could get there first. That's amusing.

—The response of the disciples to seeing the empty tomb is to go on home.

—Jesus' mother must have taught him to make his bed in the morning. His head cloth was neatly rolled up. That may be pushing it. We want lighthearted, not irreverent. You decide.

—Jesus asking Mary a patently obvious question. Why are you weeping?

—Her mistaking him for the gardener. One of the participants, Rev. Dr. Jeff Hall, pastor at Cockran Chapel United Methodist

Church in Dallas, preached a sermon on this text with the clever
title "The Gardener Did It."

John 21

—The obvious incongruity of a person you presumed dead serving
you breakfast.
—The comic plot reversal (death turned into resurrected life) without which this scene would not be possible.
—Positive homiletical connection—there are lots of scenes in our
lives and world that would not be possible without the resurrection but that now are. It's the preacher's job to flesh those scenes
out for people.
—The possibility that Jesus is messing with Peter in asking him to
profess his loyalty three times.
—Not sure how to categorize this and we don't really have to, but
it's amusing that Peter says, "What about him?" with regard to
the beloved disciple. A little jealousy here? And Jesus puts him in
his place: What's it to you? You tend to your own business. The
potential humor resides in our seeing ourselves in biblical people
acting in petty ways!

2 Kings 5:1–19

—The comic theme of the bringing low of the mighty.
—The important role in the story of persons low on the social ladder, the nameless servant girl and later the nameless servants who
intervene, with the result that this story ends on a comic rather
than a tragic note.
—The attitude of the king of Israel, taking offense at the king of
Aram for asking him to cure Naaman of leprosy. This has the mak-
ings of a tragic outcome, were it not for the intervention of Elisha.
—Elisha's actions have comic potential—he doesn't even bother to go
to meet Naaman. We might wonder if it's to put him in his place?
—Naaman's anger at not being fawned over is amusing and typical
of the haughty. His disdain for the Jordan River by comparison
with the rivers of Damascus is a hoot, and marks him even further

as a first-rate ass. The story could still end in tragedy if it were not for the intervention of his nameless servants, who basically advise him, "Take the easy way out when it's offered, for God's sake."
— His over-the-top obeisance brings the story to a comic end as Elisha offers his benediction: "Go in peace."

Having honed our knack for noticing humor in our inscape and landscape in chapter 11 and our textscape in chapter 12, we turn now to our final chapter to learn from comics how to shape our comic notes into observational, humorous segments and stories in our sermons.

NOTES

1. Ralph Milton, *The Gift of Story* (Kelowna, BC, Canada: Wood Lake Publishing Inc., 2018).

2. Terri Bednarz published her dissertation as *Humor in the Gospels: A Sourcebook for the Study of Humor in the New Testament, 1863–2014* (Lexington, MD: Lantham Books, 2015).

3. Some scholars discern in comedy, broadly understood, a framework for the Bible's grand narrative. They include Northrop Frye, Conrad Hyers, Frederick Buechner, and Brian Edgar. Northrop Frye has made the Dante-esque view key to his own approach to the Bible.

4. Francis Landy, "Humour as a Tool for Biblical Exegesis," in *On Humour and the Comic in the Hebrew Bible*, ed. Yehuda T. Radday and Athalya Brenner (Sheffield, UK: Almond Press, 1990), 99.

5. J. William Whedbee, *The Bible and the Comic Vision* (Cambridge: Cambridge University Press, 1998), 1–2.

6. Conrad Hyers, *And God Created Laughter: The Bible as Divine Comedy* (Atlanta: John Knox Press, 1987), 6.

7. This is the view set forth in Cheryl Exum and J. William Whedbee, "Isaac, Samson, and Saul: Reflections on the Comic and Tragic Visions," in *On Humour and the Comic in the Hebrew Bible*, ed. Yehuda T. Radday and Athalya Brenner (Sheffield, UK: Almond Press, 1990), 119.

8. Hyers, *And God Created Laughter*, 4.

9. From an interview with James Martin, SJ, author of *Between Heaven and Mirth: Why Joy, Humor, and Laughter Are at the Heart of the Spiritual Life* (New York: HarperCollins, 2012), 33.

10. Athalya Brenner and Yehuda T. Radday, "Between Intentionality and Reception: Acknowledgement and Application," in *On Humour and the Comic in the Hebrew Bible*, ed. Radday and Brenner (Sheffield, UK: Almond Press, 1990), 16.

11. J. Cheryl Exum and J. William Whedbee, "Isaac, Samson, and Saul: Reflections on the Comic and Tragic Visions," in *On Humour and the Comic in the Hebrew Bible*, ed. Radday and Brenner (Sheffield, UK: Almond Press, 1990), 120.

12. Brenner and Radday, "Between Intentionality and Reception," 14.

13. Elton Trueblood was an early noticer of humor in Jesus' teachings in *The Humor of Christ: A Bold Challenge to the Traditional Stereotype of a Somber, Gloomy Christ* (San Francisco: Harper and Row, 1964). He focused on Jesus' use of irony and humor in the parables.

14. Martin, *Between Heaven and Mirth,* 33. Scholars whom Martin cites include, besides Amy Jill Levine, Daniel Harrington, Gerald Arbuckle, and Margaret Silf.

15. Whedbee, *The Bible and the Comic Vision*, 7.

16. Conrad Hyers, *The Comic Vision and the Christian Faith: A Celebration of Life and Laughter* (Eugene, OR: Wipf and Stock, 1981), 152.

17. Hyers, *The Comic Vision and the Christian Faith*, 142.

18. Melissa A. Jackson, *Comedy and Feminist Interpretation in the Hebrew Bible: A Subversive Collaboration* (Oxford: Oxford University Press, 2012), 25–28.

19. Hyers, *And God Created Laughter*, 41.

20. Susan Niditch, *Underdogs and Tricksters: A Prelude to Biblical Folklore* (San Francisco: Harper & Row, 1987).

21. Radday and Brenner, *On Humour and the Comic in the Hebrew Bible*.

22. Whedbee, *The Bible and the Comic Vision*.

23. Athalya Brenner, *Are We Amused? Humour about Women in the Biblical Worlds* (London: T&T Clark International, 2003); F. Scott Spencer, "Those Riotous—Yet Righteous—Foremothers of Jesus: Exploring Matthew's Comic Genealogy," 7–30.

24. Jackson, *Comedy and Feminist Interpretation in the Hebrew Bible*.

25. Bednarz, in referring to Gospel humor, does not mean to imply a harmonization of the humor found in the Gospels. Rather, it simply denotes a presence of humor in the Gospels; *Humor in the Gospels*, 3.

26. Sometimes a preacher needs to refer to more than one text, since not every text reveals the fullness of God's mercy and justice.

27. Alyce McKenzie, "The Devil Debriefs: Reflections on the Temptation of Jesus (Matt. 4:1–11)," Patheos, March 13, 2011, https://www.patheos.com /resources/additional-resources/2011/03/devil-debriefs-alyce-mckenzie-03-07 -2011.

28. The full sermon can be found in Alyce M. McKenzie, *Novel Preaching: Tips from Top Writers on Crafting Creative Sermons* (Nashville: Abingdon Press, 2010), 118f.

13

The Preacher as Last Comic Standing
Crafting Original Comedy

"Be yourself. Everyone else is already taken."
—Attributed to Oscar Wilde

The third and last part of our book has been focused on the preacher and the comic spirit. This last chapter focuses on what preachers can learn from comics as they move from noticing humor within and around them, in life and text, to crafting it into sermonic segments using humor as one compelling way to connect the good news to people's lives.

Last Comic Standing is a reality television talent competition that aired on NBC from 2003 to 2010 and again in 2014 and 2015. The goal of the show was to select the most promising comedian from a large group of hopefuls. Among the rewards were a cash prize and a television special. It may surprise readers to learn that neither Alyce nor Owen has ever been on the program, though we each are sure the other would skyrocket to the top of the competition!

But in the process of observing comics on the show and beyond, we have learned from them about crafting original comedy. The key word here is *original*. Successful comics craft their humor from their unique perspectives and experiences. They don't pass others' material off as their own. In homiletics we often call this unique take on things the *preacher's voice*. Just as a person's physical voice is unique, so is each preacher's take on the world. It makes voice a great metaphor for both preacher and comic. In both cases, one's voice or unique take on the world is the sum total of the things one notices, in one's inner and outer worlds, through the approach we've called in chapters 11 and 12 having "soft eyes."

At the grocery store you will find long shelves of sliced bread, packaged in plastic bags, secured with twist ties. In the bakery section you will find freshly baked loaves of bread, handcrafted, perhaps with unique, locally sourced ingredients. Stores call them artisan loaves, and they are understandably more expensive than the plastic-wrapped loaves, since they take more time and individualized effort to harvest and prepare. In this chapter we learn how to use methods we've appropriated from comics—soft eyes, targeted questions, and comic notes—to craft artisan humor for our sermons, whether in the form of original jokes, observational humor, or humorous stories.

First, a lesson on how to create a short and humorous bit, an original joke. This is distinguished from a canned joke, such as, "A pair of cows were talking in the field. One says, 'Have you heard about the mad cow disease that's going around?' 'Yeah,' the other cow says. 'Makes me glad I'm a penguin.'"[1]

Remember Fred Craddock's caution about the use of standalone canned jokes, his urging that humor should be part of the sermon, not distinct from it? A joke brings a laugh, but where does one go from there in a sermon?

If the joke is borrowed from someone else or a joke collection, this runs another risk: the audience may already know the punch line. One time Owen was at a comedy night at the Comedy Museum in London. It was novice comedian open mic night. The room was filled with friends, family, and classmates from the museum's comedy class—a friendly crowd! One of the fledging comedians ended a really good set with a well-known canned joke. An audience member shouted out the punch line and some booed. Dead on stage!

Unless you can weave the message of a canned joke into your sermon you are probably in trouble. But with a little work we can teach you how to write an original, artisan-crafted short humor piece. You still need to make sure it is message-relevant—that is, connected with the theme of your sermon, directing rather than distracting listeners' attention.

HOW JOKES WORK: BENIGN VIOLATION THEORY

Jokes operate by means of what humor scholars call "benign violation theory," which we introduced in chapter 2. Some norm or expectation is overturned or violated, but in a way that does not threaten listeners with insult or damage.

With reference to the earlier cow-penguin joke, cows talking is a violation, cows' knowledge of a current disease is a violation, a cow experiencing the delusion that it is a penguin and therefore immune is also a violation. It is an absurdity and has no consequence or threat to us and therefore it is also safe or benign. In Owen's humor class he has groups of students comb through hundreds of jokes just like the cow-penguin joke and asks them to find violations of logic—and they are always there. He also has them evaluate if a joke was threatening to them, made them feel uncomfortable, or feel the subject of the joke contains a threat to themselves or a general negative impact—in this case, the cow's delusional thinking that it is a penguin could be a threat because it thinks it is not immune to the cow disease and could therefore be at risk. But since the joke's situation is so absurd, we dismiss the seriousness of it.

Racist or sexist jokes are violations of logic, but they are not benign. A person who can find humor in a sexist or racist joke perceives no threat to themselves, no personal implications because they have little empathy for the targeted other. Finding humor in a racist comment or intended joke says more about the person laughing than it does about the humor. Based on the writing of Ronald de Sousa and Henri Bergson, John Morreall makes this point in his discussion of the ethics of laughter and humor.[2] These authors suggest that laughter is a great revealer of character. We can suppress laughter or even not find a certain attempt at humor funny if we find the subject of that humor unacceptable. To not suppress the urge to laugh or rebuke the sexist joke as inappropriate is a failing. Morreall, summarizing de Sousa's thesis, comments that "Where the attitude presupposed by a joke is morally objectionable, then telling or laughing at it is also morally objectionable."[3]

A simple rule to follow: if we would tell a joke behind someone's back or laugh at it *but* feel ashamed to say it or laugh at it face-to-face, we should avoid engaging this type of "humor" at all. To laugh at the misfortune, affliction, or mistreatment of those less powerful or fortunate than ourselves is a form of emotional self-deception. To laugh is involuntary but can be suppressed and should be suppressed; to find a racist joke funny is shameful; to not try and suppress your laughter and enjoyment is disgraceful—because the aim of the joke is alienation. This parallels Kenneth Burke's discussion of aggressive, ridiculing humor as a form of scapegoating, which we discussed in chapter 7. To scapegoat a person you must first separate them from yourself completely. In Burke's opinion, such alienating humor is tragic and is not within the comic frame. We do well to remember the ancient comedy playwright Terence, as he said, "Homo sum, humani nihil a me alienum puto" (I am a man, I consider *nothing* that is human *alien to me*).[4] To alienate a person or population, even or especially under the guise of humor and laughter, is to deny their shared humanity, their being created in the image of God.

To Ponder

Suppose you want to practice creating an original short humor piece for a sermon. Here is an activity Owen uses with his students to get their creative and funny juices flowing. Owen suggests that the easiest place to start is to pick something already recognized as taboo or an antisocial behavior already recognized as a violation. Try to come up with a situation in which it would be benign and not a violation.

Owen, inspired by the annoying person sitting next to him (outside a coffeehouse) when writing up this exercise, decided the violation should be public smoking. To connect it to the book's theme, he came up with the idea of smoking in church as the violation. You can see from the diagram the location of the humor in the intersection of violated social norm and benign nature of it.

Think of ways you can make the act of smoking in church benign. List them and start playing with them: "smoking in church but. . . ." Can you create the basis for the beginnings of a joke?

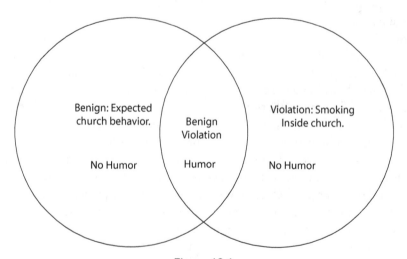

Figure 13.1

HOW JOKES WORK: SCRIPT THEORY

In a moment we return to Owen's attempt at a joke based on the benign violation of smoking in church once we have a better grasp of why jokes work linguistically. For this we can turn to the script-based semantic theory of humor (SSTH) by Victor Raskin.[5] We call it *script theory* for brevity and simplicity's sake. Script theory boils down to the fact that words have more than one meaning, and that can be a source of humor when a comic (or preacher) leads us down a path to one meaning and then flips the script.

According to linguistic scholars, any word has a large amount of semantic information that surrounds it and far exceeds its lexical (strict dictionary) definition. A native speaker internalizes these meanings and, based on linguistic or social context, innately determines which of the available meanings is most appropriate—that is, "smoking" can mean a lot of things: the act of smoking a cigarette, or smoking meat, or a smoking fire, a smoking defeat of someone overwhelming, or even slang for a very good-looking person. Sometimes we don't have enough information to determine the most appropriate meaning, and often the most common meaning serves as a default. For example, when we mentioned "smoking in church," you likely thought of cigarette smoking as opposed to one of the other possibilities.

Raskin proposes that humor in jokes happens because of this language-based sensemaking process. We need to make sense of a word. It's like a puzzle, and we naturally start to work on figuring it out as we hear or read the "script." We search for meaning, which is not just an exercise we do for fun. It is the very basis of how we think and communicate. When we think we have a word and script meaning all figured out, we are confident we are correct. But once we realize we are possibly wrong, we are then forced to reevaluate our assumption and the entire premise or logical consistency of the script. We find this forced re-sensemaking or shift humorous, which is the reaction on which comics capitalize. They offer a script that is designed to purposefully mislead you (the setup). Then they use descriptive language to make you really think the obvious meaning is the correct one (this is called *leading you*) and then *bam, crash, boom*, they shift the script (the *punch line*) and force you to go back to reinterpret all the text with a different meaning.

Humor is produced when a shift or trigger is present at the end of the joke: commonly known as the *punch line*.[6] The punch line causes the audience to abruptly shift their interpretation from the primary script (the more obvious, default script) to the secondary script (the alternative and less obvious script). Raskin uses this joke to illustrate:

> "Is the doctor at home?" the patient asked in his bronchial whisper.
> "No," the doctor's young and pretty wife whispered in reply. "Come right in."

The bronchial whisper affirms the default assumption that someone asking for a doctor is asking for medical aid. The audience assumes (more leading) that the man needs to see the doctor (the obvious script) because he is sick and probably has a bronchial illness. The fact is, we learn with the punch line, he is here to see the doctor's wife.

Alyce's grandsons Graham (eight) and Silas (four) have a favorite joke: "Taking a Penguin to the Zoo."

> A man was walking down the street one day. He saw another man walking toward him with a penguin. He called out to him, "Hey, you ought to take that penguin to the zoo."
> "Thank you, that's a good idea!" said the first man.
> The next day the same man saw the same other man walking toward him with the same penguin. "Hey," he said, "aren't you the guy I saw yesterday, and didn't I tell you to take that penguin to the zoo?"
> "Yes," said the second man. "And we had such a great time that today I'm taking him to the movies!"

The joke rests on violation of logic that a person would socialize with a penguin and the double interpretation of what it means to "take a penguin to the zoo," restoring an animal to their proper habitat versus going on a recreational outing.

Another favorite joke of Alyce's young grandsons is "Walk a Mile in Their Shoes":

> When someone upsets you or is rude to you, try walking a mile in their shoes. That way, you will be a mile away from them . . . *and* you'll have their shoes!

The joke rests on the double interpretation of what it means to walk a mile in someone's shoes: it is normally thought of as empathizing with someone, but here it mischievously refers to stealing their shoes! What is usually a motto for an inspirational poster becomes a snippet of snark!

Back to Owen's attempt to work toward joke creation using script theory and the odd, potentially humorous concept of "smoking in church." He adds a setup (leading) to the script to push the audience one way. Here is Owen's first attempt working with this concept:

> I have a strange ritual. When I have a job interview I like to attend the morning Mass at a church close by. Hey don't laugh, some people rub a dead rodent's foot for luck. [P] Seriously! A rabbit foot, and I am weird for going to church! [P]
>
> Anyway, I was in London and I looked up the Oratory, for Mass times, "8 a.m. High Latin Mass, proper attire requested." I had no idea what that was, but I'll have my suit on, and I am game for something new. I arrive early, 7:30 a.m., and I was greeted by a seriously posh Englishman at the door in a black gown. He says very formally, "Would you prefer the smoking section or nonsmoking section, sir?" [P] . . . *What!* . . . I think to myself, *Well, in for a penny, when in Rome!*
>
> "Smoking," please? [P]

See how much work Owen puts into building up the tension of the moment and still leading you to support the most obvious script meaning (smoking a cigarette as violation). He also with the rabbit's foot puts in what comedians call "warm-up comments" to signal that what follows is a joke. With this leading, Owen can add the shift or the punch line:

> Word of advice: Never say "smoking section" anywhere! [P] For the whole two-hour Mass I had priests dousing me with incense. I was in the first row right in the middle, trapped, unable to leave and being drenched with "holy" smoke.

Owen tested this joke, which got a few laughs (In testing he notes "P," which means pause for laughs). The pauses for laughs are important to avoid what comedians call "stepping on a laugh" and silencing the audience's participation in the joke process. If this joke was to become "a bit," Owen would "work it," that is, play with the scene and the lead-up before the punch line. After testing he may keep or add another throwaway line: "when in Rome." A throwaway is a witticism (clever language use, double meaning, or pun) that is intellectually playful but you don't pause on it for reaction and instead go right through to the next line, which is the punch line. Not everyone gets clever witticisms and you don't want awkward looking around; wit builds comic appreciation but rarely out-loud laughs. The throwaway is useful, it builds comic tension (further signaling this story is a joke) and pushes to the

punch line. If the punch line / joke is successful, defined as the resolution getting laughs, Owen would also consider adding on small related
jokes after the resolution to keep the laughs coming, making it the
beginning of larger bit, not just a joke.

> So I go to the job interview, first thing the recruiter does is open the
> window. . . .

Not a great joke, but a joke nonetheless. It also set up a bridge to
other interview experiences or tense situations and plenty of room for
humorous observation, especially with violation of smelling like smoke
thrown in.

Owen's second attempt involves the same violation of "smoking in
church":

> I walked into a church, and being late for the service I crept into the
> back pew. Guess what? There was a lady already there, and she was
> smoking a cigarette. I was so shocked I almost dropped my beer.

In this example, Owen one-upped the violation to the point of ridiculousness. This demonstrates the versatility of the joke-writing process.
In all this, it took Owen about five minutes to come up with two or
three passable jokes. Score one for script theory. Like any new skill,
practice makes you better.

To Ponder

— Try the exercise again. Pick a different benign violation theme
  and play with it, and then use script theory to script it.
— We mentioned in a prior chapter the workshop your authors held
  in which we broke participants into several groups, each with an
  assigned biblical text: John 21 (the resurrected Jesus making his
  disciples breakfast on the beach); John 20:1–13 (John's version
  of Easter morning); 2 Kings 5:1–19 (the healing of Namaan);
  and Luke 11:1–13 (Jesus' instructions for prayer, including the
  parable of the Friend at Midnight). We asked them to look for
  humor in the texts. What fodder for jokes, benign violations with
  a punch line, might they have found? "Don't skip breakfast!"
  (John 21); "Turning off your notifications!" or "Calling too late"
  (Luke 11:1–13); "You clean up well," or maybe "Taking the

easy way out" (2 Kgs. 5:1–19); "The Gardener did it!" (John 20:1–13). With what benign violations could a preacher use script theory to craft some brief humorous bits? Note how each idea is grounded in the congregation's common experience as well as with the text.

CRAFTING OBSERVATIONAL HUMOR
SEGMENTS IN SERMONS

In addition to creating original, traditionally formulated jokes, preachers can use this process to turn observations from their inscape and landscape (your comic notes) into sermonic humor segments, what comics call observational humor. *Observational humor* creates riffs on themes from common experiences in daily life. It works because it is true, is relatable, and questions something we all take for granted as normal. As Sid Caesar said, "Comedy has to be based on truth. You take the truth, and you put a little curlicue at the end." As a test case, almost every comedian has an observational bit based on airplanes or airports. Type in your favorite comedian and the word "flying" or "airplanes" and a humorous observational piece of humor will come up.[7] For example, Jim Gaffigan once had a bit about how companion animals have become common on planes and he takes it to the absurd level of someone bringing their horse on the plane and being indignant when questioned. What makes this more humorous now is that the ridiculous situation actually happened.[8] Comics take it at as a challenge of their craft to observe and spin something that is unique and funny from the same common source material. They also know that the audience members all have a common reference for flying—no one likes flying anymore, so the common frustration makes it easy for comedians not only to kick the pig but also to put their own curlicue on it.

Observational humor makes the normal and mundane seem odd and ridiculous or makes the odd and ridiculous seem normal and mundane. This kind of humor leaves the audience holding onto a semi-uncomfortable cognitive dissonance—two conflicting notions or behaviors simultaneously. *I'm supposed to be on a diet, but I was a guest and all they offered me was chocolate cake.* The observational content should come directly from your comic notes, experiences, and intrapersonal imaginary interactions and conversations.

For example, when Owen was a child he served as an altar boy, and one of his jobs for High Mass was to hold the incense thurible, or censer. He never forgot how it made him stink like incense after Mass. This experience became the basis for the first joke we mentioned earlier in this chapter.

When you write from what you know, your observation will be authentic. Suppose you are sitting down to write a sermon and think, *I need a way to flesh out either the human condition and its common weaknesses and absurdities or the positive experience of divine forgiveness and grace.* If you have no comic notes, you have no basis for an observational humor piece and you may find yourself searching online illustration banks for other people's material. Shoehorned into your sermon, this content often feels forced, generic, canned, dated, or even blasé.

By contrast, your own comic notes produce genuine observations because they originate with your inner thoughts (inscape) and what you notice in your surroundings (landscape). You also have an advantage in your comedy writing. There is tremendous overlap and commonality with your congregation that you can draw from: your shared space (the church) and the cultural and social environment (landscape). You and your congregation even have a shared reverence for and knowledge of common biblical texts. Note, however, that preachers need to assess their congregation's level of biblical knowledge. It may well be necessary to fill in some gaps in the treatment of texts for the congregation to draw humor from them.

In observational comedy, the observed tension between two things (cognitive dissonance) is not so great that it demands change. Observational humor is typically amusing but not corrective in nature. It doesn't often rise to the level of making us think we should change to address the dissonance or ask others to change their behavior. For example, there is little comic gold in generating cognitive dissonance in being both pro-life and pro–death penalty. When creating observational humor for a sermon, it is best to use and play with simple tensions. Here is a good example of a simple tension from Jim Gaffigan on relaxing (the most benign activity of all):

> Massages: that is how some people relax. Some people relax by sitting in sauna. Sure. Who doesn't love the feeling of being trapped inside an active volcano? I don't understand the appeal of saunas.[9]

He goes on to make many more humorous observations concerning how strange saunas are, from being naked with other people, to sweating collectively, drinking in saunas, to the hot rocks that are clearly done cooking. The common reference to an ordinary sauna and the juxtaposition of "active volcano" is humorous and creates room for more humor to follow.

Here is a good example of timely observational humor from Owen's priest in Rhode Island at the beginning of Lent in 2022. His priest uses humor to point up the shallowness of a current "sacrificial" practice (no-meat Fridays) on the way toward soliciting congregational appreciation for a deeper sacrifice made by some in their midst: first responders and essential workers.

> Okay, So the Lenten period starts today. That's wonderful and for many of us that means we will actually observe the No Meat on Friday rule. It's a big sacrifice. [laughter] No meat, but we can still eat shrimp, oysters, tuna, crab and lobster. Makes no sense: you can't have a hot dog, but you can have stuffed lobster with butter sauce! [The congregation laughs and the priest waves off their laughter with his hand.]
>
> Seriously, do what you feel you should do, but this Lent think about what real sacrifice means. Let's think about and thank health-care professionals who have been putting themselves and family at risk working incredible hours to help people during this pandemic. Are there any health-care or essential service workers here today? Please stand up. [Congregation claps.] Thank you for your sacrifice that's far more profound than no hot dogs on Fridays. If it was up to me and they made me pope [more laughs] I'd change the Friday rule first thing [Pause; more laughter] and replace it with a call to us to make a genuine sacrifice during Lent. [Pause] What would yours be?

OBSERVATIONAL HUMOR: SOFT EYES AND TARGETED QUESTIONS APPLIED TO EVERYDAY LIFE

As discussed in chapter 11, comic observation benefits from soft eyes, coming to life looking for full descriptions, questions, and curiosity. Start by describing what you see. Consider when you notice something ritualistic, anything we do without thinking, based on social norms and tacit knowledge. For example, think about the way people conform to expedite a Starbucks order. Employ some targeted questions about the ritual and our compliance: Why do we (or others) do it this way? How was it learned? If it is odd, why is not questioned? How important does it seem to be for people to say it or do it every day: does it make life more predictable (usually), and is that justification for it? Remember that all social norms require personal and social energy to maintain them. Once again, try not to make judgments too early! But once you find an edge, sharpen it. A good example of this can be seen in *Seinfeld* (season 3, episode 11) when Seinfeld discovers his reserved rental car is in effect not reserved. This is a common occurrence and source of frustration. It is one we typically accept and move on from, but not the observational comedian! Now they have found a ritual and a frustration (an edge) to which we all can relate, and comics exploit it for its effect. The clerk has explained that, in spite of Seinfeld's reservation, they have no cars:

> Seinfeld: But the reservation keeps the car HERE [change tone, louder for emphasis]. That's why we have the reservation!
> Clerk: I know why we have reservations.
> Seinfeld: I DON'T THINK YOU DO! If you DID I'd have a car. So you know how to TAKE the reservation. You just don't know how to HOLD [hand gesture of hold onto something] the reservation. And that REALLY is the most important part of the reservation, the HOLDING [same hand gesture]. Anybody can take a reservation [exaggerated gestures of snatching things in the air]!

Seinfeld in this scene doesn't win in the end. The clerk leaves Jerry to have a conversation with "her management," not in earshot. The clerk then comes back and informs him all we have is "Compact." Seinfeld accepts, and the episode moves on, with the car size becoming the basis for the next gag.

SOFT EYES AND TARGETED QUESTIONS: EXAMPLE FROM JESUS

When we as preachers apply soft eyes and targeted questions to everyday situations and find humor in them, we are taking a page out of Jesus' playbook. Realizing that he himself was a master of observational, situational humor that subverted unquestioned convention helps us recognize the humor, often acerbic, in biblical scenes we usually only view through serious eyes. He comes into situations with soft eyes, taking it all in, and then asking targeted questions like "Why is it this way? Does it have to be this way? And how should it be?" His parables, which often reverse the roles of mighty and lowly, are fueled by soft eyes and targeted questions. So are many of his encounters with individuals we normally approach with deadly seriousness. The result may not be a guffaw, or even a chuckle, but it could lead to a deeper, ironic humor as we recognize ourselves and world reflected in Jesus' words.

Consider John 8:1–11, mentioned in chapter 12, entertaining the possibility that Jesus embodied the process of soft eyes and targeted questions. He takes in the whole scene: a group of men accusing a lone woman of something of which they themselves, apparently, may be guilty. He invites them to exercise judgment, to throw a stone. He then writes something, we don't know what, on the ground. And then comes the targeted question posed to the woman: "Where are they? Has no one condemned you?" (John 8:10).

Another example comes from John 5. Jesus comes to the pool of Bethzatha with soft eyes. He takes in the many invalids lying there and focuses in on one man who has been ill for thirty-eight years. He asks him a targeted question that, on the surface, seems ridiculous. "Do you want to be made well?" There is a brusque brand of humor in Jesus cutting through the man's lengthy explanation, saying simply, "Stand up, take your mat and walk." And he does.

COMIC STORYTELLING: FOUR STRUCTURES

As preachers, you are well versed in the power that story has to help listeners engage and experience a message. There is a reason Jesus preached in parables. Storytelling and humor can be a powerful combination.

Comedians use storytelling to bring in the audience, grab their attention, and weave different observational humor bits into a coherent structure. More commonly, they make humorous observations within a story to increase the laugh rate. Stories, unlike jokes, have to be believable throughout the lead-up, authentic to the teller, and coherent in their message. They need to have a common reference point and be relatable to the audience. Observational storytelling comedians use four basic plots or frames that can be useful in sermons.

First, there is *ALL in the setup*. A mentor of Owen's named Jack McCall[10] once told him, all you have to do to capture a person's attention is simply say, "Let me tell you a story!" We can't help it; we all stop and are primed to listen. Comedians use our love of and familiarity with stories and weave in elaborate joke setups (script theory) to lead us to a punch line. This is when the comedian employs a ridiculous scene setting to build interest and anticipation and lead you through the story and then at the end unexpectedly twists it and provides an alternative and unexpected resolution to the farce-filled tale. Jesus' parables follow this structure in many cases: the Good Samaritan, the Rich Man and Lazarus, and the Vineyard Laborers are three that come to mind. They each end with a crumbling of conventional expectations.

ALL in the setup is the story version of script theory, making it more on topic and relatable than a canned joke. Interestingly, the reverse can happen when the incongruity of an obvious punch line or resolution (the shift) is so telegraphed that people find the prolonged and elaborate lead-up to be humorous in and of itself. This can be seen in the hemming-of-the-pants story mentioned in chapter 5 by pastor Zan Holmes. We all know that after he hems his pants, throughout the night, his mother-in-law and his wife will each get up and also hem his pants. But his discovery of his "walking shorts" the next morning is still enjoyable, even though we saw it coming almost from the beginning.

Second is, *Oh, I see what you mean.* This storytelling structure is saying something, usually a statement, that does not make sense upfront or is really unusual in its phrasing. Then the teller explains it through a story, or a series of scenes or examples, so that by the end the odd statement does make sense. In preaching on Job the preacher might begin with the statement, "Divine retribution is a human invention!" In a sermon on John 20, the preacher might begin by saying, "The Gardener did it!" and work backward to the giving of life in the garden of Eden and then forward to God's restoring of Jesus' life and our own in the Garden of Gethsemane.

Referring back to the comic notes landscape examples in chapter 11, Alyce might begin by saying, "I always work hard to not prepare for speaking engagements!" from Bring Your A Game or "I'm one of the few people I know who can simultaneously recycle and litter" from Best Intentions.

Comedian John Mulaney started an entire skit with, "I listen to everything my girlfriend tells me," and builds off it to create an entire hourlong special. Wanda Sykes begins by saying, "I think marriage is an institution for raising children, and that's about it!" and launches her entire thirty-minute skit on why her first marriage and other marriages don't work. Bill Burr starts a routine with, "I've come to point I wanna have a kid, and I don't think it's that hard to raise a kid."

Comedian Michael Jr. begins a skit with, "When I was a kid, laughing in church was illegal," and then goes into a hilarious set in which he makes observations about what goes on in church through the eyes of his younger self, from a lady's wig falling off, to the interminable length of services, to the idiosyncrasies of the preacher's delivery.[11]

Third, *Some stuff is like other stuff.*[12] Link two things that don't usually get associated. Tig Nataro uses this approach when he humorously illustrates how disgusting smoking is: "When I couldn't get ahold of cigarettes, I'd roll coffee grounds into typing paper and smoke that and then vomit." Or consider how Amy Schumer in a relatable way likens the company of people to the potentially destructive heat of the sun: "Being an introvert doesn't mean you're shy. It means you enjoy being alone. Not just enjoy it—you need it. If you're a true introvert, other people are basically energy vampires. You don't hate them; you just have to be strategic about when you expose yourself to them—like the sun. They give you life, sure, but they can also burn you!"

A biblical example of *Some stuff is like other stuff* is when Jesus says that rich people are like camels trying to get through the eye of a needle. Or religious leaders are like whitened sepulchers. His analogies include short sayings and longer narratives. The lead-in to many of the parables is, "The kingdom of heaven is like. . . ." Of course, powerful people of his day did not appreciate his analogies, but that doesn't stop their darkly humorous satire from stinging, even after all these centuries.[13]

Finally, there is the structure called *The Sitcom Code: Finding Humor in the Muddle.*[14] A sitcom episode by definition has to end almost where it started, or change characters and their lives very little. Characters are caricatures, and people tune in every week for basically the same thing. In the show *Friends* it took eight years, and thousands of silly conversations around the table for Ross and Rachel to finally get together. It is not easy to write a script where nothing really happens! What makes sitcoms work is that they are not dramas. They are more in the genre of escapism.

Here is a simple version of the sitcom code: there is a setup—usually a conflict or problem (called the *trouble*), a projected resolution (a small win), and the middle (called the *muddle*) where everything goes unexpectedly wrong or sidetracks especially the most obvious direct route (each deviation increases complexity that adds humor and builds tensions) until the resolution comes at the end of the episode.

LEARNING FROM COMIC DELIVERY

We began the chapter by introducing the concept of voice as a preacher's (and comic's) unique perspective on the world. One's delivery is an important contributor to a preacher's conveyance of their take on the world, their voice. We recommend that you study various comedians and learn from them, incorporating elements that fit your personality and speaking style into your preaching. One of the best comedians a preacher could watch to hone the art of comic storytelling is John Mulaney. His use of all the tools (description; language; common imagery; tone changes and exaggerated voice; long, well-timed pauses mixed with throwaway witticisms) is masterful. He starts his skit "Why Delta Air Lines Is Evil" like this:

> *I listen to everything my girlfriend tells me* [deadpan tone] . . . *because now I have someone standing next to me pointing out obvious things that are happening* [still deadpan delivery and laughter; slight smile and he pauses so as not to step on the laugh]. . . . My girlfriend will be like, "You ordered your food an hour ago, it should be here by now." And I am like, "YEAH, IT SHOULD" [dramatic louder and whiny voice, animated body language].

The story continues with more examples of his girlfriend pointing out places and situations where his outrage is justified. The performance of each situation and reaction becomes more elaborate. "Before I had a girlfriend I had no standard of how I should be treated as a human being." He uses this as an introduction to a long, involved bit on how he was mistreated and abused by an airline customer service representative and simply accepted it as normal. Though his story is exaggerated to the point of absurdity, we can all relate based on previous experience at airports.[15] We suggest finding a comedian whose delivery style best matches your own, and watch for the little things they do to signal they are being humorous or postponing a reveal until a punch line.

To appreciate the full range available for delivery of comedy, take a look at Hannah Gadsby's work. She uses PowerPoint in her comedy specials, and her flat style is an interesting contrast to that of the exaggerated Mulaney. In "How High-Function Autism Works," Hannah uses visual aids such as classic paintings and rhetorical devices such as previewing her entire act, even telling the audience her ultimate end-of-set punch line. She breaks rules but is still funny because of her cascade of wit, strange and at times jarringly honest observations, and personal and revealing truth telling.

TAKE THE RISK!

Andrew Tarvin is a humor motivational speaker who goes to office retreats and discusses the importance of workplace humor and workplace well-being. In a TED Talk, he encourages us to take the risk of incorporating more humor into our lives. He suggests that many of us fear creating humor. Tarvin encourages us as a first step to seek existing humorous content in the landscape around us (pictures, stories, posts, jokes, or quotes) and share them (in the office or with friends, not necessarily in the pulpit).[16] Your authors are asking you to do something similar in taking a note pad and writing down funny ideas and observations in everyday life, including your social media use (the more you focus in on humor in social media, the more each platform's algorithm will send you funny material . . . scary but true).

Tarvin suggests, and we think he is spot on here, that we start out by risking creating humor and see how we do. As comedians use their comic notes, so should we use a note pad to jot down ideas. Have an intrapersonal dialogue and imaginary interactions with these ideas, playing with them and seeing if they work together. Have the imaginary interaction you didn't have and make the most mundane experience even funnier. Keep in mind that our use of sermonic humor needs to be appropriate to the occasion, the congregational context, and the biblical text. It cannot trivialize serious subjects and can never objectify or denigrate another person or group. As long as we adhere to these rules of snowballing as described in chapter 3, then we can apply a motto coined by a friend of Owen's to our experimentation with sermonic humor: "There is no such thing as bad pizza, since to be pizza all you need is warm bread, sauce, and melted cheese."[17] Ted Cohen, humor scholar and philosophy professor, suggests that humor fails only if it does not increase intimacy between teller and audience, not if it failed to produce a smile or laughter.[18]

INTERNALIZE THE COMIC SPIRIT!

Trevor Noah, the comedian discussed in chapter 9 as a modern comic sage for his role on Comedy Central and the White House

Correspondents' Dinner, sees "humor as a filter you can see the world through."[19] He uses it to make sense of the news and present it from a comic frame, to see humor in things but also through satire to speak truth to power. His book, *Born a Crime*, is about his being born and raised as a mixed-race person (an outsider and a crime) under South Africa's apartheid system.[20] He realized halfway through writing the book that he was a side character and the protagonist was really his mom and her humor. He realized how they both helped him in "overcoming obstacles" and finding "acceptance and family love," which are universal themes. The lesson here: Don't be afraid to adopt the comic spirit and use a comic frame or vision as your outlook on faith and life. Use it to make sense, question and play with what you see, and inform how you use your unique preacher's "voice" to speak good news to the world.

THE PREACHER AS LAST COMIC STANDING

Owen is a very funny guy. On their student evaluations, his students regularly compliment his use of classroom humor. As for Alyce, well, she was once told by a parishioner at the back door, "I love your sense of humor! You could be a stand-up comedian!" In the interests of full disclosure, Alyce has also been told a lot of other things at the back door, like, "You have such a soothing voice. You could be a hypnotist!" (not her homiletical goal!). Or "I like your new robe." (It wasn't anywhere near new! Clearly a diversionary tactic when the sermon failed to soar.) Or "I couldn't hear a word you said!" (*Then why do you always sit in the back row?*)

Although both Alyce and Owen enjoy and employ humor in their daily lives, they stand no chance of ever being contestants on *Last Comic Standing* since the show's last season, at least for now, was 2015. And that's a good thing because preachers are not stand-up comedians, and our goal in this book is not to equip readers to win a homiletical humor preach-off, to be the last comic standing on the stage after everyone else's jokes have faltered and fallen short.

Your authors have poured our collaborative energies into this project because of the depth of our respect for the power of humor, when activated by the comic spirit. In these pages we have sought to honor the divine gift of humor that is part of our humanity as shaped in God's image and to spotlight humor's many positive effects on both preacher and congregation. We have sought to show how humor works and how we can put it to work (and play) in our sermons. We have also sought to encourage preachers to claim their identity as those who not only have a comic spirit but *are* comic spirits, internalizing the joy of the comic vision of the victory of life over death in each moment of the here and now, both within and beyond the pulpit.

The preacher as comic spirit keeps joy and laughter alive, even when the heavy pall of tragedy weighs down the present moment. When isolation and arrogance prevail in the tragic plots all around us and all appearances point to the victory of death over life, the preacher as comic spirit refuses to let the curtain fall and give death the last word. The comic-spirited preacher, though her throat is clotted with tears, stands on the stage and dares to offer a word of cultural critique, tough-minded humor, and appropriate hope.

We appreciate the comic wisdom of Father Ken Unterer's remark on the difficulty of ending sermons: "Ending a sermon is like trying to get out of a canoe gracefully."[21] The same can be said of ending books. For your sake, your authors have nobly resisted the temptation to circle the airport, to introduce a completely new topic, or to explain what we hope has already been made abundantly clear.

By mutual agreement, we are ending our tribute to the power of the comic spirit in preaching with the following story.

Several years ago, Alyce was invited to speak at a Presbyterian church in Granbury, Texas. It was a busy time, and she was mentally rather tired. Not an excuse, just a possible explanation for what happened. She had no notes, thinking she had structured her message to be easy to remember. But as she came to the end of the sermon, her mind went completely blank. As in "I got nothin." She remembered that she had planned to tell a story but had absolutely no memory of what it was. She repeated what she had just said, then said it again, and, thanks be to God, the story flooded into her mind. Jesus and the boat. Yes! The story about Earl Brockway and his famous New England boat called the Brockway scow—the boat that never sinks because it knows its true center. Whew!

Afterward, she shared what had happened with the pastor. He laughed and said, "Well, if it ever happens again, here is what you do. Just pause. Look meaningfully out into the eyes of members of the congregation, long enough to connect without being creepy, and then say dramatically, 'In the end, my friends, it all leads to Jesus!'"

And so it does. To him as the last comic standing, against whom, ultimately, there is no contest—who activates the divine power of a comic vision that is stronger than death, who imparts to us the gift of humor and the wisdom to use it in its many guises.

The Comic Spirit

NOTES

1. This joke was selected as number one of "The 100 Funniest Jokes from the Last 100 Years" submitted to *Reader's Digest* since 1922. To commemorate the hundredth anniversary of *Reader's Digest*, the "humor-loving editors combed the archives to come up with this collection of the 100 best jokes published in the magazine since 1922" (Linda Roman, *Reader's Digest,* April 13, 2022).

2. Ronald de Sousa, "When Is It Wrong to Laugh?," in *The Philosophy of Laughter and Humor,* ed. John Morreall (Albany: State University of New York Press, 1987). Also see de Sousa, "The Ethics of Laughter and Humour," in *The Philosophy of Laughter and Humor;* Henri Bergson, *Laughter* (Peter Smith Publisher, 1996). Also see Juan Carlos Aparisi, "The Features of the Ethics of Humor: A Proposal from Contemporary Authors," *Veritas: Revista de Filosofía y Teología* 29 (2013).

3. John Morreall, *The Philosophy of Laughter and Humor,* ed. John Morreall (Albany: State University of New York Press, 1987), 226.

4. See George Fredric Franko, "Terence and the Traditions of Roman New Comedy," in *A Companion to Terence,* ed. Antony Augoustakis and Ariana Traill (Malden, MA: John Wiley and Sons, 2013), 33–51.

5. Victor Raskin, distinguished professor of linguistics, was also a comedy writer in his early career and was the founding editor of *Humor: The Journal for the International Society of Humor Studies.* He first introduce SSTH in 1979, and his theory and work have encouraged and generated new linguistic approaches to understanding humor. See Victor Raskin, "Semantic Mechanisms of Humor," in *Annual Meeting of the Berkeley Linguistics Society* 5 (1979): 325–35; Raskin, *Semantic Mechanisms of Humor* (Dordrecht: Springer, 1985). For a contemporary review of Raskin's work and impact on linguistic and humor studies, see Salvatore Attardo, ed., *Script-Based Semantics: Foundations and Applications. Essays in Honor of Victor Raskin* (Walter de Gruyter GmbH & Co., 2020).

6. Raskin puts this in more technical language: he suggests that in a joke the text is compatible, fully or in part, with two different (semantic) scripts. The two scripts with which the text is compatible are opposite. Raskin argues that this is especially true when there are script oppositions in the alternative meanings: ordinary/extraordinary, possible/impossible, good/bad, actual/nonactual, obvious/obscure, and so on.

7. See Ellen DeGeneres, "Ellen Improves Your Airplane Seats," September 15, 2014, YouTube, https://www.youtube.com/watch?v=AfQT4Fz1ipI. There is a compilation (almost an hour) on different Louis CK jokes and stories about airplanes: "Stand Up Comedy—Every Airplane Joke from Louis CK—Compilation of Funniest Jokes," Comedy Clips & Humor, April 1, 2022, YouTube, https://www.youtube.com/watch?v=RqqY6WE_fiM. We could list hundreds.

8. See jimgaffigan, "'Horses'—Jim Gaffigan Stand Up (Quality Time)" YouTube, May 7, 2020, https://www.youtube.com/watch?v=e8n776ozpyA.

Also see Caitlin O'Kane, "A Woman Takes Her 115 Lbs Horse on Plane as Service Animal," CBS News, February 20, 2020, https://www.cbsnews.com/news/miniature-horse-on-plane-woman-took-service-animal-flight-could-be-his-last-airlines/.

9. See "Jim Gaffigan Doesn't Understand Winter People," YouTube, https://www.youtube.com/watch?v=OglJD_N0qxI.

10. Jack McCall's best-known wisdom can be found in McCall, *The Principal's Edge* (New York: Routledge, 2014).

11. Michael Jr., "Laughing at Church," April 5, 2016, YouTube, https://www.youtube.com/watch?v=dOHfM2jf5-k. For a biography of Michael Jr., see Rhonda Moudreax, "Michael Jr. Biography," IMDB.com, https://www.imdb.com/name/nm1143406/bio?ref_=nm_ov_bio_sm.

12. "Some stuff is like some other stuff" is a PG version of a comedy rule by Bill Maher that is a regular segment on his HBO show *Real Time with Bill Maher*: "Explaining Jokes to Idiots."

13. Scholars have executed exegetical backflips trying to take the impossibility out of this saying of Jesus, speculating that the camel was really a rope and that the eye of the needle was really a very small gate in the wall surrounding Jerusalem. See "The Camel and the Needle—August 17th, Tuesday (Mt 19:23–30)," August 16, 2010, Gospel Reflections Daily, http://davidgospeldaily.blogspot.com/2010/08/camel-and-needle-august-17th-tuesday-mt.html.

14. See Noah Charney's excellent review of the sitcom code in Noah Charney, "Cracking the Sitcom Code," *The Atlantic*, December 28, 2014, https://www.theatlantic.com/entertainment/archive/2014/12/cracking-the-sitcom-code/384068/.

15. See John Mulaney, "Delta Air Lines Is Evil," July 17, 2020, Neon Theater, YouTube, https://www.youtube.com/watch?v=-agnCrhaMmE.

16. Andrew Tarvin's work and TED talks can be found on his website Humor That Works. See "The Skill of Humor TEDx Talk—Develop Your Humor Skills," https://www.humorthatworks.com/how-to/the-skill-of-humor-tedx-talk/.

17. Inappropriate and potentially damaging humor is humor that punches down, is introduced too soon after a traumatic event, or is insensitive regarding a stressful situation.

18. Ted Cohen, *Jokes: Philosophical Thoughts on Joking Matters* (Chicago: University of Chicago Press, 1999).

19. Interview: "Trevor Noah on the Power of Humor: Recorded Live at The INBOUND Studio." INBOUND. "How Trevor Noah Challenges His Beliefs," YouTube, April 21, 2017, https://www.youtube.com/watch?v=m5WdgMAbHDk&list=PLPYoT0OlTslOOr7Jdeqk_KmhOdTAKueOM&index=2.

20. Trevor Noah, *Born a Crime: Stories from a South African Childhood* (New York: Spiegel & Grau, 2016).

21. We added the word "gracefully!" Ken Untener, *Preaching Better: Practical Suggestions for Homilists* (Mahwah, NJ: Paulist Press, 1999), 29.

Index

An *i* following a page number indicates an image on that page.
Scripture references can be found under New Testament or Old Testament.

For a list of recommended resources on preaching and humor, go to https://www.wjkbooks.com/HumorUs.

CPSIA information can be obtained
at www.ICGtesting.com
Printed in the USA
JSHW012330030523
41239JS00001B/4